Mortgage-Free For Life·

SECRETS

Banks & Lenders Don't Want You To Know!

Richard Weathington
& Beth Ley, Ph.D.

BL Publications
Hanover, Minnesota

Library of Congress Cataloging-in-Publication Data

Weathington, Richard,1960-
Ley, Beth M., 1964-
 Secrets Banks & Lenders Don't Want You To Know!
 / Richard Weathington, Beth M. Ley.
    p. cm.
ISBN: 1-890766-40-2
 1. mortgage advice 2. Saving money on mortgages 3. I.
Title.

Cover Design: BL Publications and Jerrita Gronewold

ACKNOWLEDGEMENT

Thank you to everyone who has provided stories and clarity for this most important subject. We appreciate your help in guiding our work.

We especially thank Thomas Cheng, who spent countless hours in research and preparation for this book, which would not exist without him.

"It took me a little while to understand this system, but now I do, and WOW! It's actually so simple and takes almost no effort! Now consumers have the upper hand on their finances. I am going to inform all of my past clients, as well as friends and family."
– Cheryl Caspillo (CC Mortgage)

"LEAP™ is an incredible product. More people need to find out about this loan elimination system."
– Noor Mubeen (Koe-e Noor Financial Inc.)

"I can see a reason why everyone who has loans on their houses needs to know more about this. This is great."
– Maria Dias (La Hacienda Mortgage)

"Phenomenal product, I am going to learn as much as I can about this and save my borrowers tons of money."
– Noe Longoria (Simplex Mortgage)

"It sounds too good to be true, but it is true. I can't believe it is so simple."
– Holly Ruan (Mortgage Galaxy)

"I can save my borrowers so much money it will put me at the forefront of all mortgage brokers. Thanks, Rich."
– Matt Marks (Marks Mortgage Loans)

Table of Contents

Introduction

It's Time for a Change in Thinking... Whose Money Is It, Anyway?

Imagine the first time a human being looked up at the daytime sky and saw an eclipse of the sun. Because they didn't understand, they were fearful. We would be, too!

Today when we look skyward, we see an eclipse as a wonder of nature and are not afraid.

Imagine when the now-famous Wright Brothers said they were going to fly. People must have shouted in disrespect, "Yeah, you and what dodo bird?" Soon people learned it was possible, because they saw it with their own eyes.

Today we cram ourselves into hip-hugging airplane seats with hundreds of other travelers and soar across the sky at 30,000 feet, watching hand-held movie players or typing away on our laptops.

Imagine if someone said you could learn how to build thousands of dollars in equity and pay off your mortgage years earlier (you don't have to be wealthy for this to make sense) without stress, without being a mathematical genius, and without changing your lifestyle. Would you believe?

Mortgages have been paid monthly for years. Some people make extra payments whenever they can afford to, or make two payments a month, gaining some benefit and reducing their mortgages slightly more. Others, like most of us, believe a mortgage is a mortgage, and keep faithfully paying monthly, just like our parents and their parents before them.

Stop. Good news is here!

Think about this: Our lenders and bankers make money off our homes, and they "own" them for a long, long time, until we make that final payment. Most of us don't even want to think about how much interest we have paid to own our homes. It's too overwhelming.

Getting interested?
More importantly, are you getting angry?

Mortgage bankers and lenders make money off your home sweet home. Yes, that's their business. But "your business" should be learning how to reduce your monthly payment as much as possible, saving you literally "tons" of money you can use for other things.

Learning the Secrets...
Putting Them to Work for You!

The time has come for you to look at paying your mortgage in a new and different way, one that benefits you, the homeowner, rather than those who are in the business of making money off your home.

When we learned the SECRETS the bankers and lenders didn't want us to know, we were very upset and felt embarrassed that we had let these people take advantage of us.

When we learned that an innovative mortgage payment system had been effectively used in the United Kingdom and Australia, we were very interested in the benefits for our own bank balance—and we wanted to tell others.

Are you interested? You should be — it's your money. You can save money and pay off your mortgage much sooner than you think. Once you have established and implemented the system, it becomes a no-brainer.

Sound good? Then read on. Believe what you read, and believe that you, too, can be one of the people who learns that there IS a better way to pay off your mortgage.

Then imagine how satisfied you will be with what you understand, and how good it feels to know the SECRETS — and to act on them.

If you're currently a homeowner or looking to purchase and own your home free and clear, and you want to get rid of all your debts (including your mortgage) in just a few short years, then this will be the most valuable book you've ever read in your entire lifetime.

Chapter One

The Great American Dream: Owning Your Own Home

Purchasing a home is the most important and most expensive financial transaction most people will ever make.

Owning your own home should be one of the greatest experiences in your life. There is nothing like the sense of accomplishment and security you will feel when you can truly call a place your own. Imagine having no landlords to deal with, or neighbors on all sides. No uncertainty about how long you will be able to stay in a rental, who your next-door neighbors will be or how noisy they might become. And best of all, there's nothing like knowing your home is appreciating in value and that you will get to reap the benefits of that investment instead of your landlord.

Here's the catch that too many of us have failed to consider: When you *BUY* a home, in most cases you will not actually *OWN* the home for another 30 years — possibly sooner if you manage to pay off your mortgage before then. Do you realize that the banks and lenders actually "own" your homes until you make your last payment? Think about it. If you miss two to three payments, they start the foreclosure procedure by sending you a foreclosure notice. It doesn't matter that you've been paying the bank for three, or five or 15 years on your home. Once you default a couple of times on your mortgage payment, you're at risk of losing your home. Yes, that means the 10% - 20% downpayment you worked so hard to accumulate is gone forever!

The worst part of it is the amount of money you pay them for this privilege. Bankers and lenders are making a killing off of you.

Consider this: For a typical 30-year fixed home loan of $250,000 at 5.75%, your monthly payment would be $1,458.93. Do you realize that over those 30 years you will be paying $525,214.80?! That's well over double the value of the house! The lender makes $275,214.80. Doesn't it make you wonder why we tolerate this?

A $300,000, 15-year loan fixed at 6.50% would have a monthly payment of $2,613.32. This totals $470,397.60 — not a bad profit for the lender at $170,387.60!

And these two examples are fixed loans amortized with principal and interest over 15 or 30 years! What about all the interest-only loans that are extremely popular these days? You have the 2-, 3-, 5-, 7-, 10-year fixed interest-only loans. There are even variations where you can pay interest only for the first 10 years of your loan on a 30-year fixed loan! With these interest-only loans, in which the interest rates are usually fixed for a certain amount of time and then become adjustable, you're making NO progress on building the equity in your home. If you really think about these scenarios, you'll realize that you are nothing more than a renter and the banks are the landlords! You don't really own your home until it's paid off free and clear. Only then will you have the security of knowing that the banks cannot kick you out of the home you've worked so hard to own.

This might help you understand why most lenders would rather not tell us how to pay off our mortgages faster or how to save on interest. They stand to lose a bundle! If everyone in America were to pay off their homes years ahead of schedule, lenders would stand to lose billions, even trillions of dollars.

The purpose of this book is to show you an unbelievably simple way to drastically reduce the amount of money you are paying in interest so you can pay off your principal faster and own your home sooner.

I've made the same mistakes you are probably making or have made in the past. I always made my monthly mortgage payments. And whenever I was able to free up extra money, I applied that extra amount to my principal in hopes of paying off my home faster! (And believe me, that was an extremely rare occurrence!) Like most of you, I had a tough time freeing up discretionary income. Bills were attacking my salary from all directions! There was the mortgage payment, property taxes, credit card payments, car payments, car insurance, electricity bills, gas bills, phone bills, cable bills, cell phone bills, day care, food, gasoline, medical bills and the list goes on and on!   So even if I was able to free up some money and apply it to my principal the "old-fashioned" way, I was really making NO PROGRESS.

Let's say you've been good about saving your money and making extra payments toward your principal for 10 years and you were able to pay an additional $20,000. What if there's an emergency of some kind and you need to pull that money out?   You can't just go to the bank and ask them if you can get that $20,000 back. You will have to refinance your home! And when you refinance, you will have to pay bank fees, origination fees, title and escrow fees, appraisal fees, doc fees, and all the other standard costs that are necessary in order to refinance.

If you refinance a $300,000 home, you could very well pay $6,000 to $8,000 in closing costs!   So $6,000 to $8,000 of the $20,000 you worked so hard for will be gone just like that!   This is an example of why making extra mortgage payments isn't the right answer. And — who has spare money lying around these days to make extra payments?

To further elaborate, when you refinance, the entire process starts all over again. You start at month one, and if you're in a standard 30-year fixed loan, you have another 360 months to pay until the home is yours to keep. Some other common mistakes people make are refinancing into all sorts of exotic mortgages in the hope of saving a few bucks each month. This actually defeats the purpose of owning your home.

Another big mistake is depositing money into traditional checking and savings accounts. The bank generates revenue off of your money! Yet you get paid nothing for putting money in a checking account and very little for putting it in a savings account. But if you want an account paying higher interest, you will have to tie up your money in a long-term certificate of deposit (CD) and penalties are high should you ever need that money for an emergency.

Does all of this sound familiar to you? I quickly became tired of these traps as it seemed there would be no light at the end of the dark tunnel. There had to be a better way!

I wanted to find out if there was a way to pay off my mortgage much faster, without making any additional payments or paying a little more out of my income every month. I wanted own my home free and clear.

That's when I discovered what they were doing in Australia and the United Kingdom. They were paying off their homes in 7 to 10 years on average and they didn't need to make any extra payments or change their way of life! This seemed too good to be true — I had to take a look and verify that, indeed, this was really happening! And it's true — more than 60% of homeowners in those countries are using the LEAP™ principle in order to own their homes years ahead of schedule!

There is no reason American citizens can't do the

same thing , freeing themselves of the burden of mortgage payments. Lenders practically hold us hostage through our monthly mortgage payments — which, in the first few years are primarily interest — and are not building much equity. The banks are making a killing off our hard-earned money! Why should the average, hardworking person need to pay more than $525,000 for a house worth less than half of that? Why should we hand over so much in interest to the banks when we can easily keep it in our own pockets?

This book is about making your money (whatever amount you have) work for you — instead of turning it over to a bank in interest payments. In this system, you become the bank. This is so simple that virtually ANYONE with any educational background can do it, provided he or she can at least qualify for a credit card.

The purpose of this book is to give you the confidence, skill, knowledge and tools to effectively restructure the way you handle money, thus allowing you to accomplish your financial goals.

Here is one of the most important things to know about large loans and the interest applied to them: In this country (and many others) our loans are front-weighted. This means that you are required to pay off most of the interest during the early stages of the loan and then taper off to lower amounts of interest paid later on. So most of the money from your initial payments will be going toward interest — not the principal, the actual amount you borrowed.

Imagine you have a 30-year fixed loan right now and you move in 4 or 5 years after buying the house. You can only hope that your property has appreciated in value in order to have built equity in your home, since you know that you have built NO equity by making your mortgage payments every month.

Did you realize that even after paying 15 years on a 30-year mortgage, you could still owe approximately 70 to 90% of the principal?

30-Year Amortization Loan - $200,000 @ 10%			
Time	Interest	Principal	Loan Balance
1 Month	$1,667.67	$88.48	$199,911.52
1 Year	$19,949.97	$1,111.75	$198,888.24
3 Years	$59,488.45	$3,696.72	$196,303.29
5 Years	$98,457.22	$6,851.36	$193,148.64
10 Years	$192,493.21	$18,123.95	$181,876.04
15 Years	$279,254.93	$36,670.87	$163,329.13

Take a look at the table above. This is a $200,000 30-year fixed loan at a 10% interest rate. Notice that after 3 years, you've paid a total of $59,488.45 in interest to the lender and have only built $3,696.72 worth of home equity! Do you realize that you would still owe 81% of the original principal? Even if you had the same loan at a lower interest rate, say 6%, you would still owe well over 70% of your original loan amount!

30-Year Amortization Loan - $200,000 @ 6%			
Time	Interest	Principal	Loan Balance
1 Month	$1,000.00	$199.10	$199,800.90
1 Year	$11,933.19	$2,456.02	$197,543.98
3 Years	$35,335.80	$7,831.86	$192,168.14
5 Years	$58,054.80	$13,891.29	$186,108.71
10 Years	$111,263.60	$32,628.54	$167,371.45
15 Years	$157,935.89	$57,902.32	$142,097.69

I've known people who have made their regular mortgage payments for 15 years and still owe 90% of the original amount! And these are principal-and-interest loans! Imagine all the homeowners out there with interest-only loans — They're paying interest only so they're building NO equity, especially in a downward-trending real estate market! In a negative amortization or option ARM loans, you can actually LOSE equity!

So many people are surprised when they call their lenders after faithfully paying their mortgages for a few years to find out how much they still owe. Most believe they have a lot more equity built up than they really do. This book will show you how to build your equity FAST and help you save thousands of dollars in interest payments.

This is your money. Why should you give it all to a bank? Your main goal is to get out from under the interest trap as quickly as possible. Staying focused on this goal will ease your transition to a brand new, more effective way of handling your finances.

This plan will not only produce far greater results than any mortgage-acceleration program out there (such as making extra payments, or paying biweekly), it will also teach you the power of credit and the important role it plays in financial success.

A different type of mortgage is coming to the United States. It uses home-equity borrowing and the borrower's paycheck to shorten the time until a mortgage is paid off, clearing all debt once and for all, and saving tens of thousands, if not hundreds of thousands of dollars, in interest expenses.

A Commonly Asked Question is:

I need my mortgage for deductions! Why should I pay off my home years sooner?

Have you ever been told by friends or family members that you should get the biggest mortgage possible in order to save on taxes? Yes, you'll save money in taxes, but did they also tell you that you'll be making the banks and lenders rich? I find it extremely offensive when a tax person or "financial" advisor tells me I "need" a mortgage in order to offset my taxes. Why would someone in such a position give misleading advice like this? Is it because they're just part of the overall scheme and have been brainwashed like most other Americans? When I first learned about this tax deduction, I went along with it just like everyone else! But I soon realized that this was the biggest scam ever pulled on the American public! Let me show you an example to illustrate my point:

2006 Taxes (Single)	Alan	Mary	Bob	Jane
Income	$50,000	$50,000	$50,000	$50,000
Mortgage Interest	**$0**	$24,000	$18,000	$12,000
Taxable Income	$50,000	$26,000	$32,000	$38,000
Federal Taxes	$9,058	$2,938	$4,558	$6,058
Net Income (CASH)	**$40,942**	$23,062	$27,442	$31,942

In this scenario, everyone makes the same salary and takes the same mortgage interest deduction in order for us to get an accurate comparison. Notice that Alan didn't fall for the mortgage-as-a-tax-deduction trick and owns his home free and clear. Mary, Bob, and Jane were each told to take on a mortgage and pay as much interest as possible in order to maximize the tax deduction. Notice that Mary did a great job in paying the lowest amount of taxes. However, while Alan paid the most in taxes, he had $17,880 more discretionary income than Mary!

How in the world is that possible?

Look at it this way. Mary paid $24,000 in mortgage interest in order to save $6,120 in Federal taxes ($9,058 minus $2,938). The $6,120 is the difference of what she would have paid if she didn't have a mortgage. She paid almost $4 to save $1. Does this make any sense? Why would anyone throw away $4 to save $1?

Let's take a look at another example:

2006 Taxes (Married/Joint)	Family1	Family2	Family3	Family4
Income	$100,000	$100,000	$100,000	$100,000
Mortgage Interest	$0	$48,000	$36,000	$24,000
Taxable Income	$100,000	$52,000	$64,000	$76,000
Federal Taxes	$18,115	$7,045	$9,115	$12,115
Net Income(CASH)	$81,885	$44,955	$54,885	$63,885

In this example, we have families with joint income. Although they make the same amount of money and take the same deductions, Family 1 is a lot better off financially than the other families. Family 2 had the largest mortgage payment. They saved a total of $11,070 ($18,115 minus $7,045) in Federal Taxes in 2006! Wow! But there's a catch. They have a lot less money in their pockets than Family 1. Even though they made the same salaries, Family 2 netted $36,930 less than Family 1! Where did that $36,930 go? Directly to the bank's bottom line! Even Family 4, which had the smallest mortgage, came out $18,000 poorer than Family 1.

My point: You should do everything in your power to pay off your home years sooner so you'll become wealthier and get out of debt once and for all. The financial system is set up to keep us all in the mortgage rat race! It's time that we consumers arm ourselves with this kind of knowledge and stop being lifelong slaves to the banks and lenders!

Chapter Two

Introducing LEAP™

LEAP™ stands for Loan Equity Advantage Program, a revolutionary way for you to get rid of all your existing personal debt immediately (credit cards, car loans, student loans, etc.) and leap into home ownership much faster than traditional loans and other mortgage-accelerator programs will allow. You are not required to increase your current mortgage payments or get a second job. All of your money will not be "tied up" in your mortgage, which will allow you to access the money if you should ever have an emergency.

LEAP™ not only saves you thousands of dollars on your mortgage and buys you time when you are in a financial crunch, it also gets rid of all your unsecured debt right away.

This program allows you to pay off your mortgage in as little as seven to ten years without making extra payments or changing your current mortgage. Sound too good to be true? It is true and it really works!

LEAP™ is based on making regular large lump

sum principal payments. This program relies on using a revolving Home Equity Line of Credit (HELOC) to make lump-sum payments against the original mortgage principal balance.

This powerful program is designed to reduce interest drastically without increasing your monthly payment, without altering your current standard of living and without refinancing. LEAP™ allows you to build equity FAST and have your property (home, investment property or other mortgaged property) PAID OFF in as little as seven to ten years.

LEAP™ is not to be confused with a biweekly mortgage loan (paying 1/2 of your regular monthly mortgage every two weeks). A bi-weekly loan will shorten the time it takes to pay off a mortgage, but what you're doing is making one extra payment every year. So instead of making 12 one-month payments, you're actually making 13 payments annually. The LEAP system is comparable to an approach common-ly used in Australia and the United Kingdom – in which borrowers deposit their paychecks into an account that applies every unspent dime against the mortgage loan balance on a monthly basis.

The premise is that borrowers finance a new property, or refinance existing property using a home equity line of credit, or HELOC. Borrowers then directly deposit their entire paychecks into the HELOC, via their checking account.

Monthly expenses, including mortgage payments, are funded by draws using the checking account tied to the HELOC, using bill pay, check writing, ATM withdrawals or a credit card tied to the same account.

Let's say you have a $400,000, 30-year fixed mortgage at 7% interest. If you pay off your home in 10 years, 20 years ahead of schedule, you would save yourself $329,932 in interest payments! So instead of paying $558,035 in interest payments, you would only pay $228,103! Imagine what you could do with all of the money you just saved. Imagine having your house PAID IN FULL! That's the REAL American Dream!

Classification of Loans

There are basically two main types of home loans available to the consumer. The most popular and most widely used home loan is called a "closed loan" or "closed-ended loan." The term "closed mortgage" originates from the 1980's when this type of mortgage was literally "closed." Back then, you didn't have the option of making additional payments, or paying off the entire amount during the term of the mortgage, except with the sale of your property. And you sure couldn't pull out any equity. Today, a closed-ended loan is a little different. You're allowed to make additional principal payments, and you can pay off the loan, assuming there are no prepayment penalties. However, you still cannot pull any equity out of your property without selling or refinancing your loan. With the closed-ended loan, the bank only applies money once a month to adjust the principal balance.

The most popular type of closed-ended loan is the 30-year fixed, with payments fixed at a certain amount for the life of the loan. Appendix III contains a more comprehensive list of closed-ended loans. Closed-ended loans usually have a lower interest rate than open-ended loans.

An open-end loan, on the other hand, allows you to put money in and pull it out at anytime without penalties or fees (if you choose the right type of open-end loan). Open-end mortgages usually have a 10-year term. Their interest rates are variable and usually higher than the rated for closed-ended loans with similar terms. The interest due at the end of each month is based on the daily average balance of the account during the month. The balance is updated daily whenever there are transactions. There are three main types of open-ended loans:

> Credit card
> Unsecured personal line of credit
> Home equity line of credit (HELOC).

With each of these three types of open-ended loans, the borrower will have a credit limit, or a credit line. The borrower can pull money out at any time and put money back in at any time. For LEAP™ purposes, we will be using the HELOC as our first choice. The unsecured personal line of credit can also be used to apply the LEAP™ principle. We don't recommend using a credit card as the main "vehicle" for LEAP™, but rather for support.

The Many Advantages of LEAP™:

1. Unless you spend all of the money by drawing against the home equity line of credit, your paycheck will go toward paying off your house. You'll enjoy increased cash flow and more financial flexibility.

2. You capture interest savings every month because your average balance will be less than it would have been with a conventional loan. Because you will be reducing the principal balance with LEAP™, and building equity at the same time, you'll be saving on interest payments every month! This is called reverse compounding. The interest that you'll save compounds itself month after month, accelerating the paydown of your home. Imagine compound interest, in reverse. The money you'll save will accumulate and accelerate, thereby helping you to pay off your home on a fast-track schedule!

3. LEAP™ is better than a savings account! Putting your savings and any extra income into your LEAP™, or home "bank" account makes sense and "cents" because it will save you MORE money than you will earn in interest. And, don't forget that you will have to pay taxes on that interest!

By placing this money into your LEAP™ (home "bank" account), instead of into your savings or checking account, you can be confident that your money will be working much more aggressively in repaying your loan, and that it will always be readily available if a financial emergency crops up.   If you make additional principal payments on a conventional 30-year fixed-rate loan (the "old-fashioned" way), you can't borrow that money – the money is gone. You'll have no access to that money unless you refinance again, which can cost you thousands of dollars in refinancing fees! In essence, what you worked so hard to save will be eaten up by these fees.

This is the number one question that I'm asked: "I'm making extra payments every month or two, whenever I have extra cash. I'm going to pay off my home years sooner. Isn't' what I'm doing the same as LEAP™?" I want to make it clear that yes, you will pay off your home years sooner if you make additional principal payments. If you never think you'll need the extra money you've been putting into your home to build equity, then this is fine. But statistics show that you will refinance your home in five to seven years. Will you have built up enough equity in that short period of time to make a difference? How much will you pay in fees just to refinance? And, remember, when you refinance, you'll start the cycle all over again. But even if you've owned your home for just a short period of time, you'll still build equity much faster using LEAP™.

The banking and lending industry wants to get you into a perpetual trap so they can make money off you every time you come to them for a loan. This ensures that they'll be in business forever. They need "tenants" to fill their coffers. That's right, we're nothing more than glorified tenants until we pay off our homes free and clear! I've worked for the big banks and have become privy to their true agendas. I've worked in their back offices and discovered that they only have one goal, and that's to be profitable! If there's a system out there that would allow people to pay off their homes in just an average of seven to ten years and wipe out all debt, the banks would lose a tremendous amount of revenue. I'm writing this book because I want to help consumers get out of debt for good. And of all the loan products I've seen in my 25 years as a mortgage professional, nothing has ever come close to LEAP™!

I am convinced that LEAP™ will revolutionize the way consumers look at home loans.

I'm sure by the time this book is published, there will be others who will try to copy LEAP™, and that's fine. I want as many Americans as possible to pay off their homes and own them free and clear! Just be careful if someone approaches you and wants to refinance your loan so you can pay it off faster. I wouldn't walk away from them – I'd run! If someone tries to sell me something expensive – and touts it as an advanced or premium program, I run the other way double-time!

Once you're finished reading the book, you'll have all that you need to implement the LEAP™ system yourself. This system is simple and works and there's nothing fancy about it! That's the bottom line.

However, I did develop software to help make this easier for the consumer to track progress and forecast payoff. The online software is not a necessity, but my students and clients find it extremely useful and easy to work with. (More on the software a little later in Chapter Nine.)

Note: You are in full control now. You are your own bank.

4. With this program you'll experience virtually no change in your lifestyle.

5. With LEAP™ you are not increasing current mortgage payments or making extra "out of pocket" payments.

6. With a traditional 30-year fixed loan, your mortgage payments will not change, but the way you pay them will. However, with the LEAP™ system, your monthly mortgage payments will actually decrease over time. (More on this in Chapter Seven.)

The following pages provide a few examples of how LEAP™ can work for you:

The Smiths are paying 6% interest on their $250,000 30-year fixed principal and interest (P&I) loan. Their income is $3,600 a month with $600 remaining after expenses. They applied the LEAP™ system and took out a $10,000 HELOC at 10% and opened a checking account at the same bank, and applied the principles of LEAP™. Look at their results on the following page:

SMITH LOAN PAY OFF

Loan Type	Loan Value	Years	Months	Total Interest Paid
P & I Loan	$250,000	30	0	$269,030.74
HELOC	$10,000	January 2022		$4,715.17
LEAP™	$ 250,000	14	10	$119,539.85

Total Time Saved: 14 years 9 months
Total Interest Saved: $144,775.72

The Smiths will have their house paid off in half the normal time it takes to pay off a 30-year fixed loan! They'll save almost $150,000 over the life of the loan!

The Camrens are paying 7% interest on their $300,000 30 year fixed P&I loan. Their income is $6,000 a month with $500 remaining after expenses. They took out a $10,000 HELOC and began making regular lump sum payments of $5,000 using their HELOC, using LEAP™ principles. This was the result:

CAMREN LOAN PAY OFF

Loan Type	Loan Value	Years	Months	Total Interest Paid
P & I Loan	$300,000	30	0	$405.464.10
HELOC	$10,000	January 2022		$2,136.93
LEAP™	$300,000	9	1	$105,388.84

Total Time Saved: 20 years 4 months
Total Interest Saved: $297,938.33

The Camrens will have their entire house paid off in less than 10 years!

Even if you think you don't have a lot of money left over at the end of the month, LEAP™ still goes to work for you.

Take a look at the Ryans. They are paying 8% interest on their $150,000 30-year fixed P&I. Their income is $4,000 a month with $300 remaining after expenses. They took out a $10,000 HELOC and began to apply the LEAP™ principles they learned. This was the result:

RYAN LOAN PAY OFF				
Loan Type	Loan Value	Years	Months	Total Interest Paid
P & I Loan	$150,000	30	0	$202.721.45
HELOC	$10,000	January	2022	$2,144.29
LEAP™	$150,000	6	11	$38,551.63

Total Time Saved: 22 years 6 months
Total Interest Saved: $162,025.53

That's amazing! The Ryans found that they can pay off their house in less than seven years. They won't have to change their lifestyle, get a second job or increase payments and will always have money available if they ever need it!!

How do you calculate when your loan will be paid off?

You do not need to be a financial genius. Simply enter in your financial data and our LEAP™ software will quickly and easily calculate the numbers for your individual situation. And if your situation changes or may potentially change, LEAP™ software will let you know the outcome of these changes. See Chapter Nine for more information the LEAP™ Software.

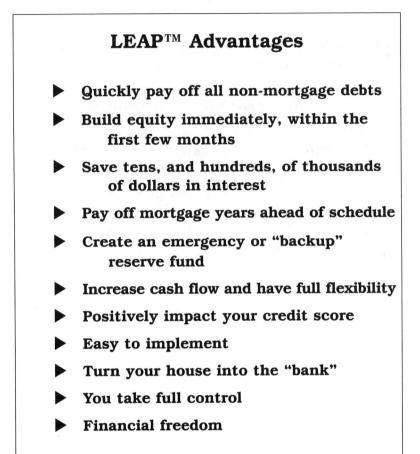

LEAP™ Advantages

▶ **Quickly pay off all non-mortgage debts**

▶ **Build equity immediately, within the first few months**

▶ **Save tens, and hundreds, of thousands of dollars in interest**

▶ **Pay off mortgage years ahead of schedule**

▶ **Create an emergency or "backup" reserve fund**

▶ **Increase cash flow and have full flexibility**

▶ **Positively impact your credit score**

▶ **Easy to implement**

▶ **Turn your house into the "bank"**

▶ **You take full control**

▶ **Financial freedom**

Keep in mind, if you have less discretionary income per month, or something happens and you need to use your discretionary income for other purposes, the LEAP™ program will allow you to do so.

The beauty of the LEAP™ program is that it adjusts to you and your lifestyle, and to changes in your financial situation. You can include other debts (for example, car loans, student loans, credit cards, etc.) into LEAP™ progam and pay them off sooner as well.

Chapter Three

Why LEAP™ Is So Important
(Pitfalls to Avoid)

There are many common mistakes people make when it comes to buying and paying off their homes. All of these errors make the LEAP™ process even more valuable. So before we get into the details of exactly how LEAP™ works, we want to point out some of the many pitfalls that await you:

1. Be Aware When House Shopping...

Did you realize there were an estimated 1.3 million foreclosures in 2006? That is DOUBLE what it was in 2004 and the 2007 figures were even worse than 2006. According to RealtyTrac™, foreclosures in January 2007 were up 25% from January 2006 and up 19% from the previous month. This trend is expected to continue into 2008, and who knows what will happen after that?

In October 2006, the U.S. Foreclosure Market Report showed that nationwide foreclosures surpassed the

$1,000,000 mark, increasing 42% from October 2005.

Why are foreclosure rates rising so dramatically? One major reason is that many homeowners are put at risk of foreclosure because of subtle, unethical practices commonly seen in the home loan industry.

Collusion between mortgage brokers and real estate agents is not legal, but it does happen. For example, a couple with pre-approved financing has a real estate agent show them various homes they can afford, but they don't like any of them. (You know the problem: "champagne taste...beer budget.")

The agent then shows them a house that is way beyond their budget – which they love, of course. The agent then suggests they see a certain mortgage broker who can work a deal with the higher price. They couple acquires an "exotic" mortgage (e.g., ARM, interest-only,

---

The U.S. Foreclosure Market Report shows a dramatic increase in nationwide foreclosure rates (34.79% nationwide average). For example:

California is up 64.49%

Rhode Island is up 2,450%

Missouri is up 96.1%

Alabana is up 715%

Minnesota is up 205.11%

CNN Money, January 17, 2007

> ## *Foreclosure rates are at all-time highs because people are not building equity.*

or pay-option-ARM) and the transaction is settled. Exotic mortgages were originally intended for financially astute, high-income borrowers. However in the frenzy of the housing boom, they have been mass-marketed to home buyers in high-cost, high-priced metropolitan markets.

While everyone seems happy in the beginning, the only true winners are the dealmakers who pocket the higher commissions from the sale of the house and the financing of the mortgage. In the long term, it is home-buyers who pay the price when certain clauses in the mortgage contract kick in that increase the payments beyond a level they can afford. At that point, the home-buyers either have to sell or undergo foreclosure.

Shouldn't prequalifying for a loan prevent this? As you know, many real estate agents ask you to prequalify before they help you search for a house. This is a good idea for a number of reasons, including and especially preventing you from falling in love with a house you simply cannot afford. It also forces you to review your finances to determine what you can comfortably afford. However, prequalification does not take into consideration the fact that you have two children you plan to send to college, or that your current vehicle is in need of replacement, or that you have been saving for years for a family vacation next summer. Neither does it figure in the fact that there is extensive water damage in your basement that your insurance does not cover, but which must be repaired before you can put your house on the market. Or that there was a big layoff at your company, leaving you (or your spouse) out of work for months. In short, prequalification is great but it does not consider the hundreds of things that come up on a regular basis and cost us our hard-earned dollars.

Unfortunately, the world banking system promotes debt. If you get into financial trouble, the bank offers you a solution like debt consolidation. This "allows" you to incur even more debt in order to pay back the money you already owe. The interest that many of us pay monthly and yearly is unbelievable. Someone else is getting rich off this interest while we are simply trying to pay back what we owe.

Sadly, this scenario plays out every day of the week all across the country. When you employ the services of a real estate agent, he or she is supposed to represent YOUR best interest first, ahead of is or she bottom line. Unfortunately, this is NOT the case in many instances. When house shopping, I was told repeatedly, "You qualify for a much better house than this. Why don't you let me show you something in your price range." I got a new agent, and another, and another, until I finally found one who WOULD show me houses in MY price range - the price I was comfortable with, not the price some bank (looking to make a lot of money) told them I could afford!

Be Careful of Exotic Mortgages

Negative Amortization / Option ARMS are still very popular these days because of the high rebates, or commissions, that banks and lenders pay to mortgage brokers as an incentive to sell these loans. Commissions can range as high as 3% to 4% of the loan amount! There are many variations of this innovative home financing product on the market. Creative wording changes perceptions:

Pay Option ARM	*Cash Flow Option ARM*
Flex 5 Home Loan	*Pick a Payment*
Option Power	*Op-Pay ARM*
Money Management Loan	

These are all basically negative amortization, adjustable rate mortgages. Example: Mortgage payments are lower and more appealing–they may be only $1,000 per month. Most of the time the payment cap is 7.5%. The rate goes up on your loan, and your new payment should be $1,200, but the cap keeps it at $1,075.00. The difference between the two is then added to your loan balance. Before you know it, the loan gets reevaluated, and you could end up paying $3,000 a month–a foreclosure waiting to happen. This type of loan also inhibits equity building. With this type of loan your principal balance can actually increase instead of decrease.

Rapid appreciation of properties allowed these loans to work for many, but today, appreciation rates are leveling off and may even be depreciating.

These loans work best in a rapidly appreciating real estate market. But when appreciation rates level off or during a housing decline or correction, these loans do NOT work well, unless you're using the LEAP™ system!

Another reason that mortgage foreclosures and personal bankruptcy filings have been steadily increasing, in recent years is the use of home-equity borrowing for purposes other than home improvement, such as debt consolidation. Despite the origination of greater numbers of debt consolidation loans, unsecured consumer debt continues to grow, indicating that credit card use is increasing.

Potentially troubling are the "125 LTV loans," junior mortgages in which the borrower is allowed an aggregate mortgage debt totaling as much as 125% of the market value of the mortgaged property. Although this junior debt can clearly benefit both the borrower and the lender, an increased reliance on credit should be recognized as a borrower behavior pattern that threatens to push up the rates of default and bankruptcy among a rapidly growing universe of overextended debtors.

Borrowers for whom mortgages were originated in 1994 and 1995 not only exhibit a greater use of credit, but also a higher delinquency rates on their unsecured credit accounts. Analyst Gordon Monsen predicted that servicers could expect higher loss levels from higher loan-to-value lending in the subprime market, a trend accelerated by aggressive home-equity lending programs of recent years.

Although such junior mortgages may be seen as a desperate measure for cash-strapped homeowners, they can provide benefits to both lender and borrower. The lender benefits through the generation of loan origination and servicing fees. The borrower typically refinances unsecured debt at significantly lower interest rates — 10% to 16% for home-equity loans vs. 18% to 21% for credit card debt.

Also, interest payments for the portion of the second mortgage that does not exceed the property value may be tax deductible. Nonetheless, the borrower is still robbing Peter to pay Paul.

Many Americans bought homes in recent years with the help of adjustable-rate mortgages (ARMs). But initial low monthly payments have skyrocketed because of interest rates have now soared, leaving borrowers struggling to pay back the loans. No doubt, ARMs are the cause of an average 38% rise per quarter in home foreclosures in 2006.

It's important to be careful of piggyback mortgages, two loans packaged together and closed simultaneously. Piggyback mortgages are one of many non-traditional mortgages that put homeowners at risk of losing their homes.

Designed for people who have little or no down payment, the amount of the first loan in a piggyback mortgage is set so it does not exceed 80% of the home's value. This allows the borrower to avoid paying Private Mortgage Insurance (PMI). The remaining loan amount is financed as a second mortgage by way of a Home Equity Loan or a HELOC and is "piggybacked" onto the first. The danger is that borrowers with adjustable rate piggybacks are not prepared for rate hikes that increase their payments.

An analysis of nearly 640,000 piggyback first-lien mortgages in bond pools by Standard & Poor's, an influential Wall Street ratings agency, discovered that first-lien mortgages connected to piggyback loans were 43% more likely to go into default than stand alone first mortgages of comparable size. The default rate increased a whopping 50% for borrowers with a FICO credit score of 660 or less.

According to SMR Research, lenders and mortgage brokers whose commissions are based on loan size have aggressively promoted piggyback mortgages because the first-lien portion tends to be larger than standard first mortgages.

What makes piggyback mortgages even more dangerous is a declining property market. If borrowers go into default in a declining property market, they can end up committing financial suicide by destroying their credit while still being burdened with debt, even after losing their homes.

A 2005 SMR Research study confirmed that many of the largest U.S. counties (in population and mortgage market size) have a huge percentage of home loans in the form of piggyback mortgages, in some instances up to 62%. These counties can be found in California, Washington, Colorado, Virginia, Arizona, Nevada, Oregon, Illinois, Georgia, Massachusetts, North Carolina, Utah, Florida, Texas and Missouri.

2. Unethical or Untrained Loan Officers

Did you know that 90% of states have NO formal training or examination requirements for loan officers?

They are NOT even required to learn about or explain to prospective borrowers the advantages and disadvantages of the many different types of mortgages now available.

Due to these lax standards, we now have 49.5% of homeowners who have taken on risky, exotic mortgages (e.g., ARMs, Interest-Only, Piggybacks, and Pay-Option-ARMs), with millions experiencing tremendous financial and emotional distress. As a result, they are being forced to sell their homes prematurely or default on their mortgages, sending their properties into foreclosure.

It is also a fact that almost 48.2% of all mortgage money originated in the first half of 2005 was through piggyback loans (80/20, 80/10/10, or 80/15/5). A recent study by Standard & Poor's found that borrowers with these types of loans have a 43% higher probability of defaulting on their mortgages compared to those with a comparable sized "standard" mortgage.

Furthermore, by the end of 2007, millions of more people with ARMs will each waste thousands of dollars in refinancing fees, when more than $1.3 trillion worth of these loans come up for readjustment. Unfortunately, these figures won't improve anytime soon - projections from 2008 to 2011 look just as grim. If you fall into this category and you look for advice from the same unqualified, untrained and unknowledgeable loan officer who neglected to give you proper guidance in the first place, you, too, will be doomed to fail.

This sorry state of affairs exists because the loan officers that set up these mortgages were NOT required to undergo any type of formal training or licensing and, as a result, are completely FREE to be INCOMPETENT and/or UNETHICAL.

They may not know about the long-term ramifications of the types of mortgages they recommended to their clients. Or they may have withheld crucial information so their clients were unable to make informed decisions.

It's important to realize that many loan officers will only sell a loan product based on the paycheck they'll receive. For example, option ARMs recently became very popular because they allow monthly payment flexibility. You can pay the 30-year or 15-year amortized payments; you can pay the interest-only payments; or you can make the minimum payment (much like you would with a credit card). Loan officers are usually great at pointing out the advantages of the four payment options. What they may fail to point out is that if you make minimum-only payments, you'll be going backwards on your principal. So instead of building equity, you'll be losing equity. Why would they leave out such an important piece of information? It could be because of the high commissions the lenders pay on these types of loans. Some lenders have paid 3% to 4% commissions

Make sure your loan officer has been trained by an accredited institution approved by a state certified bureau and department of consumer affairs that he or she understands ethics in the borrower's best interest.

on the value of a loan to brokers bringing these deals to them! Why sell a 30-year fixed loan or a 10-year interest-only loan when you can make double the commission on an Option-ARM?

Homeowners in this country should not have to resign themselves to being exploited. This is just WRONG!! We should require that those advising us about the single-most expensive financial decision of our lives be formally trained and certified, as they are in all other important professions. The only way we can receive this protection is to force legislators, at the federal level, to pass laws requiring the implementation of formal training and examination requirements for loan officers.

3. Refinancing . . . Disadvantages

Mortgage refinancing is popular, and some people do it as often as every two years. But take a good look at the current real estate market and some of the products available before you decide whether or not this is your best option.

There are significant costs involved in refinancing (including closing costs, points, origination fees, title fees, and appraisal and inspection fees). It can add up fast ($5,000 to even $15,000 in areas like California that have higher real estate values). Many times lenders will tell you they can add these costs to the loan, but it is unwise to be unaware of how much you are adding to your loan to finance these charges.

You should also consider other potential disadvantages before refinancing. For example, if you cash out some of the equity in your home, you will then "own" less of your home. And it will take you longer to own your home free and clear than it would if you had not refinanced.

In regard to equity, refinancing is like taking three steps backward. In the beginning stages of paying off a loan, you are primarily paying interest with very little going to principal (equity). If you refinance after three to five years, you'll go back to paying almost all interest again, again with very little going to principal. Some people refinance every three to five years, and after 15 to 20 years, they have hardly any equity built up.

Time is also a factor when considering refinancing costs. How long will it take for your new interest savings to pay off the property appraisal, title insurance, and other costs? You may have to live in the house longer than you planned to make the refinance worthwhile. If you move before you have recouped the refinance costs, you will lose money on the deal.

To calculate how long it will take to amortize these costs before you "break even" on your present mortgage, begin by adding up all refinancing costs. You may want to include the time you would spend locating necessary documents, calling lenders, and completing the application process. Next, call a few lenders to find out the current interest rates and what you would save in interest by taking out a new loan.

For example, let's say you have a $200,000 30-year fixed loan with 6% interest, with current monthly pay-

ments at $1,199.10. You've been making your pay-
ments for three years and you've paid down the principal $7,831.86. This means you've built $7,831.86 in
equity during these first three years, bringing your
mortgage balance down to $192,168.14. You want to
refinance to pull out some money (say, $15,000) to fix
up your home and take that long-awaited summer vacation. Here's what your refinancing costs would look like:

Fees	Amount
Origination (2%)	$4,300.00
Appraisal	$350.00
Credit report	$10.00
Tax related service	$80.00
Processing	$500.00
Wire transfer	$50.00
Lender	$1,000.00
Closing or escrow	$200.00
Document preparation	$100.00
Notary	$100.00
Title insurance	$450.00
Recording	$50.00
Total Fees	**$7,190.00**

To pull out this $15,000, you're very likely to pay
such fees. This is assuming that interest rates have
remained constant and you're still able to qualify for the
6% rate. What if you didn't have $7,190 handy to pay
these fees? That's easy! You would just wrap these fees
into the loan, thereby increasing your loan balance by

another $7,190. This is what most brokers and lenders would say: "Oh! Don't worry about it. You have enough equity in your home. Just wrap it into the loan and you won't even notice it." With a $200,000 30-year amortized loan at 6%, you've barely paid down the principal by $7,831.86!!! So it will take you roughly three years just to pay off the refinancing fees associated with this loan. That's not to mention the increase in your monthly payments. Now that your loan amount is at $214,358.14 ($192,168.14 + $15,000.00 + $7,190.00), your new monthly payments after refinancing will be at $1,285.18! Not only have you increased your monthly payments, you've also reset the amortization schedule back to 30 years, and most of the payments in the first few years will be interest.

The $7,831.00 in equity you built up was wiped away by the refinancing fees. Plus, your monthly payments went up almost $100! Double whammy!

Let's use the same example, but this time let's say you had the $7,190 to pay the bank or lender to close this deal. That's $7,190 of your hard-earned money gone! Just like that, you hand over all this cash to them! Your loan amount is $207,168.14 ($192,168.14 + $15,000) and your monthly payments are now $1,242.07. You just paid out $7,190 in order to get $15,000, netting you only $7,810.00! And you started the 30-year cycle all over again, with higher monthly payments! When did this model ever make sense? Either way, the banks and lenders are the only ones making out here. Whether you roll your fees into the loan or pay off the fees outright, you're doing nothing more than filling up their pockets!

This is why I became fed up with the system and decided there had to be a better way! We're just part of a cycle of buying our own debt while making the banks and lenders rich. The system is set up to make sure that we are perpetually indebted to them. There is no light at the end of the tunnel once you fall into this trap. LEAP™, however, will change all that! LEAP™ will revolutionize the way we look at loans in America! Our goal is to educate the American public about LEAP™ and its benefits so we can break out of this debt cycle once and for all. It doesn't need to be this way! You're just a few pages from discovering the miracle of LEAP™!

As you can see, refinancing can be a costly proposition. Refinance only if it absolutely makes financial sense! Do the calculations and don't forget to factor in the amount of time you're planning to own the property. If you're in a short-term fixed ARM, get out of it now and refinance into a longer term fixed, interest-only loan (such as the 10-year interest-only) before rates become adjustable. Watch out for those prepayment penalties: this is another way banks and lenders force you to stay with their loan for a fixed number of years. If you try to finance inside of this penalty period, the fees can be extremely hefty.

GOAL #1: Build Equity

Whether you plan to stay in your home for 2, 10 or 20 years, your goal should be to build equity as quickly as possible.

The main disadvantage of refinancing is that you are back to square one with your loan amortization. This means your payment will primarily go to interest and you will build very little equity in your home. There is a way around this, but don't worry!

Chapter Four

Ways to Pay Off Your Mortgage Sooner

I hope by now you understand the importance of paying off your home years sooner, and not falling into the trap of "getting the biggest mortgage you can afford" mentality. The interest you save is money that you keep for yourself, instead of giving it to the banks or lenders.

Remember that most of the payment in the first few years is applied towards interest, so you're really not making any progress on building equity. This means that if you refinance a couple of times, you could still owe 70%-90% of your original loan amount 15 years into the loan!

Let's go over the ways you can pay off your home years sooner.

1. Making Additional Principal Payments

This is probably the most common way people build equity in their homes, by making extra deposits toward their principal whenever they're able to free up extra income. Maybe you have an extra $100 or $200 left over every month or two, or you've received an unexpected IRS check for $500 or $1,000. You figure it's going toward your home and that it's safe there, so why not pay off the loan sooner? What harm could there be? Well, not much if you won't be needing that money for a long time, or if you're willing and able to spare it. But there are disadvantages to making additional principal payments. First of all, you may not have the extra cash sitting around to put into your home. Second, if you do but you need to take it back for any reason, you'll need to refinance. Remember that your first mortgage is a closed-ended loan, meaning that you cannot make withdrawals on the equity the way you can with a checking, savings or line of credit account. If an emergency arises and you need cash in a hurry for medical bills or whatever, you'll have to go through the process of refinancing all over again. You'll have to get all of your documents in order, and then pay all the fees associated with getting a loan. And then you'll start the mortgage clock all over again! Yes, this way will help you shave some time off the term of your mortgage. But this is probably the worst way to do it.

2. Biweekly Mortgage Payments

The biweekly system is pretty popular these days. Instead of making one full payment every month, you'll split that payment in half and make 26 payments throughout the year. In essence, what you'll be doing is adding an extra (13th) payment to your annual payments! In the case of the $200,000 loan at 6% interest, amortized over 30 years, you'll pay out of pocket an extra $46 every two weeks and pay off your mortgage in 24 1/2 years instead of 30 years, shaving off over five years. In addition, you'll save $49,624 in interest payments. Not bad, but remember you'll have to cough up an extra payment every year. And, if you want to recover what any of the equity you will have built up, you'll need to refinance. All of the costs of refinancing can easily "eat up" this equity.

Biweekly Examples:

30-Year Amortized Loan at 6% Interest

Loan Amount	$200K	$300K	$400,K	$500K
Monthly Payment	$1,199.10	$1,798.65	$2,398.20	$2,997.75
Biweekly Payment	$599.55	$899.33	$1,199.10	$1,498.88
Interest Paid	$182,052	$273,079	$364,105	$455,131
Time Savings	5 1/2 years	5 1/2 years	5 1/2 years	5 1/2 years
Interest Savings	**$49,624**	**$74,436**	**$99,248**	**$124,060**

Note: The biweekly plan is something you can do on your own. There are companies out there that "service" the biweekly plan for you at a "reasonable" fee. Do not fall for this! They charge you a fee to do all the "work" for you, when you can do it yourself. You're doing nothing more than making one extra monthly payment at the end of the year. So instead of making one payment at the end of the year, you're making two.

3. Loan Equity Advantage Program (LEAP™)

The many advantages of the LEAP system make this the best choice for accelerating loan payoff. There are no out-of-pocket expenses and no need to make extra payments. You won't have to change your current way of life. You'll build equity at a much faster pace than with the previous two methods. You won't need to refinance to access the equity you've built up and you'll have open access to these funds at any time! Best of all, with the right type of first loan, you will lower your monthly payments!

LEAP™ Example:

Let's take the same $200,000 30-Year fixed amortized loan at 6% interest. The homeowner applies the LEAP™ principle. With a salary of $4,400 a month (paid bi-weekly), and total monthly living expenses (including mortgage) at $3,400, he will pay off his home in exactly 10 years! He'll shave off a total of 20 years and save $165,254.46 in interest payments!

Comparison of Principal Remaining

Year	30-Year Fixed	Biweekly	LEAP™
1	$197,543.98	$196,264.34	$184,323.91
2	$194,936.47	$192,298.76	$167,571.27
3	$192,168.14	$188,089.12	$149,884.19
4	$189,229.06	$183,620.40	$137,639.69
5	$186,108.71	$178,876.64	$117,839.87
6	$182,795.91	$173,840.93	$96,886.00
7	$179,278.77	$168,495.29	$74,706.58
8	$175,544.71	$162,820.65	$51,259.33
9	$171,580.34	$156,796.76	$32,931.88
10	$167,371.45	$150,402.13	$6,640.78
15	$142,097.69	$112,018.17	$0.00
20	$108,007.17	$60,276.19	$0.00
25	$62,024.17	$0.00	$0.00
30	$0.00	$0.00	$0.00

Take a look at the differences between the three systems! The chart on the following page gives you a better visual.

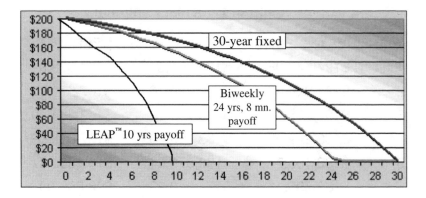

There's just no comparison! Nothing out there compares to LEAP™! Are you ready to learn just exactly how LEAP™ works?

LEAP™ actually reduces your payments AND builds your equity at a much faster rate than a traditional 30-year fixed morgage does. LEAP™ reduces your monthly payment because it is computed on the basis of your average daily balance of your home account, or HELOC.

Chapter Five

Using LEAP™...
To Save You Thousands!!!

LEAP™ (Loan Equity Advantage Program) can save you thousands of dollars on your mortgage and, perhaps just as important, can buy you time when you are in a financial crunch.

LEAP™ is based on using a revolving Home Equity Line of Credit (HELOC) which is tied to your checking account to make regular, lump-sum payments to your first mortgage balance. Basically, you're borrowing money from your HELOC to pay off your first loan. But, by using the LEAP™ system and effectively turning your house into a "bank," you will drive down the balance of the HELOC, thereby reducing your exposure to its interest payments. All of your paychecks will be deposited into your home account, or HELOC, via your checking account. This drives down the balance of the HELOC. And all of your bills will be paid out of your HELOC, via a checking account tied to the HELOC. Take a look at what this looks like on the next page:

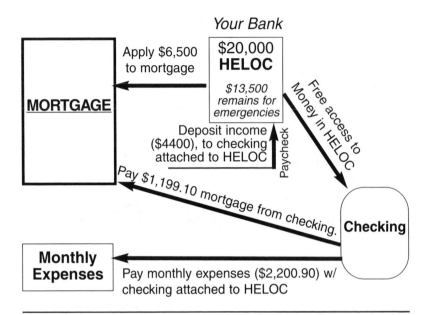

Here's an example of the numbers at work for month one:

1st Mortgage Balance, $200,000 30 -Year Fixed @ 6%	
Opening Loan Balance	$200,000.00
Principal From Mortgage Payment	-$199.10
LEAP™ Deposit from HELOC	-$6,500.00
New Balance	**$193,300.90**

HELOC Balance ($20,000 Credit Line)	
Opening Balance	$0.00
Withdraw to Deposit into 1st Mortgage	$6,500.00
Salary Income Deposited	-$4,400.00
Mortgage Payment	$1,199.10
Other Total Expenses	$2,200.90
New Balance	**$5,500.00**
HELOC interest (10% interest only)	**$46.71**

There are two accounts we need to look at. The first is the main mortgage account.

You will continue making monthly mortgage payments of $1,199.10. Notice the mortgage balance for Month One is only reduced by $199.10. Next, you put LEAP™ into action and open a HELOC and tie it to your checking account. You withdraw $6,500 from your HELOC via the checking account and make a lump sum payment to your main mortgage account. This drives the mortgage balance down $6,500!

But wait! You just incurred a new balance on the HELOC side at $6,500! This is OK. Remember that now you're the bank and in full control of your funds. Instead of depositing your paycheck into a checking or savings account and letting the money sit idle until you pay your bills, you deposit your paycheck into your HELOC account. Now your money is working for you! Notice how at the end of the first month, after depositing your paychecks and paying all of your bills, you have $1,000 left over and this keeps the balance at $5,500. All things remaining constant, the next month, your balance will be decreased by another $1,000.

Because the HELOC uses the average daily balance, your exposure to interest is barely noticeable. The bank calculates the daily amount and averages it out over the

1st Mortgage Balance, $200,000 30 -Year Fixed @ 6%	
Loan Balance 2nd Month	$193,300.90
Principal From Mortgage Payment	-$200.10
LEAP™ Deposit from HELOC	$0.00
New Balance	**$193,100.80**

HELOC Balance ($20,000 Credit Line)	
Opening Balance	$5546.71
Withdraw to Deposit into 1st Mortgage	$0.00
Salary Income Deposited	-$4,400.00
Mortgage Payment	$1,199.10
Other Total Expenses	$2,200.90
New Balance	**$4,546.71**
HELOC interest (10% interest only)	**$34.88**

full month, and this is the amount you're charged. At this rate, you would pay off this $6,500 in six short months and have paid a total of only $96.88 in interest. Wow! Can you imagine driving down the principal mortgage balance by $6,500 for just $96.88 spread out over six months? And this cycle basically repeats itself until the mortgage is paid off. In this example, the payoff is just eight years and one month! You would save $178,395.38 in interest over the life of the loan!

At first glance, this might not seem to make much economic sense. How can the HELOC, which charges a higher interest rate of 10%, work so effectively to pay off the mortgage? The reason is that you're only exposing a small portion of the HELOC to the higher interest rate. Also, the daily average balance doesn't remain at the full $6,500 throughout the month, since you're depositing your paycheck into the account and holding off on paying bills until the last possible moment. This keeps your average daily balance extremely low. And by keeping your average daily balance low, you're exposing even less to be charged interest at the end of each month.

Note: In the example above, notice that you only pay interest on the balance you withdraw from the HELOC. In this case, you withdrew $6,500 to pay down the main mortgage balance by the same amount. Now you have a $6,500 balance on the HELOC. But because the HELOC's interest is calculated on the daily average of the balance, your goal is to drive down this balance as much as possible for as long as possible. Always pay your bills online so that they leave your HELOC account on the last possible day, without risking a late payment. Also, always keep money in your HELOC as long as possible to drive this balance down. By doing this every month, you'll see a "snowball effect" in the decline of your main mortgage balance. And before you know it, you'll own your house free and clear!

Caution: Setting up your HELOC may have some additional costs. Make sure the HELOC you apply for has NO fees if possible! LEAP™ will still be effective, but those fees will mean more unnecessary out-of-pocket expenses.

See Appendix 1: Suggested HELOC Criteria Before Getting your HELOC!

Of course, you must exercise some control over your spending. For example, just because a $20,000 line of credit is available to you at any time, that doesn't mean you can spend it on unnecessary purchases. Remember that you're only charged interest on the amount you withdraw. So if you constantly max out your credit line, you'll be defeating the purpose of LEAP™. You could also be in trouble when you're ready to sell your home, as most banks require that you pay off your credit line at that time. Your home is now your bank. Don't clean out your bank unless you really need it for emergencies (medical expenses, etc.) or you're certain you can quickly replace it.

Although LEAP™ is not meant for those with reckless spending habits, the system will still work for you if you are living from paycheck to paycheck. And even though you may not be able to pay off your home in seven-10 years, you'll still be able to build equity a lot faster than if you didn't use LEAP™. In our original example, if you made $1,000 less or had an extra $1,000 in expenses, you would have no money left over at the end of the first month. But since you would be depositing all of your paychecks into your "bank," you'd be driving down the daily balance. By saving on the interest, you're actually earning money. You would save $29,684.23 over the life of the loan and in just 31 months, even when living paycheck to paycheck!

If your situation changed and you were able to generate a positive cash flow, your payoff would be accelerated to a much faster pace, saving you thousands of dollars more!

We hope you realize by now that your home cannot be a positive investment unless you build equity in it. Without equity, your home is just another debt that's hurting you, not helping you. You're doing nothing more than making rent payments to your landlord, the banks and lenders. Sure, you can wait for the property to appreciate in value to gain your equity, but why let the real estate market dictate when and how much equity you acquire? Why not take matters into your own hands so that you'll gain equity with or without market appreciation? Start using the LEAP™ program immediately so you can build the equity you need to make your home a truly profitable investment!

Take a look at the following graphs, which use various mortgages to compare the equity-building power of the LEAP™ program compared to a 30-year fixed mortgage. With LEAP™ you are literally LEAPING your way to owning your home! (instead of crawling)

Can you see how awesome this program is? Just look at how fast you can build equity, especially compared to conventional loans!

The LEAP™ Software makes this entire process easy, so you won't have to worry about any math or calculations. It takes the guesswork out of your lump sum mortgage payments and calculates the time it will take to pay off your loan quickly! Just enter your loan scenario, income and expenses, and the software will do all the work for you.

It will even tell you when to make these lump sum payments from your HELOC to your mortgage for maximum payoff time and maximum interest savings! This is the KEY! How will you know how much to inject without the LEAP™ Software? If you inject $5,000 versus $5,500, depending on the specific circumstances, you could save an additional 2 years on your way to becoming completely debt free!

The differences can be dramatic. Sure, you can do all the calculations manually on your own; after all, it's just math. But the software puts everything on "autopilot," making life much easier for you. The LEAP™

Software tells you when to make your injections and how much they should be. It can also help you forecast changes in spending habits so you can make wise and informed decisions.

You'll be much more efficient with the software and save even more money. More on LEAP™ Software in Chapter Nine.

Equity Built in 5 years on $100,000 Mortgage
LEAP vs. 30 year fixed at 6.5%

Mortgage payment: $632.07
$2,500 monthly household salary / $1,000 expenses

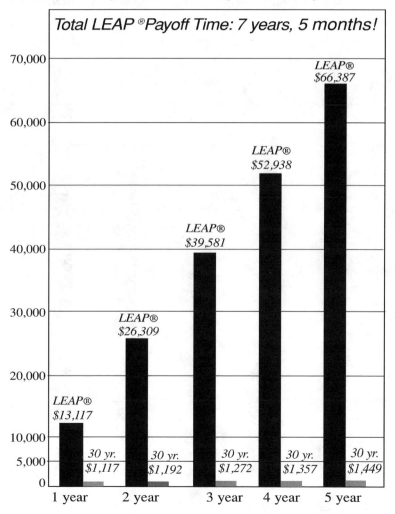

Total LEAP ®Payoff Time: 7 years, 5 months!

LEAP®
$66,387

LEAP®
$52,938

LEAP®
$39,581

LEAP®
$26,309

LEAP®
$13,117

30 yr.
$1,117

30 yr.
$1,192

30 yr.
$1,272

30 yr.
$1,357

30 yr.
$1,449

| 1 year | 2 year | 3 year | 4 year | 5 year |

Equity Built in 5 years on $200,000 Mortgage
LEAP vs. 30 year fixed at 6.5%
Mortgage payment: $1,264.14
$3,500 monthly household salary / $1,200 expenses

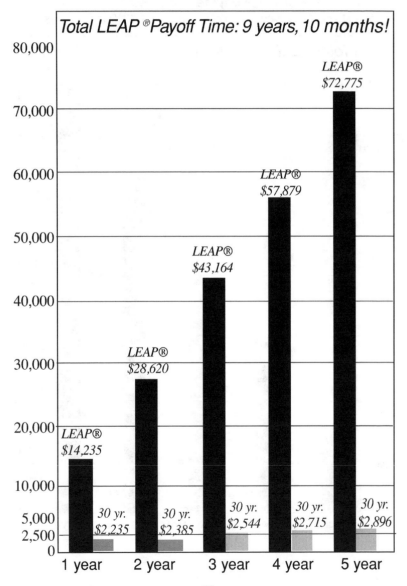

Total LEAP ®Payoff Time: 9 years, 10 months!

LEAP® $72,775

LEAP® $57,879

LEAP® $43,164

LEAP® $28,620

LEAP® $14,235

30 yr. $2,235

30 yr. $2,385

30 yr. $2,544

30 yr. $2,715

30 yr. $2,896

| 1 year | 2 year | 3 year | 4 year | 5 year |

Equity Built in 5 years on $300,000 Mortgage
LEAP vs. 30 year fixed at 6.5%
Mortgage payment: $1,896.00
$4,000 monthly household salary / $1,200 expenses

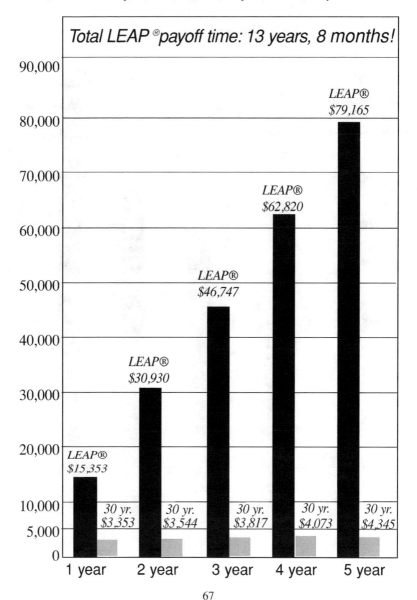

Equity Built in 5 years on $500,000 Mortgage
LEAP vs. 30 year fixed at 6.5%
Mortgage payment: $3,160.34
$7,000 monthly household salary / $2,500 expenses

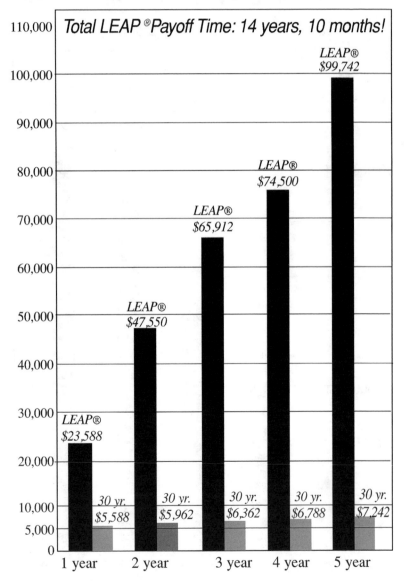

Total LEAP ®Payoff Time: 14 years, 10 months!

Got Money in Savings?

You're only making 3%-5% interest
account, which you are being taxed on. So how does one
get ahead? Why not inject that money into your
HELOC? This way it is still available at any time if you
ever do need it-but meanwhile, your money will be
working harder for you.

The interest you save on your house will far out-
weigh any interest you would earn on that savings
account. (You are taxed on interest earned, not interest
saved.)

Obtain a larger HELOC and inject that additional
amount (from your savings) into your house to bring the
principal balance down even faster.

Example: You have $5,000 in a savings account
earning 5% annual interest. You roll this every year
until the end of the 10th year and earn a total of
$2,121.44 after paying 28% taxes each year on interest
income. Now you take that same $5,000 from your sav-
ings and inject it into the mortgage principal. Using the

Secret LEAP™ Tax Savings Tip:

*You can also use the LEAP™ system to pay off all
your non-mortgage related debt: Credit cards, car
loan, student loan, etc. The interest you pay on these
other debts is not tax-deductible. When you apply
LEAP™, all these interest payments will now be 100%
tax deductible.*

_00,000 30-year fixed scenario described earlier, where the payoff was 10 years with savings of $165,282.80, your new payoff will be nine years and four months. You just shaved off an additional eight months, plus an additional $5,624.25 over these 10 years!!! Would you rather leave your money in the savings account and earn $2,121.44 or save $7,745.69 by utilizing LEAP™? Money saved is the same as money earned! Can you use that extra $5,624?

Read on to learn how to implement LEAP™.

LEAP™ Vs. Bank Savings	
Interest Saved (LEAP™)	$7,745.69
Interest Earned (Bank Savings)	$2,121.44
Net Savings/Earnings (LEAP™)	$5,624.25

Chapter Six

How To Save Thousands on Your Mortgage... and Own Your Own Home Years Sooner

A new way of handling a mortgage is emerging in the United States. It uses home equity borrowing and the borrower's paycheck to shorten the time it takes to pay off a mortgage, saving thousands in interest expense.

It's different than a biweekly mortgage loan, which shortens a mortgage by making an extra payment each year. This new way, which we refer to as the mortgage-accelerator loan program, is based on an approach commonly used in Australia and the United Kingdom, in which borrowers deposit their paychecks into an account that applies every unspent dime against the mortgage loan balance on a monthly basis.

The premise is that the borrower finances new property or refinances existing property by using a home equity line of credit, or HELOC. The borrower then regularly deposits his or her entire paycheck into a check-ing account that's tied to the HELOC. (Direct deposit is an excellent way to do this.)

All monthly expenses are funded by draws against the checking account, which can include a variety of methods such as writing checks, automatic bill paying, making ATM withdrawals or using a debit card tied to the HELOC.

As an example, let's say your monthly payment on a conventional fixed-rate mortgage is $2,000, and your monthly net income is $5,000. With LEAP™, even if you spend the $3,000 difference, your average mortgage bal-ance for the month will still be lower than that of a con-ventional mortgage. That's because the entire $5,000 will be deposited in the HELOC, or your own personal "bank," and you will only withdrew the $3,000 for expenses at the last possible moment. This will buy you a lower average daily balance, which reduces your expo-sure to the higher interest rate from a HELOC.

For the undisciplined spender, the LEAP™ system software can forecast when to make the additional prin-cipal payments from the HELOC automatically. That's the real advantage to this program. Unless you spend all the money by drawing against the line of credit, your paycheck will go toward paying off your mortgage.

Another advantage of LEAP™ is that it gives the homeowner additional flexibility, because a line of cred-it makes it easy to access cash, if it's needed in case of emergency. In contrast, if you were to make additional principal payments on a conventional 30-year fixed-rate loan, you could not borrow that money without taking out a HELOC or home equity loan (which doesn't happen overnight). With LEAP™ you already have the line of credit in place. This can give you confidence in your ability to be aggressive in repaying the loan, knowing that money will still be readily available if a financial emergency crops up.

LEAP™ incorporates interest-only minimum payments during the first 10 years, although that goes against the idea of paying off your mortgage as fast as you can. The HELOC decreases each month over the remaining loan term (20 years x 12) forcing principal repayment until the loan is paid off at the end of the loan.

The savvy part, being able to save the mortgage interest rate on idle cash instead of the low rates paid on checking and savings accounts, attracts customers that take a big-picture view of their finances. Money that isn't going toward expenses is reducing the balance on the HELOC, and thereby reducing the interest expense.

Before You Begin! Before you can decide if this plan will work for you, you'll need to calculate your monthly expenses, including mortgages, car payments, groceries, utilities, clothing, insurance, entertainment and travel. With LEAP™ you will use your credit card to pay for all of these expenses, which will free up your cash flow until the credit card bill is due.

But in order for this plan to work effectively, you'll need to have a positive cash flow. This means that your income is greater than your expenses. While you may occasionally have a month when several big bills are due at once or there is some sort of emergency expense, on average you must have a positive cash flow in order for the program to work at maximum efficiency. The size of your cash flow will largely determine the numbers you work with and how quickly you'll be able to pay down your mortgage. Obviously, if you have $150 left over at the end of the month, the program will take longer to work than if you have $1,500 left over. (More on this later.)

If you have a large amount of debt, don't give up on the LEAP™ program, as the principles outlined here will help you get out of debt. Then you can start working on your mortgage and building up your equity. You can use the HELOC to pay off your credit cards, car loans and student loans. And, as a bonus, you'll be able to write off the interest from your HELOC payments on your next tax return!

Important note: If you do have credit card bills or other high-interest debt, we recommend using the LEAP™ program to pay off these debts before tackling your mortgage. It's best to get out from under these bills as quickly as possible because they eat up your income. This will allow you to focus solely on paying off your mortgage.

Now, on to the LEAP™ program! We think you'll find it's easy to implement, and in the sections below, we'll show you how to do so in just five simple steps:

Evaluate Your Primary Mortgage, Set Up Your Home Equity Line of Credit (HELOC), Set Up Your Program, Select a Credit Card to Pay For Monthly Expenses, and Put LEAP™ into Action.

To get started, we have outlined the program in five simple points:

First Step:
Evaluate Your Primary Mortgage

Take a look at your current mortgage situation. If you're looking to refinance or purchase a home, make sure you find the right home loan for your individual circumstances. Ask yourself: What is your current and projected financial situation? How much of a down payment can you afford? What are the current interest rates? How long do you plan to stay in your new home? You should consider these factors, plus others, to help you find the right home loan for you. Failure to evaluate the financing for your home can have grave consequences that come back to haunt you later. For our recommended loan choice for LEAP™, read Chapter 7. But please be sure to read all material thoroughly leading up to Chapter 7.

How long will this be your address?

While no one can predict the future, you can probably make a good guess as to how long you'll stay in your new home. If you know your job will require a transfer in a few years or if you realize that you're part nomad, this should affect the type of home loan you choose. If, however, your job doesn't require that you move around and you are the type who likes to put down roots, a different type of home loan may be better for you.

If you think you may move again within 3 to 5 years, you'll want to consider current interest rates. If rates are low, you may want to opt for a short-term fixed rate mortgage (such as a 5 or 10-year fixed interest-only loan). It doesn't make sense to get a fixed loan, since you're not building much equity during the first 3 to 5 years, unless you're using LEAP™.

We highly recommend staying away from anything that requires a piggyback loan, or anything with negative amortization or Option ARMs. Unless you know exactly what to do with an Option ARM/Neg AM loan, stay away. Making the 1% minimum payments, especially in a negative real estate environment, can be a setup to future foreclosure.

It's okay to make those minimum payments only when you're in a temporary jam, not as a regular monthly habit.

Although you're only paying 1% (or less) interest rate on your monthly payments, the difference of this 1% and the interest-only portion of your payment (i.e. 6%) will be taken away from your equity. For example, let's say you have a $250,000 loan amount. Your minimum payment of 1% is $208.33. Your interest only percentage is 6%, or $1,250. The difference of $1,250 and $208.33 is $1,041.67. This $1,041.67 is added to your loan amount. So next month, your balance is $201,041.67. By the next month, you would have lost $2,506.25 in equity! You're going backwards on your loan in order to make those lower 1% payments. Before you know it, you'll be maxed out on your LTV and the bank will call you on it. Foreclosure! It's ok to make those minimum payment only when you're in a temporary jam, or when the market is hot, but not as a regular monthly habit.

There are now hybrid option ARMs (negative amortization) loans that will fix your minimum payments for 3 to 5 years. We prefer these hybrids over the traditional option ARMs that start out at 1% or less in many cases. If you are in an option ARM loan and can't refinance out of it, you definitely need to start LEAP™ as soon as possible. By using the LEAP™ system, the negative amortization portion of the loan will not be as dramatic.

Take at look at this chart which examines the difference between LEAP™ and no LEAP™ on a NEG AM

Months	Option ARM(Negative Amortization Loan 1%)		
	LEAP™	versus	**Without LEAP™**
	Loan Amount		Loan Amount
Month 1	$244,000.00		$250,000.00
Month 3	$246,516.28		$252,506.25
Month 6	$244,343.06		$256,312.81
Month 12	$246,200.91		$264,098.96
Month 24	$244,752.44		$280,388.00
Month 36	$250,484.25		$297,681.72

(Option ARM) loan if you only make minimum payments. LEAP™ will help you build equity much faster if you have an option ARM.

Notice the right column shows how it would look if you had a "NEG AM" loan and not using LEAP™. After one year, you would lose $64,098.96 in equity if you didn't use LEAP™. Now take a look at the left side and see what happens if you use LEAP™ while making monthly minimum payments on a "NEG AM" loan. After one year, you would have gained about $4,000 in equity. The difference between using LEAP™ and not using LEAP™ is $68,000!!! This truly shows you the power of LEAP™ in action! Again, we highly discourage making monthly minimum payments on an Option ARM loan. But if you have no other option, you should definitely use the LEAP™ principle to offset losses in equity.

If you know you won't be moving again anytime in the near future, a fixed rate mortgage may be the right loan for you. A 15-year or 30-year fixed rate mortgage can be the perfect fit if you plan to stay in your home for a longer period of time and you prefer the security of knowing what your interest rate and monthly payments will be each month. Ideally, you'll be able to lock in a good interest rate that will be guaranteed for the 15 or 30-year term of the mortgage. However, if you're looking to lower your monthly payments using LEAP™, an interest-only loan, such as the 10-year interest only, may be the way to go. (See Chapter Seven.)

Finding the right home loan also means evaluating options for your down payment. The 20% down payment is not necessarily the standard these days. Even with a market downturn, you may still be able to find a lender willing to take a 10% down payment. If you have an excellent credit rating, you may even qualify for a 0% down payment. Keep in mind, though, that having little or no equity in your home can be dangerous if home prices should fall, unless you're using LEAP™ to build equity.

FHA Loan

The government has established a program to help first-time homebuyers realize their dreams. An FHA (Federal Housing Administration) loan can help you buy a home with as little as 3% down.

Here are some key questions you should ask your lender or broker:

1. What types of mortgages do you offer?

2. What are the discount points and origination fees?

3. What are the closing costs?

4. What is the minimum required down payment?

5. Is there a prepayment penalty?

6. How long will it take to close and fund the loan?

7. What documentation will I need to provide?

These are just some of the many factors involved in finding the right home loan. Know your financial situation and fully understand all of your mortgage options so that you can get the right home loan for you. If you're unsure of your needs, or need a professional, ethical opinion on your loan situation, please call (800) 240-4514 or go to www.leapequity.com/loan and input your information. One of our trusted and preferred lenders will guide you in the right direction for your particular set of circumstances. These lenders are not only top-notch but extremely trustworthy. In order to become one of our trusted and preferred LEAP™ lenders, the loan officers in the firm need to go through our mortgage broker and training facilities and be LEAP™ certified. Our trusted and preferred lenders fully understand LEAP™ and how it relates to a borrower's needs. They also fully comprehend all the different types of loans currently available and can select those that will provide maximum benefit to the borrower. Remember: You don't need to refinance if you're in a good loan scenario already. You should only refinance if your current loan is unfavorable. Do not let unethical loan officers, mortgage brokers or lenders talk you into unnecessary refinancing. And make sure the broker or banker you seek fully understands the LEAP™ principles.

Second Step:
Set Up Your Home Equity Line of Credit (HELOC)

Once you've chosen the proper loan, you'll need to secure an open-ended line of credit. To reap the maximum benefits of LEAP™, you should set up a Home Equity Line of Credit (HELOC). If you already have a line of credit tied to the equity in your home (HELOC), you're ahead of the game!

If you have no equity in your home or you've maxed out your home equity (as a result of a piggyback loan), don't worry. The principles of the LEAP™ program still apply and you can use LEAP™ to pay this debt off. There is an alternative to using the HELOC as your primary source of line of credit that we'll discuss in this chapter.

For the HELOC, you will need to get an updated appraisal (this usually costs around $300 to $400, depending on the size of your home), as the banks will base your HELOC loan amount on this figure. Depending on the bank and how high your credit score is, you may get a loan-to-value (LTV) as high as 90%. This means you can borrow up to 90% of the equity in your home. For now, 100% LTV's are hard to come by, but if you're persistent, you may still find one at a bank in your area.

The good news is that there are no fees associated with the HELOC, other than the cost of an updated appraisal of your home and the paperwork is minimal (compared to the paperwork required for a primary mortgage). If anyone tries to charge you for setting up a HELOC, move on. You can even do it on your own. But if you don't feel comfortable with this, your local banker can help you out. Be sure to check Appendix I before you secure your HELOC.

If you don't qualify for a HELOC, you'll need to open up a personal line of credit (PLOC) with your local bank. Dozens of organizations offer credit lines to consumers, but try your own bank first. They know you and your history, and you will be able to negotiate better terms with them. If they won't cooperate, then go online. Some websites will allow you to apply for lines of credit from several lending institutions at once. Be aware that the criteria for personal lines of credit vary from bank to bank, and some lenders specialize in loans to people with less-than-perfect credit scores.

LEAP™ works equally well with a personal line of credit (PLOC). A key difference is you will not be able to deduct the interest fees generated from a PLOC that you would in a HELOC. Unless you live in Texas, you should convert your PLOC into a HELOC once you've built enough equity in your property to apply for a HELOC. In short, nothing is better than the HELOC, but if you don't qualify for one initially, a PLOC is the next best choice and will perform equally well.

If you have an extremely low credit score and you're not able to qualify for a HELOC or a PLOC, you will need to start working on building your credit as soon as possible! See more about increasing your credit score starting in Chapter 12. If you have a tough time getting any credit at all, there are banks that are willing to give credit cards regardless of credit history. Check www.insidercreditcards.com for the latest offers. Once you build your credit profile and can qualify for a line of credit, you'll be on your way to becoming debt-free in just a few short years.

If you need additional information on other topics such as getting rid of your bill collectors, settling your credit card debt for pennies on the dollar, avoiding bankrupcty or foreclosure, you can get additional information at www.insiderdebtsecrets.com.

Note: *For Texas homeowners, the only option you have with LEAP™ is a personal line of credit. Texas law prohibits homeowners from making payments from a HELOC into their primary mortgage.*

VERY IMPORTANT LEAP™ TIPS

▶   Look for a HELOC that includes an attached free checking account and free overdraft protection for your checking.

▶ Obtain the largest HELOC possible, based on your appraisal value. Getting a large HELOC does not mean you're charged interest on the entire amount. You only pay interest on the amount you withdraw. By getting the largest amount you qualify for, you'll receive a much lower interest rate. Example: Rates for a $10,000 HELOC may start at around 9.49%. A $50,000 HELOC may start at around 7.99%. A $100,000 HELOC could start at about 7.875%. You get penalized 1.5%+ with a smaller HELOC.

▶ Never expose your entire home value to the HELOC. This is a risky proposition as HELOC rates are usually adjustable. You may run into special promotions where the rates are fixed for a certain period of time, but they will adjust once the promotional period is over. Nobody can predict future interest rates. It's better to play it safe and never use a HELOC as your primary loan. It has come to our attention that there are other companies trying to sell HELOC's as the primary mortgage. Steer clear of such companies.

▶   Only max out the HELOC amount in case of an emergency. Even though the money is readily available and tempting at times, remember why you're doing this in the first place. Once your home is paid off and you have so much extra cash sitting around because you're debt free, you will be able to do anything you want!

Third Step:
Setting Up Your Program

Depending on your credit history, you may qualify for a line of credit that is large or small. If you're unable to secure much credit, that's not a big deal. The results produced by LEAP™ will be the same, whether you have a credit line of $10,000 or $100,000. You just need to use it wisely.

Note: The following is an overall view of the strategy. As you read further, we will go into greater detail, allowing you to understand the cycling theory better.

Let's say you've secured a line of credit with a $10,000 limit, and that your income is $3,600 per month. To utilize the LEAP™ principles, you will use $6,000 of your credit line to pay toward your mortgage, and leave $4,000 in reserve to pay off unexpected expenses or for emergencies. This is a major advantage over traditional pre-payment plans. The reserve money in your line of credit supplies a buffer in case of financial emergencies. No other early pay-off programs allow for this. If you were to assign all of your monthly surplus money directly to your mortgage principal, you would be without money to handle financial emergencies.

But you must be careful. Don't use your reserve unless you really have to! It is important you never use your reserve for impulse purchases. In fact, it's best if you never use this reserve money at all. You don't NEED a home theater system or a speedboat. You NEED to get your mortgage paid off early and THEN you can play with all your extra money! Don't let yourself be tempted.

It will only delay the process and cost you more money.

If you must dip into your reserves, you can always use the LEAP™ Online Software to calculate the impact of using your reserves. For example, if you need to take out $5,000 for an emergency, you can plug in the numbers in the expense section and the software will automatically recalculate the payoff of your home, and all other numbers affected by this change. (More on LEAP™ Online Software in Chapter 9.)

When searching for a HELOC line of credit, look for a bank that charges no fees and offers online banking to pay your bills and transfer funds via a checking account attached to the HELOC. See our recommended criteria in Appendix I.

The checking account is an extremely important part of LEAP™. For maximum efficiency, the checking account should reside at the same bank as your HELOC.

You may also be able to qualify for discounts when you have multiple accounts at the same bank. For example, the bank may lower interest rates by .25% if your accounts have a combined net worth of $25,000 or more. This is easy to achieve if you have a first mortgage or a HELOC plus a checking account at the same bank. The bank may then waive all applicable checking, transfer and overdraft protection fees. Make sure the checking account has overdraft protection tied directly to your HELOC. Then, when you write checks, money will automatically be pulled from your HELOC to pay your bills. You must also arrange for your paychecks to be automatically deposited into your checking account, and then you must transfer the funds to your HELOC online. Direct deposit saves you time and interest by getting the money into your account faster. The goal is to keep your checking account empty, and your HELOC as full as possible. Your HELOC is now your personal bank. You want "your bank" to contain the largest possible amount of money, just like a major banking institution wants it's own banks to have as much as possible!

Once you've set up the credit line, choose one credit card that you will use to pay your monthly bills and expenses. (This process will be explained in detail later). And be aware that you must pay off this card in full every month. Don't leave even one dollar on the card or this strategy will not be as effective.

Remember, if you have many different debts, you'll need to pay off those with the highest interest rates before beginning to use the LEAP™ program. This will save you time and money, as this program is designed not only to help you become mortgage-free, but also debt-free!

If you have existing credit card debts, student loans and car loans, zero in on the one with the highest debt and apply the LEAP™ principle to each debt, in turn, until they're all paid off. It won't be long until you're completely free of these personal debts and can start tackling the big mortgage debt. You can use the LEAP™ software to project payoff of your personal debts as well.

LEAP™ Tips on Paying Off Non-mortgage Debts:

LEAP™ is equally effective in paying off non-mortgage related debts. Let's say you have $10,000 in student loans, $5,000 in credit card debt, and a $15,000 auto loan. You apply the LEAP™ principle and follow the steps needed to set everything up. And you wrap this $30,000 debt into the HELOC. Now the interest on your $30,000 debt is completely tax deductible! Although this debt will be gone relatively quickly, while you're in the process of eliminating these debts, you'll be able to write off the interest charged. This only holds true if you're using HELOC as your primary open-ended line of credit.

The LEAP™ Online software will automatically calculate the payoff of these non-mortgage debts as well!

Even if you're not able to get a large line of credit – let's say you only qualify for $10,000 or less, you can still make small injections to pay off these other debts.

Note: The LEAP™ Online Software is an extremely useful tool that calculates exactly how much to inject and when, for optimum mortgage and debt payoff. However, it is not required in order for LEAP™ to work. In fact, you can still see great

results without using the software. The disadvanage
is that you'll be "blind" and won't know how much to
inject from your HELOC to your primary mortgage,
and when. And you won't be able to project when
your ultimate payoff date will be. By using the software, you'll know exactly how much to inject and
when, and when the payoff date will be for all your
debts. The software does all the work for you, and
takes just three to five minutes a month to maintain
after your initial setup. Also, anytime your financial
scenario changes, you can enter the updated information into the software and your numbers will be
automatically recalculated. The state-of-the-art
LEAP™ Online software is a highly recommended
tool, but is not a requirement of LEAP™.

To be debt free should be the goal of everyone.
Even the Bible gives us wise counsel to be debt free:

*Render therefore to all their dues: tribute to
whom tribute is due; custom to whom custom;
fear to whom fear; honor to whom honor. Owe
no man any thing, but to love one another: for
he that loveth another hath fulfilled the law.*
Romans 13:7-8

Fourth Step:
Select a Credit Card to Pay Monthly Expenses

Depending on your situation, you may want to use one of your existing credit cards to handle your monthly expenses or you may want to get a new card. If your current cards have high interest rates, put them away. Don't cancel the cards. Use a card (or get a new one) that has the highest credit limit and lowest interest rate you can possibly get. You need to have a high enough spending limit in order to pay all of your monthly expenses, with the exception of your mortgage payment.

No matter which card you use, it must have a zero balance when you start and you must pay off the balance in full every month. If you do not pay the entire balance, you will end up wasting your hard-earned money and this program will not work as effectively. Check www.insidercreditcards.com for best credit card offers and terms.

If you need to shop around for a new credit card, you'll need to consider several important questions before you apply.

Q: What is the interest rate and billing cycle? The billing cycle may not coincide exactly with the time of the month that your bills are due or you send the payment to cycle your mortgage. If there is a mismatch, you could be charged interest. Draw up a time line of all monthly bill due dates and incorporate them into an efficient cycle.

Q: How is the interest calculated? Some credit cards will accrue interest based on your daily balance, which means that you may be charged interest just for using the card. Be sure to read the fine print CAREFULLY along with any new terms and conditions sent to you by the credit card company. Cash advances also charge interest based on your daily balance. Do not use a card that calculates the interest in this manner.

Q: Is there a grace period? The card should have at least a 25-day grace period and offer the lowest possible interest rate. Be aware that many credit card companies have great introductory offers, but watch out for the rates when this period ends! Again, read that fine print. When reading the fine print on one of my cards, I found that when the no-interest period ended, the interest was computed on the 6-month average balance instead of the actual balance. I had to call the credit card company to find out exactly what I needed to pay to avoid charges of over $100 in interest. There are so many scams out there!

Q: Any other tips for getting the right credit card? Avoid cards with annual fees. That's an extra expense you don't need! Some credit cards offer bonuses that allow you to acquire air miles or cash back, which can be a great incentive. Also, make sure you pick a reputable bank.

Calculate Monthly Expenses

The following is an example list you can put together to help determine your monthly expenses.

Association Fees _____ | _____

Auto Insurance _____ | _____

Auto Lease/Payment _____ | _____

Auto Maintenance _____ | _____

Auto Registration _____ | _____

Cable/Satellite _____ | _____

Cell Phone/Phone/Internet, etc. _____ | _____

Child Care _____ | _____

Clothing _____ | _____

Contributions _____ | _____

Dining Out _____ | _____

Dry Cleaning _____ | _____

Electricity/Utilities _____ | _____

Entertainment _____ | _____

Garbage _____ | _____

Gasoline _____ | _____

Gifts (Christmas, birthdays, etc.) _____ | _____

Groceries/Toiletries _____ | _____

Health Insurance _____ | _____

Misc. Household Expenses _____ | _____

Supplements _____ | _____

Travel _____ | _____

Taxes and Insurance (property) _____ | _____

Other _____ | _____

                              Total

Plus Mortgage _____ | _____

Fifth Step:
Putting LEAP™ into Action

The power of LEAP™ comes from the ability to apply large payments against the principal balance of your first mortgage. This reduces your principal which, in turn, reduces the calculated interest on your loan. When you reduce the interest in this manner, your equity rises quickly and easily. (This is something other mortgage accelerator programs cannot do.)

In the past, the LEAP™ Online software was a required step in setting up the LEAP™ program. It's no longer required, but is highly recommended. Since the LEAP™ principle is so powerful, it will work even without the software. However, you won't know the precise amount to inject into your primary mortgage for maximum payoff. And you won't know the exact date that you'll own your home free and clear and become completely debt free and financially independent. The software takes all of the guesswork and the difficult math calculations out of the process. And any time your financial situation changes, the software can easily recalculate these figures!

The LEAP™ Online software used to be one of the required steps of setting up LEAP™. It's something we don't require, but highly recommend. Since the LEAP™ principle is so powerful, it works even without the software. However, you won't know the precise amount to inject into your primary mortgage for maximum payoff. And you won't know the exact date you'll own you home free and clear and become completely debt free and financially independent. The software really takes out all the guesswork and the difficult math calculations and puts the LEAP™ system on auto-pilot month after month. And any time your financial scenario changes, the software will recalculate your individual circumstance at any given time!

LEAP™ Tip:

After you have set up your HELOC/LEAP™ account, consider taking advantage of some of the promotional credit card offers such as 0% interest for 12 to 15 months. You can use that credit to pay bills or pay off a higher interest card. Max out the card. It's interest free for 12 to 15 months.

Another favorite is the 5% cash back card with 0% interest for up to 12 months! Everyone should use these cash back cards to pay ALL expenses! Why should you have to pay for the monthly expenses? Why not get 5% cash back just for charging your expenses!

Make minimum monthly payments on the card. Before the promotional period ends, pay off the entire card balance with your HELOC—you have just borrowed money interest-free for 12 to 15 months.

Understand that your credit score may drop a few points once your credit card is over 50% of the credit line. But once you're fully operational with LEAP™, and don't need a loan in the near future, you should be fine. Just pay off the balance 90 days before you anticipate needing some type of loan and your score will go back up to its previous levels.

Visit <u>www.insidercreditcards.com</u> to apply for featured 5% cash back cards and the best 0% introductory offers to use to your advantage. For those with less than perfect scores, this site also features credit cards that will help you build your score back up. Tip: Do not apply for too many credit cards at one time. A few here and there is fine. But too many inquiries will lower your score over a 6-month time period.

Here is a Step-by-Step Guide to LEAP™:

1. Establish a Home Equity Line of Credit (HELOC) or a personal line of credit. (See Appendix 1 for HELOC characteristics needed.)

2. Open a checking account at the same bank as the HELOC. Tie the checking account to the HELOC with "no-fees" overdraft protection. Always leave your checking account balance at zero. Use online banking transfer features to transfer funds (such as your paycheck) from your checking account to your HELOC. When you make a payment from your checking account (i.e. when you write a check), the overdraft protection will kick in and pull the necessary money from your HELOC to cover the check. This procedure ensures that your money will be used to pay down your HELOC as soon as possible and for as long as possible, until you need the funds to cover a check.

3. Make your first payment to your primary mortgage account from your HELOC. The amount you pay will depend on your level of income and your total monthly expenses, including your loan payment. We generally recommend anywhere from $4,000 to

> **Note:** When making a payment from your HELOC to the main mortage loan via checking account you MUST write "principal ONLY" on the check.

$10,000, depending upon your individual circumstances.

The LEAP™ software is a valuable asset at this stage, as it helps you calculate the correct amount to infuse into your primary mortgage to maximize your mortgage payoff. You don't need to use the software, as LEAP™ will work perfectly well without it. However, unless you can build your own mathematical algorithms, it will be tough to forecast and calculate your optimal payment.

4. Keep at least 20% to 30% of your reserves in your HELOC in case of emergencies. If you're only able to qualify for a $10,000 HELOC, keep at least $3,000 available. If you have a $20,000 HELOC, you should be okay with $10,000 in reserve. This doesn't mean that if you have a $100,000 HELOC you should take out $70,000 and apply it to your mortgage! Rarely do you need to infuse more than $10,000 at any one time. Having that $100,000 HELOC will allow you to have the best interest rates possible (based on your credit rating) and provide emergency funds, should you need them. Regardless of the size of your HELOC, remember that the outcomes don't change.

5. Sign up for direct deposit through your employer so your paycheck will be automatically transferred into your checking account every payday. Once these funds are deposited into your checking account, go online and transfer them into your HELOC, especially before the weekend arrives. If you need to withdraw some spending cash, go to the bank or ATM as you normally would and use your checking account, not your HELOC. The overdraft protection will then kick in, if necessary. Remember that your income will offset your expenses, lowering the balance on your HELOC.

6. Pay off all of your monthly expenses with your credit card, using a card with 5% cash back and/or 0% introductory period of 12 months. (See LEAP tip in box on page 105.) Once you've paid off your bills, you will have a grace period (usually 25 to 28 days) before you must pay off your credit card, to avoid finance charges. Use online "billpay" to pre-schedule your credit card payment date so you won't be late. Schedule the payment to arrive one day before it's due, to give it a little cushion.

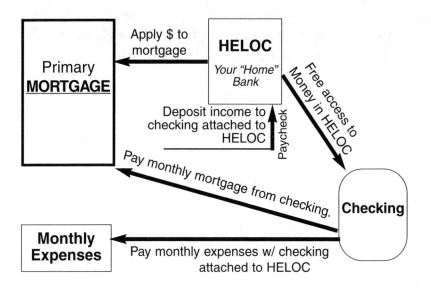

By doing this, you've just kept your money in your HELOC an extra 25 days or so. If you don't have a 0% interest card, be sure to pay your credit card balance off in full every month so you don't incur high interest charges. If you do have a 0% introductory period, pay all of your bills on this card and make only minimum payments.

Be sure to mark the date on your calendar when this introductory period ends, so you can pay off the entire amount before the high interest rates kick in. By doing this, you've just borrowed money from the credit card for free! Either way, you save extra money by using this credit card tip!

7. Be careful not to pay mortgages with your credit card. Some credit card companies view this as a cash advance and will charge you the exorbitant 24% or more. And there's NO grace period for cash advances! Some may classify this as a balance transfer and hit you with the balance transfer fee. Be sure you know all the rules and have read the credit card application's fine print.

8. Repeat this cycle every month. Once your HELOC balance nears zero, that's your cue to make another lump sum payment from the HELOC to the primary mortgage. Never allow your HELOC balance to reach zero or a negative amount. The HELOC must always carry a balance in order for your money to work for you.

Example: The Andersons

The Andersons, a family of five, recently purchased a home for $375,000, putting down 20% and paying the rest with a 30-year fixed mortgage at 7%. The monthly payment on the $300,000 loan is $1,995.90. Their monthly non-mortgage related bills equal another $2,500. Their net income is $5,800 a month. They found out about the LEAP™ program through some friends and knew this would be a perfect fit.

They put the LEAP™ program into action and opened a HELOC account through their local bank, receiving a $37,500 line of credit with a 9.5% interest-only rate. At the same bank on the same day, they opened a checking account and set up overdraft protection linked to their HELOC.

About a week later, the Andersons received a welcome package containing information about their HELOC, some checks and a debit card. They put the checks and debit card away, as they knew they would only be using the checking account to pay bills. The Andersons already had a few credit cards, but read about the value of a card with 5% cash-back and a 0% introductory rate for up to 12 months. They went online to www.insidercreditcards.com to find cards with these features, applied online and were accepted. Also, they signed up for the direct deposit program at work so paychecks would go directly into their checking account. Lastly, they went online and signed up for the LEAP™ Software and plugged in their information. The software forecasted their home would be completely paid off in 10 years and seven months, which would save them

$293,713.19! They were extremely excited. Now they were ready for LEAP™!

Here's how they put their plan into action:

1st Loan Balance, $300,000 30 -Yr Fixed @ 7%	
Opening Loan Balance	$300,000.00
Principal From Mortgage Payment	-$245.90
LEAP™ Deposit $6,300 from HELOC	-$6,300.00
New Balance	**$293,454.10**

HELOC Balance ($37,500 Credit Line)	
Opening Balance	$0.00
Withdraw to Deposit into 1st Mortgage	$6,300.00
Income	-$5,800.00
Mortgage Payment	$1,995.90
Other Total Expenses	$0.00
New Balance	$2,495.90
HELOC interest (9% interest only)	$20.14

Month 1

1. Paid $6,300 from checking account to primary mortgage.

2. Used their new credit card to pay all bills, except their mortgage, a total of $2,500.

3. Paid their mortgage online, $1,995.90.

4. Transferred their paychecks from checking to HELOC for the entire month, a total of $5,800.

Notice the "Other Total Expenses" on the HELOC side. Since the Andersons paid all of their bills using their credit card, they bought themselves time and more money! Also, notice that they borrowed $6,300 to pay down their first mortgage at the cost of only $20.14 in interest!

Month 2

1. Logged on to their LEAP™ account to check any updates.
2. Paid their mortgage from the checking account.
3. Paid last month's credit card bill.
4. Transferred income from the checking account to HELOC.
5. Paid new bills using credit card.

1st Loan Balance, $300,000 30 -Yr Fixed @ 7%	
Loan Balance 2nd Month	$293,454.10
Principal From Mortgage Payment	-$247.34
LEAP™ Deposit $7,500 from HELOC	$0.00
New Balance	**$293,206.76**

HELOC Balance ($37,500 Credit Line)	
Opening Balance	$2,495.90
Withdraw to Deposit into 1st Mortgage	$0.00
Salary Income Deposited	-$5,800.00
Mortgage Payment	$1,995.90
Other Total Expenses	$2,500.00
New Balance	$1,191.80
HELOC interest (9% interest only)	$8.83

Notice that their balance on their HELOC is only $1,191.80, and they incurred a mere $8.83 interest charge. And while the 1st loan balance is shrinking, the equity is growing!

During month 3, according to the LEAP™software, it was time to make another payment from HELOC to the primary mortgage loan.

If the Andersons continued following the LEAP™ program, here's what the results would look like compared to the traditional approach:

Traditional Primary Loan vs LEAP™		
Year	Primary Loan Balance WITHOUT LEAP™	Primary Loan Balance WITH LEAP™
1	$296,952.57	$277,601.98
2	$293,684.84	$259,848.62
3	$290,180.88	$234,321.98
4	$286,423.63	$213,515.81
5	$282,394.76	$184,639.77
10	$257,437.15	$28,937.98
11	$256,942.95	$0.00
15	$222,056.59	$0.00
20	$171,900.23	$0.00
25	$100,797.30	$0.00
30	$0.00	$0.00

As you can see, the Andersons would be able to pay off their home in 10 short years using LEAP™. If they didn't use LEAP™, after 10 years they'd still owe a hefty balance of over $250,000 -- 85% of their original loan value! Imagine only shaving off 15% of the original loan value after making monthly mortgage payments for over 10 years!

What if they wanted to take a summer vacation in the third year? They budgeted $10,000 for a two-week European vacation. How would this affect their mortgage payoff?

In this situation, their mortgage payoff would be 11 years and 1 month, instead of 10 years and seven months! And the actual cost of their trip would be $6,688.82, instead of $10,000! How can the actual cost be only $6,688.82? Because of the LEAP™ system! Remember, when you use LEAP™, you're the bank. You can borrow $10,000 or even more against your bank, or HELOC, at extremely low interest rates! How? By applying the LEAP™ principle and keeping the average daily balance of your HELOC extremely low!

What if the Andersons get a raise the year after their wonderful European vacation?

Let's say they receive a small raise of $200 net, per month. This changes their mortgage payoff situation. Now, they can own their home free and clear in 10 years and 5 months instead of 11 years and 1 month, saving a total of $295,694.13 over the life of the loan!

These are just a few examples of the many changes

You don't put money back into the HELOC, you leave it in the HELOC—this is the home account.

The HELOC allows homeowners to be their own bank—they borrow against their HELOC through their checking account, etc

---

that can occur over the life of a loan. The LEAP™ Software can help you forecast and accommodate any planned spending or any unexpected financial outcomes, good or bad. With the LEAP™ system, you will have full flexibility with your funds, won't have to worry about locking up all your emergency money in your home, and will never need to worry about refinancing and incurring costly fees again!

Important:

Since your HELOC account is your bank now, make sure all of your liquid assets are transferred to this account. You will ALWAYS earn more through your HELOC than you would through a traditional savings account. Your paychecks and other sources of income should always be deposited into this account. The key to maximizing the power of the LEAP™ system is keeping your average daily balance in the HELOC as low as possible. This way your money will work for you, instead of you working for your money. And the greater your cash flow, the faster you'll build equity and the sooner you'll own your home. But even if you don't generate positive cash flow right away, the LEAP™ program can be the jumpstart you've been waiting for to turn your financial life around! And the best part is that LEAP™ just keeps getting better and better!

HELOC Tips

▶ Be sure to refer to Appendix 1 as your guide to the type of HELOC you should open.

▶ Start out with the largest HELOC the bank is willing to give you. (You tend to get a lower interest rate on a larger HELOC, even though you won't be using the entire line.)

▶ Never expose (use up) the entire HELOC amount! You should always leave a reserve in case of emergencies and unexpected events when you may need cash in a hurry.

▶ Injections (payments) to your primary loan should be in small "chunks." We recommend anywhere from $4,000 to $10,000 at a time, depending on your individual circumstances. The LEAP™ Software will calculate the right payment amount for maximum pay-off and earnings. (For larger loan amounts or higher income earners, your injections may need to be greater than $10,000.)

▶ Increase your credit line as you start building more equity in your home. You should review your situation at the end of each year to determine whether to raise your HELOC limit. In the Anderson Family example, the HELOC should be around $40,000 by the second year and $80,000 by the fourth year. The more equity you build in your home, the higher your credit limit should be in your HELOC. This is simply to provide you with full flexibility and access to that equity at any given time, so that you won't have to refinance.

More LEAP™ Examples

The Roberts are paying 7% interest on their $150,000 P&I. Their income is $5,000 a month with $1,500 remaining after expenses (not including their monthly mortgage). They took out a $10,000 HELOC with a 9% interest rate, and began making regular lump-sum mortgage payments of $6,000 from their HELOC. Their regular P&I payment is $997.95. This was the result.

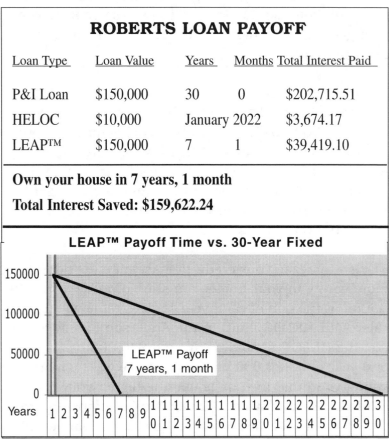

ROBERTS LOAN PAYOFF

Loan Type	Loan Value	Years	Months	Total Interest Paid
P&I Loan	$150,000	30	0	$202,715.51
HELOC	$10,000	January 2022		$3,674.17
LEAP™	$150,000	7	1	$39,419.10

Own your house in 7 years, 1 month

Total Interest Saved: $159,622.24

LEAP™ Payoff Time vs. 30-Year Fixed

LEAP™ Payoff
7 years, 1 month

The Johnsons are paying 6.5% interest on their $300,000 fixed loan. Their income is $5,500 a month with $2,703 remaining after expenses (not including their monthly mortgage). They took out a $10,000 HELOC with a 9% interest rate, and began making regular lump-sum mortgage payments of $6,000 from their HELOC. Their monthly payment is $1,896.20. This was the result.

JOHNSON LOAN PAYOFF

Loan Type	Loan Value	Years	Months	Total Interest Paid
P & I Loan	$300,000	30	0	$372,164.12
HELOC	$10,000	January 2022		$5,885.79
LEAP™	$300,000	9	1	$147,939.51

Own your house in: 9 years, 1 month

Total Interest Saved: $218,338.82

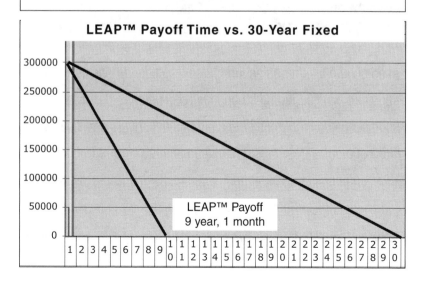

LEAP™ Payoff Time vs. 30-Year Fixed

LEAP™ Payoff
9 year, 1 month

Take a look at the next two charts. Compare the difference in savings between paying off your mortgage in seven years, 10 years and 15 years, over the life of a traditional 30-year fixed loan. The larger the loan amount, the more you save if you pay off your home sooner.

The larger the loan amount, the higher the discretionary monthly surplus that's needed in order to pay off your home sooner. But even if it took you 15 years to pay off your house, look at how much money you'd save!

What will you do with all of this extra money once you're completely debt free and you own your home free and clear?

Interest Saved Using LEAP™

Loan Amount	Paid in 7 Years	Paid in 10 Years	Paid in 15 Years
$100,000.00	$93,728.48	$84,337.88	$64,634.41
$200,000.00	$185,653.90	$166,199.27	$128,211.69
$300,000.00	$279,257.96	$248,075.75	$192,033.13
$400,000.00	$371,804.42	$329,932.00	$257,019.15
$500,000.00	$465,903.15	$413,164.78	$321,249.15

Based on 30-Year Amortized Loan at 6% Int. Rate

Interest Saved Using LEAP™

Loan Amount	Paid in 7 Years	Paid in 10 Years	Paid in 15 Years
$100,000.00	$113,213.88	$100,698.13	$79,258.40
$200,000.00	$225,995.24	$201,541.46	$155,636.15
$300,000.00	$337,229.00	$301,290.15	$233,436.08
$400,000.00	$449,879.33	$401,138.28	$310,353.32
$500,000.00	$563,042.73	$500,108.31	$387,921.57

Based on 30-Year Amortized Loan at 7% Int. Rate

Chapter Seven

How to Reduce Your Monthly Payments with LEAP™

Interest is calculated on the principal balance of your loan. With LEAP™, by making the injections from your HELOC, your principal balance will drop quickly. Therefore, you'll pay less in the long run.

If you have a 30-year fixed loan, your payments are unchanged for the life of the loan. With LEAP™, you'll be able to pay off your home years sooner by making regular injections from your HELOC into the first loan. The injections are applied toward principal at the back end of the loan. Even though your principal is being reduced every time you make these injections from your HELOC, your payments will remain the same.

With an interest-only loan, however, your interest payments are tied directly to your loan balance. Let's look at a 10-year fixed, interest-only loan with a 6.625% interest rate on $400,000. With LEAP™, as you make injections into your first loan, your balance decreases. Because the interest-only monthly payments are calculated from your principal balance, every time you make injections, your balance will decrease and so will your monthly payments!

See the chart below. Notice that as time goes by, the amount of your monthly payment continues to drop. Notice how it really starts to accelerate toward the end. Your equity is building at a rapid pace and your payments are decreasing!

Just take a look at how your mortgage payment amount drops using LEAP™! There's no other system that will allow you to lower your payments AND build equity so quickly, helping to pay off your home years ahead of schedule!

Principal Balance	Monthly Payment Due	Year of Loan
$400,000	$2,208	1 year
$376,000	$2,075	2 years
$358.000	$1,976	3 years
$334,000	$1,843	4 years
$316,000	$1,744	5 years
$292,000	$1,612	6 years
$268,000	$1,479	7 years
$238,000	$1,313	8 years
$214.000	$1,181	9 years
$178,000	$982	10 years
$148,000	$817	11 years
$112,000	$618	12 years
$70,000	$187	13 years
$34000	$419	14 years
Paid off in less	**than 14 years!**	**WOW!!!**

Here's an example of a 10-year fixed interest only loan with a 6.625% interest rate on $300,000. With LEAP™, as you make the $6,000 injections into your first loan, your balance decreases. Because the interest-only monthly payments are calculated from your principal balance, every time you make injections, your balance will decrease and your monthly payments will decrease. Using LEAP™, your loan will be paid off in less than 12 years!

Principal Balance	Monthly Payment Due	Year of Loan
$300,000	$1,656	1 year
$276,000	$1,523	2 years
$252.000	$1,391	3 years
$228,000	$1,258	4 years
$198,000	$1,093	5 years
$168,000	$927	6 years
$138,000	$761	7 years
$102,000	$563	8 years
$66.000	$364	9 years
$30,000	$165	10 years
$6,000	$33	11 years
Paid off in less	**than 12 years!**	**WOW!!!**

Here's a 10-year fixed, interest-only loan with a 6.625% interest rate on $200,000. Every time you make your $6,000 injections, your balance will decrease, your monthly payments will decrease and your loan will be paid off in less than nine years!

Principal Balance	Monthly Payment Due	Year of Loan
$200,000	$1,104	1 year
$176,000	$971	2 years
$152.000	$839	3 years
$134,000	$739	4 years
$110,000	$607	5 years
$80,000	$441	6 years
$56,000	$309	7 years
$26,000	$143	8 years
Paid off in less	**than 9 years!**	**AWESOME!**

Interest-only loans are great if you want to lower your monthly payments fast, while building equity at the same time. But how about a 30-year fixed payment loan? Your payoff time is the same, whether it's for a 30-year fixed or an interest-only type loan. If we look at the Anderson scenario from the previous chapter and change their loan to a 10-year fixed interest-only loan at 7%, they would still pay off their mortgage in 10 years and seven months!

So be wary of loan officers, mortgage brokers or bankers who try to tell you differently. These people are motivated by profit when selling you a loan. If possible,

try not to get a short-term loan, unless
be moving within that time period and y
a better rate. If you think you're going
home for a long period of time, try to get a 10 year interest-only fixed or a standard 30-year fixed loan. Then, if
you utilize the LEAP™ system, there's no reason why
you can't be mortgage free in seven to 10 years!

If you know you're going to stay in your home for 5
years or less, we recommend a 3 or 5-year interest-only
loan. You'll get great rates and maximum benefits of
lowering your monthly payments while building equity.
If you need to refinance, please look at interest-only
loans as your first option. No other loan allows you to
accelerate the payoff of your loan while reducing your
monthly payments at the same time!

Go to <u>www.leapequity.com/loan</u> and fill out a simple application and a LEAP™ specialist will assist you
with your loan needs.

Chapter Eight

LEAP™ Advantages:

▶ **No extra out-of-pocket mortgage payments.**

▶ **You always have "emergency" money if needed.**

▶ **You do not have to change your current lifestyle.**

▶ **You build equity at a much faster rate.**

▶ **You will pay off your mortgage (and OWN your home free and clear) very quickly!**

▶ **You may have a lower monthly payment as well, because your principal balance decreases rapidly.**

▶ **You can also use LEAP™ to pay off student loans, car loans, medical bills and credit cards. The interest you pay on the HELOC is all tax deductible, but the interest you pay on these others is not.**

▶ **Better than bi-weekly payments.**

Increasing your BANK ACCOUNT

One key advantage to the LEAP™ system is that you'll have emergency money available anytime you need it. You don't need to refinance in order to access that money. You can withdraw it from your own bank (your HELOC) via a check drawn on your checking account, an ATM, or a debit card (not recommended). If you're ever in a bind or you're unemployed, having access to this money will give you peace of mind until the problems have been solved. Or, if you ever want to go on that exotic vacation, the money will be readily available. Of course, this will alter your mortgage payoff. And that's where the LEAP™ Online Software can help. You can enter your new financial information and the software will recalculate your new projected payoff. Similarly, if you get a raise or a bonus, you can also input these numbers and the software will create new projections.

In order to expand your bank account (via your HELOC), it's important to increase your credit line every 12-15 months. As you start building equity in your home, you'll need to increase your HELOC amount. Let's say you started with a HELOC of $10,000, and you were able to knock down the principle from your primary mortgage by $10,000 the first year. You should then go to the bank that holds your HELOC and ask for an increase to $20,000. Remember that the bank will pull your credit report

again to determine your new rate, s[...]
maintain a high credit rating.

Go to www.insidermoneysecrets[...]
Credit Reports tab for best offers to [...]
ratings. Having a top notch credit rating will save
you lots of hassles and ensure that you get the best
rates and product offers from major banks and lending institutions.

So, continuing with our example, at the end of
year one your HELOC has a limit of $20,000. At the
end of the second year, let's say you gained an additional $20,000 in equity. You'd then go back to the
bank and ask to increase your HELOC to $40,000.
Repeat this cycle until your house is completely paid
off. This way, you'll always have access to cash,
without having to refinance. And you'll never need to
worry about foreclosure. LEAP™ will provide you
with the true financial independence you deserve.

Chapter Nine

The LEAP™ Software

Now that you know how easy it is to slash years off your mortgage and save tens of thousands of dollars in interest payments, you'll undoubtedly want to create your own personalized LEAP™ profile and apply the LEAP™ principles to your own financial situation. Remember, every day that you're not using LEAP™, you're losing money and adding years to your mortgage! The most important, time-saving and efficient way to utilize the LEAP™ program is through the LEAP™ software.

This software program is the most innovative and powerful mortgage reduction and personal financial management tool available nationwide. You can manipulate your finances to create any number of "what-if" scenarios in order to find one that will help you make the best financial decisions and avoid going into default. You can also pinpoint EXACTLY how much time and interest you will save when you use the LEAP™ program in a variety of scenarios.

Once you enter your information, LEAP™ Software will run an algorithm in the background and instantly provide a forecast of your loan scenario. You'll be able to see a month-by-month cash flow spreadsheet that tells you exactly how your financial situation will look in the future. You will find out when to make additional injections from your HELOC into your primary mortgage loan, and the exact amount these payments should be. Another section will provide a graph with the forecasted final payoff date, plus total interest paid and saved over the life of the loan.

LEAP™ Software takes all of the guesswork out of the loan payoff equation. You don't need to perform any calculations. Once you set up your account, maintenance takes just three to five minutes a month. This software will put your LEAP™ system to work on auto-pilot!

With LEAP™ Software, you'll get the maximum potential savings possible. You'll know exactly when to make the injection from your HELOC to your primary mortgage and how much to inject.

These are the keys to making LEAP™ work at the optimal level in your individual financial situation. Without LEAP™ Software, LEAP™ will still work. But wouldn't you rather pay off your home in seven years instead of eight or nine? Wouldn't you rather pay off your home in five years, instead of six? Without the software, you'll be operating blind. You can randomly pick a number of injections to make, but you won't know how many will produce the fastest payoff and maximum savings. Sure, you can probably work out the scenarios manually on an Excel spreadsheet. But why would you do all of that tedious work when the LEAP™ Software can do it for you? LEAP™ Software does the math, so you can concentrate on getting rid of your debts, including and especially your mortgage. And because it's web-based, you can use LEAP™ Software 24/7 from anywhere in the world, as long as you have a computer with Internet access. There is absolutely no excuse not to do this. There is no way you can lose.

If you did not receive a software disc with this book, you can order one by calling 800-503-1801 between the hours of 8:30am and 5:00pm Pacific Standard Time, Monday thru Friday.

1. LEAP™ Software shows you exactly how much time and interest you can save by creating a direct relationship between your income and expenses, and the effect these variables can have on the term of your home loan.

2. LEAP™ Software puts you in total control of your finances by giving you specific, measurable, achievable goals for your closing balances EVERY month. This crucial information will help you stay on track and pay off your home loan years earlier.

3. LEAP™ Software gives you the power to make informed decisions about allocating your hard-earned money in the most efficient way. You will be able to create any number of "what if" scenarios and see their effects on the term of your home loan. For example, you can see the financial ramifications on your home loan caused by taking a $10,000 vacation in June 2011, spending $25,000 to renovate your home in August 2009, increasing/decreasing your income and/or your expenses by $X per week/ month/ year, and more.

4. LEAP™ Software demonstrates the real "time value" of your money. It also helps you gauge when it's a good time to invest, because you'll know when you have built up enough home equity to do so safely and effectively.

5. LEAP™ Software is truly unique. MS Money, Quicken, Excel, and any number of other financial programs currently on the market DO NOT have features that can help you keep track of your mortgage and pay it off years sooner!

6. LEAP™ Software will help you PREPARE and PROTECT your home from an uncertain housing market as well as SAVE YOU more than $5,000 in refinancing costs in the years to come.

WARNING!

As is the casewith any successful product that has the potential to help mankind, there will be others who exploit and take advantage of the LEAP™ system. Other companies will try to copy the LEAP™ system and profit from it. Be wary of any company trying to sell you this at an outrageous price! We've spent countless hours working out the calculations and making it what it is today. If someone tells you they have something superior, don't fall for their fancy marketing pitches. At best, it will probably only have a higher price tag. We've made every effort to provide this at a reasonable price for everyone.

Skeptics may claim that making extra payments directly to your primary mortgage is just asgood as using LEAP™. We've seen resistance to our LEAP™ system from various mortgage brokers trying to protect their own interests. These same brokers can't stand it when we tell others that they don't need to refinance. Brokers make a living refinancing others' homes. The lending industry is designed to entice homeowners to refinance every five to seven years. LEAP™ puts an end to this.

Chapter Ten

Commonly Asked Questions About LEAP™:

Q: What is LEAP™?

A: LEAP™ stands for Loan Equity Advantage Program. It is designed to help you, the homeowner, build equity FAST so you can pay off your loan years sooner. This breakthrough system consolidates your checking and savings accounts and restructures your finances so that your money works hard for YOU! You'll have the ability to pay off your traditional 30-year mortgage in as little as one-third to one-half the time! There is NO NEED to refinance (assuming you currently have a good loan), and there's no need to make extra payments or lifestyle changes.

For a free evaluation of your current loan situation by a trusted and preferred LEAP™ certified professional, fill out and submit the form found at www.leapequity.com/loan.

Q: Why do I need to apply for a home equity line of credit?

A: The LEAP™ system uses the home equity line of credit (HELOC) or a personal line of credit as the main vehicle or tool to drive this system. A line of credit is an open-ended loan that allows free access to your money without refinancing.

Q: What makes the loan pay off sooner?

A: Direct-deposit of your income into the HELOC has an immediate and dramatic impact on your principal HELOC balance. (With this loan, interest is based on your daily balance, so when your paycheck is deposited, you'll start saving interest compared to a traditional loan.) This leaves more of your income available for paying down the principal on your home mortgage, accelerating the buildup of equity with no change to your spending habits. Naturally, the more positive cash flow you have, the more your loan paydown will accelerate.

Q: If I pay off early, will I lose my tax deduction?

A: Yes, and this is a good thing because you will no longer have a mortgage. We believe that "interest is not in your best interest." How does paying $4,000 in interest to get approximately $1,000 in tax deductions make for a good long-term strategy? LEAP™ can help you get rid of your mortgage faster. And, of course, while you're still paying down your balance, the interest you're paying IS deductible.

Q: Why is the interest rate slightly higher with a HELOC than with other loans, and what if rates go even higher?

A: Here is where we're changing the way mortgages are viewed. It's no longer about the interest rate. It's about how many dollars of interest you'll end up paying on a given principal balance. Your HELOC balance is continually forced down by your direct deposit, which in turn, lowers the amount of interest you must pay. This can even offset the effect of higher rates -- even if the current rates double!

Don't believe it if someone tells you that you "need" to get the biggest mortgage possible for the tax write-off. Ask them to show you just how your bottom line will benefit from this. They won't be able to do it.

Q: Who is the ideal customer for this program?

A: This program is ideally suited for the responsible homeowner who has a positive cash flow and understands that putting cash against the mortgage balance can earn a much higher effective return than if it lingers in a low-interest checking or savings account.

Q: How do I know how much I need to inject from my HELOC into my first mortgage?

A: Please refer to page 105. You can arbitrarily pick a number from the range as discussed on page 105 and you'll be able to see outstanding results! However, with the LEAP™ Software, you'll know precisely (to the penny) how much and when to inject payments from your HELOC to your primary mortgage. The software puts LEAP™ on auto-pilot so you won't need to perform any difficult math calculations. The software will also tell you the exact date of your payoff. Most of our customers find the LEAP™ Software to be an invaluable tool that they wish they had when they purchased their homes years ago. The returns on your minimal investment will be staggering! Nothing else compares!

Q: I have a bad credit score. Can I qualify for LEAP™?

A: Most banks require a 620 FICO score in order to obtain a HELOC. For example, Wells Fargo will pull your credit score from Experian in order to determine your eligibility as a borrower. Shop around your local banks to see what the credit score requirements are. Each bank has its own guidelines. If you cannot find a local bank, check online. Just make sure that you set up a checking account with the same bank that provides you with your HELOC. Again, check Appendix 1 for HELOC requirements in order to maximize the potential of LEAP™.

Q: Why can't I make extra principal payments to my primary mortgage and achieve the same results?

A: Simply put, the algorithms in the proprietary LEAP™ system are designed to create the highest interest savings possible in the least amount of time. The math engines programmed in the LEAP™ system calculate the specific timing and dollar amounts required to produce optimum savings. Also, if you simply make extra principal payments, you would no longer have access to that money. With a HELOC or personal equity line of credit, you will have access to this money at any time.

Q: If I am not increasing the monthly payments on my mortgage, how can it work?

A: The LEAP™ system makes a connection between your bank account, the HELOC and your primary mortgage. You are simply restructuring the way your money works for you. Each time you transfer income into your account, it registers as a decrease to your mortgage balance. This, in turn, lowers the amount on which interest accrues, decreasing the amount of interest you will pay. By decreasing the amount of interest you must pay, you will increase the portion of your monthly payment that is credited toward the principal. The LEAP™ system determines the specific timing and amounts required for each transfer to produce the quickest pay-off time and highest interest savings possible.

Q: Can I make extra lump-sum payments in addition to my payroll deposit?

A: Yes, anytime, and this can be beneficial. Moving funds from low-interest deposit accounts or poorly-performing assets into your HELOC will reduce your principal instantly, and save you even more interest, allowing you to pay off your mortgage even sooner. And, you will have access to the additional equity this creates through your HELOC.

Q: Should I put all of my available cash into the mortgage?

A: Putting "all of your eggs in one basket" is usually not a good idea. If your cash is earning less interest than you're paying in mortgage interest, it could be an excellent idea to move a portion of your cash into the mortgage. Instead of "earning" 3% to 5% on your deposits, for example, you'll be saving 7% to 10% on your mortgage via your home bank account, the HELOC. In effect, you'll get the same advantage the banks now enjoy with your money. Again, you'll have access to your available credit line if you do need it.

Q: Should I close my old checking and savings accounts?

A: No. But to maximize the effectiveness of the product, you will want to infuse as much of your cash into the HELOC account as possible. The more funds you place in the HELOC, the lower your average daily balance, and the more interest you'll save.

Q: Does it make sense to move my savings accounts over to my HELOC?

A: Yes. In moving your savings accounts into your HELOC account, you'll decrease the amount of time left to pay off your mortgage. Use the LEAP™ software to help you understand the effect that transferring the money from your savings account into your HELOC will have in decreasing the amount of time it will take to pay off your mortgage.

Q: Are my payments FDIC insured?

A: No. This is a line of credit mortgage, not a savings account, and therefore not FDIC insured. You are paying down your mortgage, not making a deposit in the traditional sense.

Years of traditional banking has trained us to think we need to have a "pile" of money somewhere to insure us against loss, when in reality the banks are loaning our money to others. We lose by simply handing our hard-earned money over to them.

Q: What is the risk involved?
A: From a financial standpoint, there is very little risk. No stock market crash or extreme interest fluctuation can alter the expected outcome dramatically.

Q: How do my house payments get paid? Do you make them for me?
A: No. We do not have any access to your accounts. You will be initiating all transactions. You are in complete control.

Q: Do you have access to or control of my money?
A: No. You are the only person with access to your accounts.

Q: Do I pay interest on the home equity line of credit?
A: There is interest charged on the HELOC, but because your income is deposited into this account at regular intervals, the bank will adjust the amount of interest they charge you by offsetting the average daily balance. As a result, the interest charged is minimal.

Q: What happens when I pay off the loan EARLY?
A: If you pay off your home loan early, you still have access to the accumulated equity, up to your credit line maximum, until your 30-year term is complete. If you continue to make deposits into the account and your loan

is paid in full, those deposits will earn interest at a competitive rate. If your home is paid off, imagine what you could do with all of the money you were paying on your mortgage. This is a great way to prevent foreclosures.

Q: What happens if my home loses value?
A: With any type of home mortgage you owe the amount you've borrowed, regardless of what happens to the value of your home. When a home devalues, some people can end up owing more than the house is worth. However, since LEAP™ allows you to pay down principal faster, you'll stand a better chance of avoiding being "underwater" on your loan than you would with a traditional loan.

Q: How do I find out how fast my loan should pay off?
A: Simply refer to your LEAP™ Software. It performs all the calculations for you.

Q: How do I access the home equity line of credit for expenses?
A: Just like you access your bank account. You have online access to view your account balances and transactions, and you can access funds via checks, debit card, ATM, EFT, ACH and bill-pay. For paying bills, we recommend using the main checking account set up with overdraft protection tied to the HELOC in order to pull the money from the HELOC.

Q: Is there a maximum amount I can draw from my HELOC account?

A: You can draw up to your credit line; the amount you have available is the difference between your principal HELOC balance and the credit limit

Q: Do I need to change my spending habits?

A: No, you do not. As long as you have positive cash flow, changing your spending habits will not be necessary. However, if you can find a way to trim expenses even more, you'll pay off your loan even earlier. Make it a goal to use the maximum amount only for emergencies, or when withdrawing for a short duration. Look at it this way: You're borrowing from your own bank. The effective interest rate you're paying on this money is extremely low, especially with the LEAP™ system working for you. But always be sure to use the LEAP™ Software to calculate how this will affect your financial situation before you act.

Q: Isn't access to all that equity a bit dangerous?

A: As with any of your finances, you need to be disciplined. You probably already get several credit card offers each week, and can easily open a HELOC to access your home's available equity. You can get into plenty of financial trouble through either option.

Q: Can I use this loan as a platform from which to make other outside investments?

A: Absolutely. Sophisticated investors will see it as an opportunity to "borrow" money from their available equity and "reinvest" it in an outside investment at a higher rate of return, netting the difference between the two.

Q: What happens if I move?

A: The HELOC that LEAP™ uses will have no effect on your ability to sell your home. Once you have sold your home and purchased another residence, you can put LEAP™ back into action on the new residence. In addition, the equity that you've built up in the account, as well as any equity built up through market appreciation, will make a great down payment on your next purchase!

Q: Can I use just one LEAP™ program for several investment properties at once, or do I need one for each property?

A: LEAP™ is most effective when used to pay off one property at a time. As each property is paid off, your overall discretionary income can increase, creating an accelerated payoff period for each subsequent property. Once the "snowball effect" kicks in, the acceleration intensifies.

Q: What portion of the interest I pay is tax deductible?

A: Since this is a mortgage and it represents the acquisition debt on your property, under IRS pub. 936, the interest you pay may be tax deductible.

Q: Do I have to refinance my existing mortgage loan to make this work?

A: No, but some first loan programs work better than others. You may choose to refinance your existing mortgage loan for additional interest savings, but refinancing is not required in order for LEAP™ to work.

Q: Will LEAP™ work with an interest-only or negative amortization payment on my primary mortgage?

A: Yes. In fact, LEAP™ helps you to take control of the outcome of these types of loans that will benefit you substantially.

Q: How does LEAP™ compare to interest-only or 30-year fixed loans?

A: With an interest-only loan, you're making no progress on building equity. With a 30-year fixed loan, you're building equity in an excruciatingly slow manner. For example, after 15 years of making monthly payments, you could still owe up to 90% of your original loan amount. There's one more loan we should mention. If you make the minimum payment option on Neg/Am or Option ARM loans, you're actually going backward on your loan and losing equity. LEAP™ minimizes the loss of equity for Neg/Am or Option ARM loans. For the 30-year fixed or interest-only loans, LEAP™ helps you pay off your home in just a few short years! There's no difference in payoff time and savings between the 30-year fixed and interest-only type loans. They both perform equally well when applying the LEAP™.

Q: Can I use this system to pay off current credit card bills, car loans, or other debt?

A: Absolutely. You can and you should. The interest you pay on these other debts is NOT tax deductible. Interest paid on homes is tax deductible! If you have other debts, this system should be used to clear other debts first, then work on the mortgage.

Q: Can I get a HELOC at any bank?

A: No. Not all mortgage companies and banks are designed to handle this type of loan. See Appendix 1 for HELOC requirements.

Chapter Eleven

Significance of Your Credit Score

If you're in the market for a new home, a refinance or a loan, and your credit score is marginal, your private mortgage insurance (PMI) rate might be hundreds of dollars higher per month than you expect.

Credit scores affect interest rates on all types of loans, but their effects reach far beyond loan rates, resulting in additional expenses that can run into thousands of dollars per year.

The sticker shock of a sky-high PMI payment is bad enough, but some borrowers don't find out that their PMI will add hundreds of dollars to their payments until they are sitting at the closing table.

Mortgage lenders require PMI on loans where borrowers are financing more than 80% of the price. Unlike other types of insurance, PMI is designed to protect the lender, not the person paying the premiums. There are ways to structure mortgage loans to avoid PMI, but because the effect of a poor credit score is so pervasive, the costs of alternative transactions can equal the cost of higher PMI.

If your credit score is in a range where you fall into a subprime category, you will pay a higher PMI rate. This is not just based on your credit score, but it is a basic principle of risk management. If your loan is deemed as risky in terms of your ability to repay, you will pay more in interest on the loan, PMI and in your closing costs.

Basically, your terms will be more restricted than a borrower with a higher credit score because the company that is lending the money needs a higher rate of return to compensate for the increased risk.

Most Americans have credit scores that fall between 600 and 800; the range of all FICO scores is 300 to 850. However, those with credit scores below 620 are frequently categorized as "subprime borrowers," meaning that creditors view them as more likely to default on loans. They get hit with higher interest rates and fees on virtually every loan, from mortgages to car loans to credit cards.

Other determining factors:

• Size of the down payment. Your PMI premium will be higher if you put down 5%, vs. putting down 15% (this is also known as the "loan-to-value ratio").

• Potential for property appreciation. Your premium may be higher if you live in a city with declining property values. PMI companies monitor real estate prices and economic trends that affect them as they set PMI rates.

• Type of loan. The rate can vary depending on whether you are getting an adjustable or fixed-rate mortgage, or an interest-only loan. The riskier the loan, the higher the PMI.

• Interest rate. A higher interest rate can, and usually does, mean a higher PMI rate because borrowers with poorer credit scores are frequently offered higher-interest loans that carry higher PMI payments.

• Borrower occupancy. If you are borrowing to purchase an investment or rental property, your premiums will be higher than if you borrow for a home you plan to occupy.

Types of PMI

There are two types of PMI: borrower-paid and lender-paid. Borrower-paid PMI is by far the most widely used, but PMI companies are touting lender-paid as an alternative to piggyback loans, which are popular with borrowers.

Here's a rundown of PMI options:

• Borrower-paid PMI. This is the traditional type of PMI. The loan premium is added to the mortgage payment and the mortgage company transmits the PMI payment to the insuring company.

• Lender-paid PMI. The payments are wrapped into the overall loan rate so you don't make a separate PMI payment. Instead, you pay a higher interest rate, and the lender pays a portion of your overall payment to the insuring company. The advantage of this type of PMI is that you can deduct the mortgage interest from your taxes. PMI isn't deductible. Some lenders will tell borrowers they aren't paying PMI with their loans, but they are—indirectly.

• Piggyback loan: Named because a second mortgage is "piggybacked" onto the original mortgage, a piggyback is a second mortgage that closes simultaneously with the first. There are variations, but a popular product is the 80-10-10 loan, where the consumer takes out an 80% first mortgage, thus avoiding PMI, a 10% second mortgage and pays 10% as the down payment.

Chapter Twelve

SECRETS to Miraculously Increasing Your Credit Score

• Are you in "bad-credit" hell?

• Do you wonder if you will ever be able to get credit again?

• Does paying higher interest to get loans make you angry?

• Have you had your car or house repossessed?

• Are you tired of the hassle (and embarrassment) bad credit brings?

• Are you ready to live the life you want?

• Do you need a miracle to get out of debt and to repair and raise your credit score?

OR...

Like many other American families, do you just

want to know how to increase your credit score?

If you are knee deep in debt, and the level of your financial difficulties shocks even you—just because you have poor credit report doesn't mean you won't be able to get credit again.

You are NOT ALONE—your situation is not hopeless. Have we got great, eye-opening news for you!

Read on . . .

Poor credit is nothing to be ashamed of because it is more common than most Americans realize. Often we wait too long before we react and try to solve the problem—and then we are in too deep. We are struggling and juggling the money we have, but without professional help we don't always do what will benefit us.

But before we announce the "good news," we will give you some credit report history and how valuable that 3-digit FICO number is to get car loans, mortgages, insurance and even jobs.

You need to understand how you got into this situation before you can learn how to get out of it.

How do individuals get into a credit crisis?

Here are some ways:

1. Job loss/long unemployment

2. Medical bills from major emergency

3. No savings or emergency fund

4. Business failure

5. Divorce

6. Identity theft

7. Spending more on entertainment/eating out than on rent

8. Poor money management/debt control

About Debt

Most people think of being in debt as irresponsible. There are thousands of different reasons for being in debt. It can happen to anyone and when it does, it's tough. The world today is designed around credit, credit cards, and loans, making it very difficult to go through life without credit cards or debt.

Many people experience the depression and anxiety of debt while trying to survive the daily stress of life. Debt can be controlled with a little discipline and help from the right people, but, surprisingly many people just never get good advice when it comes to getting rid of debt. Numerous people file for bankruptcy when their debt problems could have been solved in less than half the time a bankruptcy would stay on their record.

Do you know how you got to this uncomfortable place of bad-credit debt?

For many people, it is because they spend MORE than they MAKE. Soon you are not able to pay even minimum monthly payments. Once bad debt equals a poor credit report score, you can be denied a credit card, leasing/renting an apartment or—bigger still, a loan for your dream car or new family home.

You have to change your "want" thinking into what you actually "need." Making smart choices and decisions will help you pay down debt.

Financial stress affects every part of your life. A 2002 study by the Filene Research Institute (an organization that works with financial institutions and credit unions) found that as many as one-third of all employees are stressed by personal finance problems, and one-half of those individuals are so impaired that job performance is affected.

Can you relate?

Identity Theft

Before we tell you more, let's talk a little about identity theft. If you are a victim of identity theft, you must act quickly, perhaps even before the bad guys can use your information.

Identity theft happens when someone somehow gets your private information, like your Social Security number, date of birth, address, and phone number—and then uses them, without you knowing, to commit fraud or theft.

If you become a victim of identity theft, be sure to document every move you make in clearing your name. If someone opened a fraudulent account in your name, contact the creditor immediately and file a police report. If you place a "fraud alert" notice, you are entitled to a free copy of your credit report from each of the three bureaus (listed on page 146).

Much of identity theft today is done electronically. However, all of us need to watch our personal information and property, and to shred items such as charge receipts, checks, bank statements, expired credit cards. Also, don't carry your Social Security card on you.

Organizations/corporations are compromising our confidential data such as our Social Security number, which can be used to open accounts in our name.

The first sign of identify theft might be denial of credit or a call from a collections agency. Another clue is if you have not received a bill you expect. Maybe the thief has diverted it to a new address. You must immediately inform the creditor. Many states now have "security freeze" laws, which allow consumers to indefinitely prevent anyone from issuing credit in their name.

As recommended by the FTC, immediately:

1. Place a fraud alert on your credit report and review the credit reports.

2. Close the accounts that you know or believe have been affected.

3. File a report with your local police or the police where the theft occurred.

4. File a complaint with the FTC's Identify Theft Hotline, toll-free: 1-877-IDTHEFT (1-877-438-4338) or write Identity Theft Clearinghouse, Federal Trade Commission, 600 Pennsylvania Avenue, NW, Washington, DC 20580.

Be vigilant. Proving you are a victim of identity theft can be a time-consuming battle. The credit that gets ruined can be yours. Much is written about identity theft, so do research on the Internet and know your rights. But if it happens, it will be your credit and life that is turned upside down!

BOTTOM LINE:

A high credit score can save you money and a low credit score can cost you money
— Sometimes LOTS OF MONEY!

A Poor Credit Report Can Cost You a Job, Promotion and More!

You can be denied a job as all government agencies and some inter-related businesses check credit scores on potential employees and consultants. If you are up for a high-paying job, those companies often check your credit report. Also, bad credit can prevent you from starting that business you've always wanted.

About 35% of companies surveyed by the Society for Human Resource Management have pulled a credit report for current or potential employees last year, up from 19% in 1996. They add the credit report to the criminal check and identify verification. Employers use credit reports to verify employment history and Social Security number. Some also use it to decide whom to hire, fire or promote.

Credit reports are also checked if you are applying for a job that pays more than $750,000 or more than $150,000 worth of credit or life insurance.

• Case Example •

Sam had been working hard and looked forward to getting a better job. He saw the perfect job advertised, applied and was interviewed. He knew this company did "checks" on all prospective employees—especially those with direct access to cash—but he wasn't worried. He had never been fired, his resume was 100% factual, he had no criminal record and would get good references from his present employer. What he didn't know was that his FICO score was lower than their standards . . . and he was denied the position.

Was he a victim of identify theft, did he have delinquent accounts he was not aware of, or did he have something else on his credit report that caused the problem? If he had checked his FICO score regularly, he would have been able to correct the problem before this important job was offered to someone else.

The 3-Digit Score That Controls Your Life

The FICO score (so named from the software developed by Fair, Isaac and Co. that calculates the score) is one way lenders decide whether to give you credit. Credit scores do not show your age, gender, color, religion, marital status and employment history.

According to Fair, Isaac and Co., credit numbers fall into these categories.

- Under 620 - 20%
- 620-690 - 20%
- 690-745 - 20%
- 745-780 - 20%
- 780 plus - 20%

Lenders like credit scores of 700 and up (that is about half of all applicants). People with credit between 500 and 600 can get credit, but they pay for it with higher interest rates. Ultimately, specific lenders use their own guidelines, but the FICO score helps determine what kind of risk you are.

Fair, Isaac and Co. Estimates:

- 35% of your credit score is based on your loan payment history (On time? Bankruptcy, liens, wage garnishment, collection or delinquencies?)

• 30% is based on how much you owe (How much of a credit line is being used)

• 15% is based on the length of your credit history (How long open, activity of accounts)

• 10% is based on new credit (How many open accounts, and what type, and whether any effort is being made toward positive credit)

• 10% on type of credit

A free guide that will help you understand your credit report is available at www.Consumer Reports.org or www.MyFICO.com.

These things determine your score and count against you:

• Delinquents/late payments

• Length of credit history

• If you recently obtained other credit

• Your credit mix

These money-management steps can boost your FICO score:

• Personal cash flow: Create a chart of how much money comes in and goes out

• Personal budget: Use it to find ways to cut expenses and use that extra money to repay debt.

• Work directly with a creditor to find a solution—a debt-repayment plan.

• Apply for a secured credit card, one that you back with a secured savings account or some other way agreed to by the lending institution.

Credit Reports

Most people applying for a home mortgage need not worry about the effects of their credit history during the mortgage process. However you can be better prepared if you get a copy of your Credit Report before you apply for your mortgage. That way, you can take steps to correct any negatives before making your application.

A Credit Profile refers to a consumer credit file, which is made up of various consumer credit reporting agencies. It is a picture of how you paid back the companies you have borrowed money from, or how you have met other financial obligations.

Making a Major Purchase?

Your creditor immediately pulls a credit history file. If you are below 650, they will examine your credit file to see why it is so low.

– Are you exhibiting poor debt management?

– Did you know that 14% of credit-worthy Americans have a FICO score below 600?

Here's how it works: ("real life" example provided by Fair, Isaac & Co.)

Bob and Mary both apply for a home mortgage.

Bob has a FICO of 600

Bob's interest rate would be 8.631%

Mary has a FICO of 720

Mary's interest rate would be 5.702%

On a $300,000 mortgage

Bob's monthly payment (principal and interest) would be $2,313.

Mary's would be $1,742.

Difference: $571 in Mary's checkbook at the end of every month.

There are five categories of information on a credit profile:

– Identifying information

– Employment information

– Credit information

– Public record information

– Inquiries

NOT included on your credit profile is race, religion, health, driving record, criminal record, political preference, or income.

If you have had credit problems, be prepared to discuss them honestly with a mortgage professional who will assist you in writing your "Letter of Explanation." Knowledgeable mortgage professionals know there can be legitimate reasons for credit problems, such as unemployment, illness or other financial difficulties. If you had problems that have been corrected (reestablishment of credit), and your payments have been on time for a year or more, your credit may be considered satisfactory.

The mortgage industry tends to create its own language and credit rating is no different. BC mortgage lending gets its name from the grading of one's credit based on such things as payment history, amount of debt payments, bankruptcies, equity position, credit scores, etc. Credit scoring is a statistical method of assessing the credit risk of a mortgage application. The score looks at the following items: past delinquencies, derogatory payment behavior, current debt levels, length of credit history, types of credit and number of inquires.

The FICO score was developed for the three main credit Bureaus; Equifax (Beacon), Experian (formerly TRW), and Empirica (TransUnion). FICO scores are simply repository scores meaning they ONLY consider the information contained in a person's credit file. They DO NOT consider a person's income, savings or down payment amount. The scores are useful in directing applications to specific loan programs and to set levels of underwriting such as Stream-line, Traditional or Second Review, but are not the final word regarding the type of program you will qualify for or your interest rate.

Want to know your score?

There are many companies selling you services to allow you to see your fico scores. There is usually a monthly fee associated with keeping a tab on your credit ratings and reports. For maximum savings and best offers, go to www.insidermoneysecrets.com and click on the credit report tab. We constantly look for the best offers and will update and feature them at this site.

Many people in the mortgage business are skeptical about the accuracy of FICO scores. Scoring has only been an integral part of the mortgage process for since 1999. However, the FICO scores have been used since the late 1950s by retail merchants, credit card companies, insurance companies and banks for consumer lending. The data from large scoring projects, such as large mortgage portfolios, demonstrate their predictive quality and that the scores do work.

The following are some of the ways you can improve your credit score:

- Pay your bills on time.

- Keep balances low on credit cards.

- Limit your credit accounts to what you really need. Accounts that are no longer needed should be formally canceled since zero balance accounts can still count against you.

- Check that your credit report information is accurate.

- Be conservative in applying for credit and make sure that your credit is only checked when necessary.

The following are common borrower classifications with respect to bankruptcy and foreclosure:

A+ None allowed within 10 years

A- Minimum 2 years with re-established credit

B Minimum 2 years with some lates

C Minimum one year

D Discharged

E Current bankruptcy possible

• A borrower with a score of 680 and above is considered an A+ borrower. A loan with this score will be put through an "automated basic computerized underwriting" system and be completed within minutes. Borrowers in this category qualify for the lowest interest rates, and their loan can close in a couple of days.

• A score below 680 but above 620 may indicate underwriters will take a closer look in determining potential risk. Supplemental documentation may be required before final approval. Borrowers with this credit score may still obtain "A" pricing, but the loan may take several days longer to close.

• Borrowers with credit scores below 620 are normally locked out of the best rate and terms offered. This loan type usually goes to "sub-prime" lenders. The loan terms and conditions are less attractive with these loan types and more time is needed to find the borrower the best rates.

All things being equal, when you have derogatory credit, all of the other aspects of the loan need to be in order. Equity, stability, income, documentation, assets and more, play a larger role in the approval decision. Various combinations are allowed when determining

> *Do NOT CANCEL your oldest credit card if possible, as length of credit is very important to FICO.*

your grade, but the worst-case scenario will push your grade to a lower credit grade.

Late mortgage payments and bankruptcies/foreclosures are the most important. Credit patterns, such as a high number of recent inquiries or more than a few outstanding loans, may signal a problem. Since an indication of a "willingness to pay" is important, several late payments in the same time period is better than random late payments.

The Fair Debt Collection Practices Act

This new law requires that each of the three nationwide consumer-reporting companies (listed below) must provide you one FREE copy of your credit report every 12 months at your request. Three easy ways to order:

1. Order online at www.annualcreditreport.com IMPORTANT: This is the ONLY authorized online source for your free annual report.

2. Call 1-877-322-8228

3. Complete the Annual Credit Report form and mail it to Annual Credit Report Request Service, P.O. Box 105281, Atlanta, GA 30348-5281.

4. You can print the form, which is available on www.ftc.gov/credit.

Order from each of the three national bureaus with this one form. DO NOT contact each of the reporting agencies individually—at the same time.

If you need more than the one FREE report each

year, the charge will be about $10 for another copy within that 12-month period.

This Act restricts bill collectors as follows:

• You have the right to tell a collector to not contact you again. If they call again, they can say only that collection efforts have ended or you are going to be sued.

• If you don't come to an agreement, they will hand your case back to the creditor or creditor's attorney.

• Collectors cannot threaten violence or use obscene or profane language.

• Collectors cannot call you at work and can call you at home only between 8 a.m. and 9 p.m. and cannot harass you.

• Collectors cannot put any markings on any mailed communications that indicate they are trying to collect a debt.

• Collectors cannot mislead you into repaying a debt.

Watch out for "imposter" sites—make sure that you land on the Federal Trade Commission (FTC) Website and not some other site that "offers" free credit reports (but you must order other products).

Fair Credit Reporting Act–Fall 2004

Under the Fair Credit Reporting Act, only you or someone with your permission can see your credit history. Some bureaus also provide business customers with "risk scores" that are based on facts in your report, indicating the likelihood of you having financial troubles. Businesses pay a fee to have the right to order reports, but the bureaus are very careful about their members' legitimacy.

Negative items can stay on the report from months to years:

- Lender inquiries: minimum of six months

- Employer inquiries: two years

- Credit information requested because job has a salary of $750,000 or more: no time limit

- Credit information requested because more than $150,000 in life insurance or credit has been requested: no time limit

- Delinquencies, wage garnishments, repossessions, court orders, evictions for non-payment, and missed child support: seven years or until the statute of limitations has run out

- Bankruptcy: seven or 10 years (depending on type of bankruptcy) from date of filing

Credit Reporting Agencies

The big three national bureaus control the national reporting systems, holding the financial records of millions of Americans are listed below.

Equifax Credit Information System
P.O. Box 105873
Atlanta, GA 30348
1-800-685-1111
www.eqifax.com

Trans Union Corporation
Consumer Disclosure Center
P.O. Box 1000
Chester, PA 19022
1-800-916-8800
www.transunion.com

Experian (formerly TRW)
P.O. Box 2104
Allen, TX 75013-2104
1-888-397-3742
www.experian.com

Each one may have different information, thus you have three credit histories, not just one. They collect information, store it in a database and charge a fee for the information. In addition to these three national bureaus, smaller ones serve local markets. It is a good idea to request a copy from each one once a year.

Free from the Government

The U.S. Government has very helpful booklets available for $1.00 by mail, or you can download them FREE onto your computer. Check out www. pueblo.gsa.gov.

- ID Theft: What It's All About #341N

- Building a Better Credit Report #311N

- Choosing a Credit Card #309N

- Consumer Handbook to Credit Protection Laws #310N

- Healthy Credit #622N

- Identity Theft and Your Social Security Number #519N

- Preventing Identity Theft: A Guide for Consumers #651N

- Your Credit Scores #313N

What Information Is in Your Credit Report?

Credit reports outline your borrowing, charging and repayment activities and abilities. They list your credit cards and loans, balances and paying history as well as any legal action against you for unpaid bills. Information included is:

Personal information: Name, current and previous address, marital status, Social Security number, date of birth, spouse's name, number of dependents, and employment record. Review this information for accuracy because all kinds of errors can happen.

Credit history: Includes status on current and past loans, account numbers, lender's name, amounts borrowed, amount of last payment, amount still owed or credit limit and timeliness of payments. Any late payment of over 30 days goes against you. If a collection agency had been used, that will be a mark against you, even if paid.

Public records: These are anything that has involved the courts such as tax liens, mechanics leans, court judgments, overdue child support and bankruptcy. Even if handled, they are still "negatives."

Inquiries: This is a list of anyone else who has inquired and can go back two years. Too many inquiries (if you are seeking help from many places) may indicate problems to future lenders. You can ask to have unauthorized inquiries deleted.

What If You Find Errors?

To avoid unwelcome surprises, before you apply for a loan for a car, mortgage or credit card, check for human errors like misspelling of your name, or error in street address as well as out-of-date information. Mistaken identity and errors can occur quite easily.

You can dispute information. First contact your reporting agency immediately. They must research and then change or remove the incorrect information—that can take up to 45 days. A corrected report will be sent to anyone who received your credit report within the past six months, or employers within the past two years—*but you must request it.*

If you are denied credit because of an error, the lender must give you the name and address of the credit bureau. Then you have up to 30 days to request a free copy of your report.

If the credit bureau stands by the original report, you can write them a brief (100-word) letter of explanation that they might attach to future requests, unless they believe the information you presented was insignificant.

People who have had serious errors on their reports say one undisputed error can wipe out years of good credit. These errors may be mistaken identity, identity theft or administrative error, for example.

Remember: Put everything in writing when you deal with credit bureaus, and NEVER send them any original (only copies) of important documents. Send the letter by certified mail, return receipt requested so you know they got it.

The time to check your credit report is before you apply for credit. You don't want any surprises that might deny you credit. You may need time to clean up any incorrect information.

You can also request that the reporting companies send notices of any corrections to anyone who received your report in the past six months, or two years for employment purposes.

The Fair Credit Reporting Act gives you the right to sue if the credit bureau refuses to remove inaccurate information from your file. Look for an attorney with experience working with credit reporting cases. Try the National Center for Consumer Advocates, www.naca.net, or the National Consumer Law Center, www.nclc.org.

Sample Dispute Letter

The FTC recommends a letter like that on the next page. The FTC is a U.S. Government organization that works for consumers to prevent fraudulent, deceptive and unfair business practices. They also educate consumers on how to avoid them. Check out www.ftc.gov or call toll-free, 1-877-FTC-HELP (1-877-382-4357); TTY: 1-866-653-4261.

Date
Your Name
Your Address
Your City, State, Zip Code

Complaint Department
Name of Company
Address
City, State, Zip Code

Dear Sir or Madam:

I am writing to dispute the following informa-tion in my file. The items I dispute also are encir-cled on the attached copy of the report I received.

This item (identify item) disputed by name of source, such as creditors or tax court, and identify type of item, such as credit account, judgment, etc.) is (inaccurate or incomplete) because (describe what is inaccurate or incomplete and why). I am requesting that the item be deleted (or request another specific change) to correct the information.

Enclosed are copies of (use this sentence if applicable and describe any enclosed documenta-tion, such as payment records, court documents) supporting my position. Please investigate this (these) matter(s) and (delete or correct) the disput-ed item(s) as soon as possible.

Sincerely,
Your name

Enclosures: (List what you are enclosing)

Educating Your Children of All Ages— Even College Bound . . . and Beyond

As parents we need to tell our children when they are young (before becoming teenagers or even college students) about how to establish and maintain good credit. Today, college students are aggressively marketed to by credit card companies. Also, the government has withdrawn some financial aid for student loans.

Too many college students today graduate with huge student loans and tremendous credit card debt. It can take these young graduates several years to repair their credit and pay off their credit card bills because they used credit cards like cash, paying for everything from cell phones to pizza. They graduate with bills that sometimes seem insurmountable!

College-bound young adults can control their credit-card spending with some simple steps. College students receive credit card offers in the mail—even if they have no income. Their parents, however, had to "earn" the right to get a credit card by showing they had a low-risk factor—once they had their first full-time job.

The 30-somethings and younger are the first generation marketed to on TV, radio and the Internet. They have access to credit, and they spend, spend, spend. They will be known as the generation that is the most indebted in modern history. Credit cards have been their "right of passage," and this sense of entitlement is causing them big problems and will for years to come as they pay off student loans and credit cards.

Many of those 30-something feel unduly burdened

by their financial obligations. Often their parents attended college they paid for mostly with a summer job or with some help from their parents. Since the mid-1980s, though, tuition has been growing far faster than many families can afford.

• The price of public colleges, which about 80% of all students attend, increased 28% in the past five years alone, far more than in any five-year period since 1975.

• At private colleges, the total cost increased 17%.

• Those figures already consider the rate of inflation.

At the same time, outright grants have been shrinking as a proportion of total financial aid. "The costs of education are moving from the government to families, and in families from parents to kids," says Melanie E. Corrigan, associate director of national initiatives and analysis at the American Council on Education in Washington.

A shocking statistic:
• The median debt for college graduates in 2004 was $15,162—an increase of 66.5% since 1993. That may not seem like a crippling sum, but plenty of individuals owe much more.

• In 1993, only 4.2% of graduates had loans exceeding $25,000. A decade later, 17% had loans that exceeded that amount.

Nov. 14, 2005 "Business Week" special report, "Thirty & Broke: The real price of a college education today"

"A college education doesn't protect you from the vicissitudes of global competition," says Jared Bernstein, director of the living standards program at the Economic Policy Institute in Washington. Real earnings for full-time workers between the ages of 25 and 34 who have only a bachelor's degree have, in fact, dropped by almost 10% since 2000, by 5% in 2004 alone. This exaggerates the burden of their debt. For many in their early 30s, establishing themselves takes longer and is more complicated than they thought it would be.

According to Maryland-based payment-cards research firm CardWeb.com (see *Business Week*, 11/14/05, "Thirty and Broke: The Real Price of a College Education Today" and 2/06/06, "Up Against It at 25"), the average credit card debt in 2004 of 25- to 34-year-olds was $5,200, 98% higher than in 1992.

"It's so much more difficult to achieve the adult milestones today than it was 30 years ago," says Draut of the think tank Demos. "There is some sense of betrayal," also reported in the *Business Week* report.

• Case Example •

At 18, Johnny went to college in another state. He knew his parents were putting a lot of money into his education and living costs. He felt bad asking them for "fun money."

That's where the many credit card offers that bombarded him caught his eye. He jumped at the offer for one in his own name that his mom and dad didn't have to know about.

After four years of college, this new graduate will be quickly confronted by student loan payments and the ever-growing credit card balance. Soon he might not be able to pay EVEN the minimums—even though he has a decent paying full-time first job.

The debts he incurred in college will haunt him every month when the bills come. When he wants to rent or lease, get a mortgage or a new car, his credit score will be low, based on his paying history of late and minimum payments.

What can Johnny do now to improve his credit, get a lower interest rate and even be considered for a mortgage or new car loan at a decent rate?

Where can he turn to get help bringing his FICO score up 50, 100 or even 200 points?

How Much Debt Can You Handle?

How much debt can you handle? The answer is different for everyone. How you handle debt can affect you for a long time. Pay close attention to the advantages, pitfalls and consequences of debt.

Many experts recommend that:

• No more than 15% to 20% of your monthly household take-home pay be committed to credit card minimum payments and other loan payments, excluding rent or a mortgage.

• No more than 40% of your monthly take-home pay should go to paying all debts, including rent or mortgage.

What is right for the lender? Lenders will lend you only as much as they feel they can risk, typically:

• Less than 40% of your current income

• Less than 30% for a home

• Less than 10% for other debts

Credit ratio analysis is the measurement of your financial abilities, calculated by dividing your monthly expenses into your income.

– LOW is under 20% = a good job of managing finances

– MODERATE is between 21% and 40% = the person should look closely at their monthly payments and expenses and start decreasing their overall level of debt, including credit cards

– HIGH is over 40% = stop immediately accumulating debt and look for ways to decrease total debt level

Use this formula to determine what is right for you.

Income: Add up all income for one year: job (after taxes), loans, scholarships, parental or spousal support or other sources. Divide by 12 to get monthly income.

Expenses: Include monthly payments for rent, loans, car and insurance payments, clothing, transportation, utilities and other expenses.

Extra: Subtract what you spend (expenses) from what you make (income) to determine how much you have left over each month.

For example, if your family has a $2,500 monthly income and $1,500 in expenses, you have a $1,000 positive balance.

Getting Help

If you can't resolve a debt directly with a creditor, consider getting help from a credit counseling service.

Credit Counseling Organizations

• Consumer Credit Counseling Service (CCCS) is supported partly by the credit industry. For a small fee (waived in hardship cases), a counselor acts as a go-between with your creditors and helps set up a workable repayment plan. They help with budgets, education, debt management and housing. You can find information at www.cccsintl.org.

• The National Foundation for Consumer Credit (NFCC) is dedicated to educating consumers on how to use credit wisely. It is a parent group of CCCS. DebtAdvice.org is a service provided by Members of the National Foundation for Credit Counseling (NFCC), most of them known as Consumer Credit. Find them online at www.nfcc.org

• Credit Counseling Agencies—www.nfcc.org/memberserv/membserv_01.html

• Credit Counseling Constituents—www.nfcc.org/mo/partners/index.cfm

• Bankruptcy Reform—www.nfcc.org/bankruptcy/index.cfm

• Keys To Home Ownership—www.nfcc.org/publications/index.cfm

Get help quickly.

Waiting usually makes the situation worse.

• Debt Counselors of America (DCA) is the first Internet-based nonprofit credit-counseling firm. Check out www.americancredit.org/Debt-Counselors-of-America.asp

• Genus Credit Management is a non-profit, nation al service offering free debt counseling over the phone. It offers debt management and educational programs to help financially distressed families and individuals effectively manage their finances. Clients are asked to   make a contribution to AFS-Genus if they can afford to. All contributions are voluntary. www.genus.org

• Universities, military bases, credit unions and housing authorities may also offer low- or no-cost credit counseling programs.

Beware of illegal debt consolidators who charge a fee to combine your debts and help you manage paying them off. Many are prohibited in most states and highly regulated in others.

People with lower credit ratings might receive appeal letters and mailers from organizations claiming to be able to remove negative information from your credit file—doing what you could do yourself for FREE. In fact, if the negative information is legitimate, the only way to handle it is to deal with your debt.

Some "experts" charge a high fee for work you could do yourself, causing problems and delaying payments. Often their efforts lead to more trouble for you in addition to the high fees.

Other options in addition to consumer credit counseling are:

- Mediation—use of a third party to resolve a dispute.

- Arbitration—use of a third party (usually a judge or lawyer) to handle the dispute. You are bound by the decision.

- Litigation—The most expensive and aggressive choice is when you have a lawyer fight the battle for you. This is appropriate if you want to tell collection agencies to talk to your lawyer and stop harassing you at home.

The best way to reduce debt is to earn extra income and reduce expenses.

IMPORTANT:
What Clues Tell You a Credit Repair is a Scam?

These companies may:

1. Ask you to pay for credit repair services before you receive any service.

2. Not explain your legal rights or tell you what you can do yourself for free.

3. Recommend that you do not contact a credit reporting company directly.

4. Tell you how to invent a new identity to get credit.

5. Suggest actions that you feel are illegal.

Always check with the local Better Business Bureau or local consumer protection agency in the company's location.

Debt Management Plan . . . Proving your Creditworthiness!

How do you improve your credit report? Through time, conscientious effort and a payment plan.

A counselor creates a workable budget with you and then they negotiate with creditors to reduce your monthly payments and extend the time to make payments you've already missed. They may be able to get lower interest rates. You send your counselor a designated amount each month, and the counselor pays the creditors with this money that is held in a special account for you. You will be required to close existing credit lines and receive no new credit until your debts are under control.

Too Much Debt?
Nothing is Going to Change Unless You Do!

What if you feel like you're in over your head in debt? Find a way to get out of it. Making an effort to pay your bills will help lenders see that your promise is still worth something. Many experts suggest these are some ways to control debt:

- Assess the situation and itemize your financial obligations.

- Refinance high-cost loans.

- Build an emergency fund.

- Make a budget.

- Pay off high-interest debt first.

- Use credit cards cautiously.

- Find ways to save.

- Contact your lenders and tell them your situation.

- Talk with creditors and set up payment plans. They want their money and may be more flexible than you expect.

How Do You Rebuild Credit?

First of all, unless your bad credit is caused by something beyond your control (such as major illness, family member's death, job loss or divorce), you must change your bad spending, buying and charging habits. No one set out to have bad credit, but when it happens, it takes time and perseverance to fix it. It is worth the effort.

Here are some simple tactics others have used successfully to improve or rebuild their credit:

1. Establish and then carefully limit your use of a low-limit or secured credit card. Perhaps a credit union or other "agreeable lender" would give you such a credit card. It means that you "secure" the credit card with your own money that you charge against. Try to keep the limit at 50% or less of maximum. New accounts like this will greatly improve your score—if you have a solid record of on-time payment for a few months.

2. You can also get a passbook loan using your own money in a savings account. If you get this through your local bank or credit union, make sure they report accounts to the three national reporting agencies.

3. Take the money from the passbook loan and open a savings account in a second bank. You can do this at more banks to establish new credit. Make sure there are no "early-payment" penalties.

> *You may not need credit today, but if you don't think ahead, you will have NO options when you do!*
>
> *Every incident of bad credit stays with you for up to seven years. So, what you do today will impact your life later on.*

4. See if a local retail store will issue you a card, which usually has a low limit. Charge only what you can pay for at the end of each month. Most national department stores and bank credit cards are reported, but some travel, entertainment, gas, local stores and credit unions are not reported. If you have any of those cards, make sure that credit history on the cards is reported.

5. Sign up for automatic bill payment. Being 30 days late can mean 100 points.

6. Limit credit card applications. Sometimes credit card companies offer a low introductory rate—for a certain period of time. Then the interest rate increases considerably. If you take such a card's offer, watch for that increase date and decide if you really need that card. Read the offer carefully.

7. Don't cancel all credit cards. The ones you have had for a long time help you establish a credit history. If

you want to get rid of a card, maybe it's the one that charges an annual fee or one you never use. Just don't ever close the oldest accounts!

8. Make sure the credit limits are obvious and listed so you always know.

9. Spend less! Look at where you spend money, and look for ways to change your lifestyle that reduce outgoing cash.

Be careful if you are considering taking out a consolidation loan—not all consolidators are reputable. Also, spending the money you saved by consolidating debts will only increase your monthly payments again.

Many employers check your credit before they make you a firm offer for a position (or even a promotion). Jobs where you will be handling money require you to have good credit.

Be aware that insurance companies review your credit before giving you an auto loan or personal insurance—and your FICO credit score may determine what rate you will pay. *Most consumers do not know this fact.*

Work toward maintaining good credit, or repair damaged credit. Pay everything on time, every month: credit cards, utilities, insurance, and rent or mortgage.

If your money problems are serious—and cutting up credit cards is the only way you can stop using them—your credit score may suffer. But that's the least of your problems. You have to learn to control your spending.

Remember: If you have a friend or relative co-sign on a loan or credit card, their credit will also be affected by your payment history.

If you have a lifetime of slow pay and other debt problems, it will cost you hundreds of thousands more in mortgage, car loan and credit card interest over your lifetime. Some credit crises come on slowly after years of poor debt management. Others occur because of other kinds of financial setbacks.

Secured and Unsecured Loans: The creditor can repossess your car under most vehicle financing agreements if you are in default—because the car is the security for the loan. You may still have to pay the balance due on the loan, plus towing and storage in order to get your car back. If you cannot make car payments, you'd be better off selling the car yourself rather than having it repossessed.

The same is true with your home as security for a mortgage. If you are behind on payments, the lender can foreclose and you lose your home. Again, it is better for you to be honest and tell them about your situation, and see what flexibility there is. Waiting only worsens the problem.

Bankruptcy: Consumer debt is at an all-time high. In 2003, 1.6 million Americans filed bankruptcy. According to an FTC report, bankruptcy is the last resort because it stays on your credit report for 10 years, and bankruptcy can make it more difficult to live your life, to do everyday things like getting credit, securing life insurance, buying a home—or even getting a job.

In October 2005, a new law went into effect making it harder to file bankruptcy. In 2005, 2.1 million people filed for bankruptcy, many were part of the last-minute surge before the law took effect. This was up 30% from 2004—making 2005 a record-breaking year for bankruptcy filings. It is estimated that one of every 53 households filed. In 2004, 1,597,462 people filed for bankruptcy, and in 2005, 2,078,415 filed. *Stats from:* www.uscourts.gov/bnkrpctystats/bankruptcystats.htm .

Chapter 13 allows employed persons to keep their property as the court approves a repayment plan involving future income to pay off the default during a three-to-five-year period. In 2005, this type of filing actually went down 6% from 2004.

Chapter 7 liquidates all assets that are not exempt (cars, work-related tools and basic household items). A court-appointed trustee may sell your property and use the proceeds to pay off creditors. Chapter 7 bankruptcy filings increased 17% in 2005.

Personal bankruptcy does not eliminate your responsibility to pay child support, alimony, fines, taxes and some student loans.

> ***30 million Americans have less-than-good***
> ***credit scores: Below 620 FICO scores***
> ***AND MOST TIMES,***
> ***the #1 reason is:***
> ***Late payments***

<u>Good News - Good News - Good News!</u>

Have you been embarrassed, frustrated or limited by your credit score and some of the credit issues you have been dealing with? Have you been unable to get decent interest rates for your home or car loans?

Are you ready to start living the stress-free credit life you deserve?

We have the answer for you—and it's so simple you'll want to start working today toward getting a credit score of 700+. Guaranteed!

Does that sound good to you?

If you answered "YES," this is the first day of a better financial life for you and your family.

Secrets Insiders Don't Want You to Know

The Credit Enhancement Network is so confident this easy-to-do solution will change your life that we will just blurt it out (no more buildup!). Here's the "secret" plan that works.

Who in Johnny's life will allow him to tie onto their credit score? Could it be a parent, grandparent, sibling or friend? This person will need to work with Johnny in this one-way credit repair solution.

IMPORTANT: It is absolutely essential to understand that when parents, grandparents or friends offer to help raise someone's credit score, the other person's score in NO WAY affects their good credit. Also, the person they list as an additional user CANNOT affect the score of the "host" account.

The person(s) who help must:

1. Have excellent credit

2. Have a 700+ credit score

3. Have no-balance credit card(s) that are paid off every month

4. Have credit lines of $5,000, $10,000 or $20,000 (the higher the better)

5. Have never been late with a payment

6. Have a long credit history (10 years+) in good standing with the merchant, which is also beneficial.

• Case Example •

Bill and Suzanne got married about 15 years ago and quickly had two children. For years Bill was a hard-working blue-collar worker who put in a full day, every day. Suzanne stayed home when the children were younger. When they started school, she went back to work.

Actually, Bill was hardworking until he was laid off and, for many months, could not get a new job. And then Suzanne got a serious illness shortly thereafter.

The family had about $2,000 in savings, had been conservative with their spending and had quite good credit—when the roof fell in, twice. First with Bill's unemployment where he lost the family's low-cost medical benefits and then Suzanne's inability to work.

They owned their home and had monthly mortgage payments, one new truck they owed money on and, of course, living expenses for four people.

Soon they were not able to pay their mortgage and not even the minimum on their credit card balance. They were in debt, and even though Bill finally got a job and Suzanne recovered, it was taking them forever to get back their good credit ranking.

Bill and Suzanne were not the kind of people who bought everything they wanted, and were proud people. Unemployment and serious illness were emergencies most cannot plan or prepare for.

How can they get a better credit score?
Who can help them raise their credit score?

Easy Steps to a Better Financial Future:

If you meet the criteria listed on page 172, you can help them.

1. Add Bill to your credit card as an "additional user" name. His Social Security number is given to the credit card company (Citibank works but some bank cards don't).

2. Understand that Bill never actually gets to use your credit—he just gets your credit "reputation" as he is now tied into your excellent credit score. His negative score will not affect yours in any way.

3. Add Bill's name to your $10,000 line of credit a few times, and this will SUPERCHARGE his credit.

Your high FICO score will show up on his report, increasing the amount of credit available to him and deceasing his overall debt ratio. (Individual situations vary, depending on the number of derogatories.) In "The 3-Digit Score That Controls Your Life" section earlier, it

---

Word of Warning:

Using a person who does not meet every criteria on page 172, could negatively affect Bill even more.

shows that 35% of your credit score is based on your loan payment history. But the other 65% (how much you owe, length of credit history, new credit and types of credit) is also important.

Your good credit score, your perfect payment history, length of history (date opened), and credit line, will show up on his credit report within 90 days, increasing Bill's credit score 50, 100 or even 200 points—a miracle in Bill's credit life! For every credit line Bill's name is added to, he can expect a 30-to 50-point increase.

BREAKING NEWS UPDATE

All good things come to an end sometime. If it's too good to be true, it probably is. But in my entire career, I've never seen a strategy as fast and effective as this one (for increasing one's credit score.) Since it is so good for the consumers, and hurts the banks, FICO (or Fair Isaac and Company), will be shutting this down soon and changing the way they score additional card holders. This will only help banks charge higher interest rates to those with lower scores in hopes of keeping them indebted to them perpetually. We don't know when this will happen, so if you need to utilize this technique, do it as soon as possible before this window is shut forever.

Additional Ways to Improve Your Credit Score

Remember, the keys to obtaining and keeping good credit include your perfect payment history (DON'T BE LATE), the length of your credit history (date loan or credit account opened), and credit line.

There are additional things you can do to improve your credit score. AND it will only take a few weeks for you to see results.

1. Add non-reported accounts to your report. Things like your utilities, (phone, electric and gas companies) insurance, car payments actually do not show up on your credit report, unless you are delinquent. To add a non-reported account to your report, contact the credit bureaus and give them a list of companies you do business with and that have extended you credit, and that you have had no problems with. The bureaus will call these companies and ask for a reference on your account, which will be added to your file.

2. Open a secured card to help you build credit if you have none. A secured card is a bank granted credit card that is backed by a deposit of collateral at the bank. To be approved, all you have to do is make a security deposit at the bank. The bank then issues you a Visa or a MasterCard with a spending limit equal to the amount of the security deposit. You will not be able to use the money in the account as long as you have the card. If you do not pay your bills, the bank will seize the money in your account to make the payment. They will then close your account. The best place to go is a bank where you already are doing business. If you do not already have a checking account, then go to the largest bank in the neighborhood.

Secured cards look just like a regular credit card. No one can tell that it is any different. Secured cards also show up on your credit report, except they are marked with a code that means secured. Most creditors do not differentiate between secured and regular bankcards, This makes it easier for you to qualify for other cards and credit.

There are scams out there, so make sure you go to a reputable bank where deposits are FDIC protected.

3. Cosigning....our advice is be careful. If you are having difficulty obtaining a loan due to lack of credit, you may consider having someone cosign with you. Realize that a large loan can actually hurt the other person's credit.

Also, cosigning a loan for someone else may hurt your credit, so be careful who you cosign for. You will also be legally responsible for that account if they do not pay. If they do not pay, your credit will be damaged.

Chapter Thirteen

Commonly Asked Questions Regarding Mortgages

Q: How much down payment is required?

One of the first questions that home buyers ask is "how much down payment are we going to need?" Unfortunately, there is no standard answer. Down payments vary from 0% (with a Veteran's Administration loan) to upwards of 25% (with certain "non-conforming" loans). On average, most home buyers make down payments in the 5%–15% range, although your personal situation may dictate more or less of a down payment. When you are factoring money for a down payment, don't forget about closing costs, which will total in the 2% to 5% range, payable in cash at the time of closing.

Q: What is prequalification? Does it mean the loan is approved?

Prequalification is the initial step in securing a mortgage. It does not mean the loan is approved. A lender will analyze your current income, debt and basic credit history situation in order to qualify you for a maximum loan amount. This gives you a clear picture of your financial parameters and a maximum housing price (the mortgage amount plus your down payment). With preapproval, the lender verifies your income, debt and financial picture, and approves the loan subject to a favorable appraisal of the property you select. See the discussion on mortgage prequalification and preapproval for more information.

Q: What are the differences among mortgage prequalification, preapproval and final loan approval?

Prequalification is the process where the lender looks at a basic copy of your credit report and uses the information you supply to determine how much mortgage you can afford based on your income. No accounts or employment information are verified. Preapproval occurs when all credit and employment are verified and the mortgage is approved, subject to the appraisal of the property you have chosen to buy. Final loan approval occurs when the property has been appraised, all documentation is in the lender's hands, and all contingencies have been met. For more information, see the section devoted to prequalification and preapproval.

Q: There are many mortgage programs and offers available. How do I compare them?

To avoid confusion consult a few sources, including a local bank that has a mortgage broker who will deal with several different lenders. In addition, you may want to use an online source such as LendingTree, which deals with numerous lenders throughout the U.S. Through a single brief loan request form, you can get up to four offers from lenders competing for your business.

Q: Can I use my IRA retirement funds for a down payment on a house?

For most first-time buyers, you can use the funds in these retirement accounts without penalty.

According to the IRS, if both husband and wife are first-time homebuyers, they each can withdraw up to $10,000 penalty-free for qualified acquisition costs of a first home. A first-time homebuyer is, generally, any individual (and his or her spouse, if married) who had no present ownership interest in a main home during the two-year period ending on the date the individual acquires the main home to which these rules apply.

Qualified acquisition costs include the following items:

- Costs of buying, building or rebuilding a home.
- Any usual or reasonable settlement, financing or other closing costs.

Q: What mortgage options are there for those with poor credit?

There are lenders available for many people with tarnished credit records. One of the mistakes commonly made by homebuyers involves their credit report. Some buyers assume that their credit is worse than it really is, and they may well have been able to secure a more advantageous mortgage. Other buyers are unaware of problems in their credit report and have to scramble to resolve the problems. You can avoid many of these hassles by getting a copy of your credit report up front and examining it for errors that need to be corrected and for accounts that need to be handled.

Q: What are front and back ratios when qualifying for a mortgage?

Part of the mortgage application process is the determination of how much house you can afford based on your income. The two ratios computed are the front ratio and the back ratio.

• Front Ratio: The total mortgage payment including principal, interest, taxes and insurance (PITI) as well as any condominium or homeowner association fees, divided by your total GROSS income. Traditionally, this ratio must be below 28%. Example: With a gross income of $3,700 per month, a total mortgage payment (PITI) of $973, the front ratio would be 26%.

• Back Ratio: The total mortgage payment PLUS car payments, credit card and any other loan payments divided by your total GROSS income. Traditionally, this ratio must be below 36%. Example: With a gross income of $3700 per month, a total mortgage payment of $973, a car payment of $212, one credit card payment of $59 and one credit card payment of $43 for a total of $1,287, and a back ratio of 35%.

Q: What options are there for buyers with no money down and no cash for closing costs?

Although there are some new programs that allow buyers to purchase a home with little or no cash, you will generally need some funds for down payment, closing costs or both. Since a mortgage payment will take a good percentage of your income, lenders will usually want you to be "involved" (meaning having your money involved) from the very beginning. There are options for low down payment (5% or less) mortgages such as FHA mortgages, and there is always the possibility that the seller could absorb some of your closing costs, which are usually 3% to 5% of the selling price. However, to buy a home with no cash down is a rare occurrence. If you have cash for closing costs, though, and excellent credit, there are new options in the conventional loan arena.

Mortgage Hints

• **Don't build yourself a mortgage mountain.** It's fine to want the best home you can afford, but be certain that it is comfortably affordable. Although you may find mortgage lenders who will stretch your qualification ratios (the ratio of your total mortgage payment to your total income), the traditional ratios—the mortgage payment as 28% of your income and the total of your mortgage payment plus your monthly debt payments as 36% of your income — are good basic guidelines.

• **Get your budget under control**. Spend time reviewing your budget (or developing one if you don't have one) and sharpening your money-saving skills—it can bring big rewards later. A coordinated budget allows you to get the most home for your money, without strapping yourself while eliminating wasteful spending.

• **Prepare to pay off small debts.** Having three credit card balances, for example, one with a $225 balance, a second with a $155 balance and a third with $190, will only cloud the picture. Even though the total is only $570, all three will have minimum payments, credit lines, etc. If possible, pay them down to zero balances and close any unnecessary cards.

- **Begin to gather documentation**. It is not necessary that you have all items on hand before you apply, but there are a number of documents you will need eventually. The approval process will go much smoother if you begin to gather them now. Examples are: W-2s and income tax returns from the previous few years (especially if you are self-employed), bank statements for possibly up to two years for checking and savings (especially for stated income loans), copies of pay stubs, a copy of your credit report, records of any child support or alimony (either going out or coming in).

- **Closing costs.** In addition to your down payment, you will need to reserve funds for closing costs. Depending on the type of loan and your location, closing costs can range from 2% to 5% of the mortgage amount, and they must be paid in cash at the closing and cannot be borrowed funds.

- **Compare.** There are many sources for mortgage funds—be sure to make comparisons. Your local bank or credit union, mortgage brokers and Internet resources are all available. Be certain to compare equal terms, down payments and loan types.

- **Consider points when comparing.** Your total mortgage cost will be determined by three factors:

the interest rate, the term and the number of points.

• **Get educated!** Securing a mortgage is not that complicated, but if you approach it blind, mistakes can be very expensive! Get as much information as possible.

• **Adjustable Rate Mortgages (ARMs).** If you are certain that you are going to be in the house for a short time (less than five years, for example) strongly consider an adjustable rate mortgage (ARM). You will take full advantage of the lower initial rate and not be as concerned about rate increases since you will have moved when they begin to take effect. Tailor your ARM's first adjustment period to the time you will be in the house.

Loans are available in various arrangements. Some have variable interest rates, others have attractive low introductory rates, and a few have fixed rates. You also may find that most loans have large one-time upfront fees, others have closing costs, and some have continuing costs, such as annual fees. You can find loans with large balloon payments at the end of the loan, and others with no balloons but with higher monthly payments.

No one loan is right for every homeowner. The challenge, then, is to contact different lenders, compare options, and select the ARM best for your needs.

Q: What about home equity credit lines?

If you need to borrow money, home equity lines may be one useful source of credit. Initially at least, they may provide you with large amounts of cash at relatively low interest rates. And they may provide you with certain tax advantages unavailable with other kinds of loans.

At the same time, home equity lines of credit require you to use your home as collateral for the loan. This may put your home at risk if you are late or cannot make your monthly payments. Those loans, with a large final (balloon) payment, may lead you to borrow more money to pay off the debt, or they may put your home in jeopardy if you cannot qualify for refinancing, and if you sell your home, most plans require you to pay off your credit line at that time. In addition, because home equity loans give you relatively easy access to cash, you might find you borrow money more freely.

Q: How much money can you borrow on a home equity credit line?

Depending on your credit and the amount of your outstanding debt, home equity lenders may let you borrow up to 85% of the appraised value of your home, minus the amount you still owe on your first mortgage. Ask the lender about the length of the home equity loan, whether there is a minimum withdrawal requirement when you open your account, and whether there are minimum or maximum withdrawal requirements after your account is opened. Inquire about how you gain access to your credit line—whether with checks, credit cards or both.

Find out if your home equity credit line sets a fixed time when you can make withdrawals from your account. Once the draw period expires, you may be able to renew your credit line. If you cannot, you will not be permitted to borrow additional funds. Also, in some plans, you may have to pay your full outstanding balance. In others, you may be able to repay the balance over a fixed time.

Q: What is the interest rate on the home equity loan?

Interest rates for loans differ, so it pays to check with several lenders for the lowest rate. Compare the annual percentage rate (APR), which indicates the annual cost of credit. Be aware that the advertised APR for home equity credit lines is based on interest alone. For a true comparison of credit costs, compare other charges, such as points and closing costs, which will add to the cost of your home equity loan. This is especially important if you are comparing a home equity credit line with a traditional installment (or second) mortgage, where the APR includes the total credit costs for the loan.

In addition, ask about the type of interest rates available for the home equity plan. Most home equity credit lines have variable interest rates. These variable rates may offer lower monthly payments at first, but during the rest of the repayment period the payments may change and may be higher. Fixed interest rates, if available, may be slightly higher initially than variable rates, but fixed rates offer stable monthly payments over the life of the credit line.

If you are considering a variable rate, check and compare the terms. Check the periodic cap, which is the limit on interest rate changes at one time. Also, check the lifetime cap, which is the limit on interest rate changes throughout the loan term. Ask the lender which index is used and how much and how often it can change. An index (such as the prime rate) is used by lenders to determine how much to raise or lower interest rates. Also, check the margin, which is an amount added to the index that determines the interest you are charged. In addition, ask whether you can convert your variable rate loan to a fixed rate at some future time.

Sometimes, lenders offer a temporarily discounted interest rate—one that is unusually low and lasts only for an introductory period, such as six months. During this time, your monthly payments are lower, too. After the introductory period ends, however, your rate (and payments) increase to the true market level (the index plus the margin). So, ask if the rate you are offered is "discounted," and if so, find out how the rate will be determined at the end of the discount period and how much larger your payments could be at that time.

Q: What are the upfront closing costs?

When you take out a home equity line of credit, you pay for many of the same expenses as when you financed your original mortgage. These include items such as an application fee, title search, appraisal, attorneys' fees and points (a percentage of the amount you borrow). These expenses can add substantially to the cost of your loan, especially if you ultimately borrow little from your credit line. You may want to negotiate with lenders to see if they will pay for some of these expenses.

Q: What are the continuing costs?

In addition to upfront closing costs, some lenders require you to pay continuing fees throughout the life of the loan. These may include an annual membership or participation fee, which is due whether or not you use the account, and/or a transaction fee, which is charged each time you borrow money. These fees add to the overall cost of the loan. Be sure to shop around.

Q: What are the repayment terms during the loan?

As you pay back the loan, your payments may change if your credit line has a variable interest rate, even if you do not borrow more money from your account. Find out how often and how much your payments can change. You also will want to know whether you are paying back both principal and interest, or interest only. Even if you are paying back some principal, ask whether your monthly payments will cover the full amount borrowed or whether you will owe an additional payment of principal at the end of the loan. In addition, you may want to ask about penalties for late payments and under what conditions the lender can consider you in default and demand immediate full payment.

Q: What are the repayment terms at the end of the loan?

Ask whether you might owe a large payment at the end of your loan term. If you do, and you are not sure you will be able to afford the balloon payment, you may want to renegotiate your repayment terms. When you take out the loan, ask about the conditions for renewal of the plan or for refinancing the unpaid balance. Consider asking the lender to agree ahead of time and in writing to refinance any end-of-loan balance or to extend your repayment time, if necessary.

Q: What safeguards are built into the loan?

One of the best protections you have is the Federal Truth in Lending Act, which requires lenders to inform you about the terms and costs of the plan at the time you are given an application. Lenders must disclose the APR and payment terms and must inform you of charges to open or use the account, such as an appraisal, a credit report, or attorneys' fees. Lenders also must tell you about any variable-rate feature and give you a brochure describing the general features of home equity plans.

The Truth in Lending Act also protects you from changes in the terms of the account (other than a variable-rate feature) before the plan is opened. If you decide not to enter into the plan because of a change in terms, all fees you paid earlier must be returned to you.

Because your home is at risk when you open a home equity credit account, you have three days to cancel the transaction, for any reason. To cancel, you must inform the lender in writing. Following that, your credit line must be canceled and all fees you have paid must be returned.

Once your home equity plan is opened, if you pay as agreed, the lender, in most cases, may not terminate your plan, accelerate payment of your outstanding balance, or change the terms of your account. The lender may halt credit advances on your account during any period in which interest rates exceed the maximum rate cap in your agreement, if your contract permits this.

APPENDIX I

Suggested HELOC Criteria:

The "right" HELOC is one into which you can transfer funds online from your checking account so you can access those funds to pay your living expenses.

The necessary components include:

• **HELOC** (with same lender as you have your checking account)

• **Checking account** (with same lender as HELOC)*

• **Online banking**

• **Two debit cards** (one to access your HELOC, the other to access your checking account)

* NOTE: The reason you want to have your HELOC and checking account with the same lender is that it ensures smooth and quick transactions. By using the lender's online banking, you can see that your funds are transferred back and forth properly. If you use different lenders for your checking and HELOC, you'll increase the chances of your funds getting lost. Remember: The key to making the program work is keeping money in the HELOC as long as possible. If you're transferring funds between banks, the process is delayed, while fund transfers within the same bank are posted that very evening.

In a Nutshell: How to Make the HELOC Work for YOU

1. Arrange for your HELOC bill to be automatically paid from your checking account on its exact due date every month so you'll never "forget" to make the payment. Late mortgage or HELOC payments are frowned upon by the credit bureaus and will dramatically decrease your credit score and ability to secure favorable financing terms. But by waiting to make the payment until its due date, you'll keep the maximum amount of money in your HELOC most of the time, which is the key to making the LEAP program work optimally.

2. Make sure your income is deposited into your checking account, as you cannot make direct deposits into the HELOC.

3. As soon as your income is deposited into your checking account, use online banking to transfer that money into your HELOC. Remember that you want to keep the daily balance of the HELOC as low as possible. When transferring to your HELOC, you'll most likely have two options: "regular payment" or "principal only." Always choose "principal only." This way, more money goes toward paying your principal and lowering your interest fees.

4. Pay your normal living expenses using a credit card within the grace period so you are not charged interest.

5. At the end of the billing cycle, when you get your

credit card statement, use online banking to transfer funds from the HELOC back into your checking account. Then use your checking account to pay the credit card in full.

What You Want in a HELOC:

Use the questions and answers below as a guide to help you find the correct type of HELOC to use with LEAP™ strategy.

1. Is there an application fee for the HELOC and/or additional closing costs?
You want: Zero application fees and zero closing costs.

2. Are there any upfront fees in the form of points?
You want: Zero upfront fees in the form of points.

3. What is your maximum loan-to-valuation (LTV) ratio?
You want: The best LTV you can get. Some banks allow up to 125% LTV, depending on your FICO score. Most banks will go up to 100% with a decent score.

4. If the LTV is above 80%, are there any penalties such as higher application fees, closing costs or interest rates? If so, are these penalties avoidable?
You want: A lender that gives you options for reducing your interest rates. Some do this if you have multiple accounts such as a checking or savings account, online banking or bill pay.

5. What is the interest rate for the HELOC?
You want: Prime interest rate plus a margin if your LTV

exceeds 80%.

6. What is your maximum debt-to-income ratio (DTI)?
You want: A 50% DTI is typical. However, if your DTI is greater, you can always apply for a HELOC at institutions that don't require you to prove your income. You'll pay a higher rate, but at least you'll be able to get a HELOC.

7. Can I make interest-only payments?
You want: Interest-only terms and a 10-year loan period.

8. Do you have annual membership or maintenance fees?
You want: Zero annual membership/maintenance fees.

9. Are there per-transaction fees and/or charges for deposits and/or withdrawals?
You want: Zero transaction fees and charges.

10. Can I make withdrawals via check and ATM card from the HELOC?
You want: The ability to withdraw HELOC funds via check and ATM debit card.

11. Can I make an unlimited number of withdrawals/draw-downs (advance) from the HELOC?
You want: The ability to make an unlimited number of withdrawals/draw-downs from your HELOC.

12. Is there a limit on the size of withdrawals/draw-downs? If so, what is it?
You want: NO LIMIT on the size of withdrawals/draw-downs.

13. Am I required to take out an initial advance when I first get the HELOC?

You want: NO requirement to take out an initial advance.

14. Can I have a FREE checking account, FREE online banking and FREE Bill Pay?

You want: ALL THREE.

15. Can I get a discount on the HELOC interest rate if I have other accounts or products with your institution?

You want: The discounted rate.

16. Can I have my checking account linked to the HELOC via online banking?

You want: Your checking account and HELOC linked so you can transfer funds between the two accounts.

17. Can I make unlimited deposits/payments into the HELOC?

You want: Unlimited deposits/payments.

18. Is there a limit to the size of deposits/payments that I can make into the HELOC?

You want: No limit.

19. Can I have the monthly interest charges automatically deducted from the HELOC?

You want: Monthly interest charges automatically deducted. If this isn't possible, get them deducted from your checking account, since the HELOC will provide overdraft protection.

20. What is the draw period of the loan?

You want: At least 10 years.

21. Are there any early payout/termination fees on this HELOC?

You want: NO early payout or termination fees.

22. Can I renew the HELOC at the end of the contractual period at no charge?

You want: To be able to renew the HELOC at the end of the contractual period at no charge.

23. Can the HELOC be used against investment or income-producing properties?

You want: To ask for this only if you need it.

APPENDIX II

Additional Ways to Save $

If you're like many of us, you probably spend a good chunk of your monthly income on little things that you really don't need. If you could cut out some or all of these items, you could probably stash away enough to take a fun family vacation or pay down part of your mortgage.

Start thinking carefully before you spend, instead of writing a check or getting out the credit card every time you want something. Saving money is a state of mind that requires you to renounce excessive spending and realize that you don't really need a lot of the stuff you buy. Sure you want it, but that's no reason to buy it when you REALLY don't need it. The next time you want something, take the $50 or $100 that you would have spent on it and stash it somewhere. That's what we call saving. You won't end up with stuff; you'll end up with MONEY. Money that you can put into your house.

Be frugal. Remember the things you did back in the days when you had no money? Play Frisbee in the park. Eat out only occasionally and choose affordable places. Go for a bike ride instead of shopping. Turn off the lights in the rooms you're not using. Decrease the heat or air conditioning in the house when you're not home. Look into ways to save on gas mileage with fuel additives such as acetone. (Check out our book "Secrets the Oil Companies Don't Want You To Know" by Louis LaPointe). Try fixing things around the house, rather than replacing them.

Seek inspiration for living less expensively. Go to your favorite search engine and type in "living cheap," "frugal living" or "save money." You'll find lots of websites devoted to living on less, including www.thefrugalshopper.com and www.simpleliving.net. There are many painless ways you can economize without decreasing your quality of life.

Go veggie. If you can do three meatless days a week, you can save $25 a week, which equals $100 a month, which equals $1,200 a year! Eat beans! You'll be healthier, and if you need recipes, check out my favorite healthy recipe book, "Recipes for Life" at www.blpublications.com.

Play money games. Whenever you get a $5 bill, put it aside. Or put aside $1 bills, quarters or all your spare change. You'll have a nest egg before you know it.

Never spend a windfall. Take your income-tax refund, holiday money from your folks, rebate checks, refunds and any other extras and apply them to your principal.

Haggle. You'll be amazed at how often you can get a cut in prices, fees and interest rates from cable companies, Internet providers, airlines, hotels, credit card companies, computer and appliance salespeople, and many others.

Brown bag it. Instead of eating out for lunch, take a sandwich, an orange, some raw almonds, soup in a thermos, and anything else that sounds good. You'll save a bundle.

Re-evaluate. One dinner out can cost more than you

spend on groceries in a week. One pair of designer shoes is worth half (maybe more) than a commuter pass. Learn what your money is worth, and you won't be so quick to dispose of it on things you really don't need.

Don't impulse buy. If you are shopping for a new pair of comfortable black shoes that you do need, why are you trying on the jeans and pumps that you saw in the window? Stick to the program.

Never pay full price. If you must shop, buy things out of season when they are marked way down. Or shop the outlet mall—and don't even pay (their) full price—wait for the item you want to go on sale. Discover the online world of discount web sites. eBay, www.half.com and www.craigslist.org are excellent sources of "lightly used" goods, everything from books to office furniture.

Don't overpay your taxes. If you are getting a hefty refund from the IRS every spring, you're effectively lending money to the government interest-free. Go through your tax return and see if you can plan your withholding so you get to December 31 maybe getting a $100 refund. That way you can use your money NOW. (And bank the refund when you get it.)

Brown bag it. Instead of eating out for lunch, take a sandwich, an orange, some raw almonds, soup in a thermos, and anything else that sounds good. You'll save a bundle.

Do a reality check! One dinner out can cost more than you spend on a week's worth of groceries. One pair of designer shoes can be worth half (or more) of a yearly commuter pass. Think about what your money can buy in necessities, and you won't be so quick to blow it on frivolous things.

Don't impulse buy. If you are shopping for a much-needed pair of comfortable black shoes, why are you trying on the pumps that you saw in the window? Stick to the program.

Never pay full price. Buy things out of season when they are marked way down. Or shop the outlet mall and don't pay their full price. Wait for the item you want to go on sale. Discover the online world of discount websites. eBay, www.half.com and www.craigslist.org are excellent sources of "lightly used" goods, including everything from books to clothes to office furniture.

Don't overpay your taxes. If you are getting a hefty refund from the IRS every spring, you're effectively lending money to the government, interest-free. Go through your tax return and see if you can adjust your withholding so you'll receive a refund of around $100. That way you can use your money NOW. (And don't forget to apply the refund to your mortgage when you get it.)

Raise your insurance deductibles. Reassess the deductibles for various kinds of insurance and decide which ones you can reasonably increase. If you can raise them, your premiums will drop.

Don't pay unnecessary fees. Avoid the $1.50 you pay just because an ATM is right there, right now, while your bank's ATM (which carries no charge) is two blocks away.

Avoid fees for paying bills late or forgetting to return videos, and fines for bouncing checks. These are all needless expenses.

Get help from your friends and neighbors. If you can fix the neighbor's car, and she can paint your bathroom, make the trade.

Pay less for long distance. Evaluate your phone bill and see how much you're paying per minute. Some dial-around codes or cheap calling cards (one without a per call surcharge) may give you a better rate. Use your cell phone only when the minutes are free.

Keep your credit score in tip-top condition. The better your credit, the better deal and interest rates you'll be able to negotiate on purchases you may want to make in the future.

Get rid of it! Have regular garage sales to get rid of unwanted items, clothes you haven't worn in two or more years, and toys the kids don't play with any more. Then, put the proceeds toward your principal.

APPENDIX III

General Mortgage Information

Your mortgage payment consists of two primary portions: principal and interest.

Principal refers to the repayment of the original amount borrowed, made on a monthly basis. Interest refers to the cost of borrowing the principal amount, and is repaid on a monthly basis.

When setting up your financing, you will have the option of including property taxes and insurance at the same time that you pay your principal and interest. The advantage is that you will not have to pay your tax and insurance bills all at once when they become due. If you choose this option, the total cost of your tax and insurance for the year will be estimated and divided by 12. The money will then go into escrow (a holding account) until the payments are due, when the bank will pay them for you. This is called PITI (principal/interest/taxes/insurance).

Types of Mortgages

Fixed: This refers to a fixed term of the loan (usually 15 or 30 years), as well as a fixed interest rate, both of which are set when the mortgage is acquired. The monthly payment of principal and interest will not change for the life of the mortgage.

Adjustable: Often referred to as ARMs (Adjustable Rate Mortgages), these are mortgages with interest rates that can be adjusted up or down during the loan term. Thus, the monthly payment of principal and interest will go up or down in accordance with these rate changes. These mortgages may include "Interest-Only" type loans.

There are many types and sub-types of mortgages. Here are some examples:

- 1%-Down Programs
- 100% Financing
- Access Gold
- Adjustable Rate Mortgages (ARMs)
- Chaffa
- COFI Loans
- Fannie Mae
- Farm Loans
- Freddie Mac Gold
- Future Value Loans
- High-Debt-Ratio Loans
- Jumbo Loans
- Manufactured Homes
- MTA Loans
- Option ARM/Negative Amortization
- Pers
- Self-Employed Loans
- Stated Income
- VA
- Zero-Down Programs

APPENDIX IV

Glossary: Important Mortgage Terms You Need To Know BEFORE Obtaining a Mortgage

Adjustable Rate: An interest rate that changes periodically in relation to an index (such as the Cost of Funds for the Eleventh Federal District of banks). Payments may increase or decrease accordingly.

Adjustable Rate Mortgage (ARM): Mortgage loans with interest rates that are periodically adjusted to conform with the current interest rates.

Alternative Documentation: The use of pay stubs, W-2 forms, and bank statements in lieu of verifications of employment (VOE) and verifications of deposit (VOD) to qualify a borrower for a mortgage.

Amortization: A repayment method in which the amount you borrow is repaid gradually though regular monthly payments of principal and interest. During the first few years, most of the payment is applied toward the interest owed. During the final years of the loan, the majority of the payment is applied to the principal.

Annual Membership: A fee charged annually for access to a line of credit. It's often charged regardless of whether or not the line of credit is used. This is also referred to as a "participation fee."

Annual Percentage Rate (APR): A term used in the Truth-in-Lending Act to present the percentage relationship of the total finance charge to the amount of the loan. The APR reflects the cost of the mortgage loan as a yearly rate. It could be higher than the interest rate stated on the note because it includes, in addition to the interest rate, loan discount points, miscellaneous fees and mortgage insurance.

Application: A statement of personal and financial information required for loan approval.

Application Fee: Fees paid upon application. An application fee may frequently include charges for the property appraisal ($200 to $400) and a credit report ($30 to 50).

Appraisal: A report made by a qualified person (appraiser) setting forth an opinion or estimate of property value. (Appraisal also refers to the process involved in determining the value of the property.)

Appraisal Amount or Appraised Value: The fair market value of a home as determined by an independent appraiser. The appraisal uses local real estate market sales activity as a major basis for valuation.

Appreciation: An increase in the value of a property due to market conditions or other causes. The opposite of depreciation.

Assumption of Mortgage: The agreement of a purchaser to become primarily liable for the payments on a mortgage loan. Unless otherwise specified by the lender, the seller may remain secondarily liable for payments.

Balloon Mortgage: A mortgage with a fixed interest rate for a set number of years which must then be paid off in full in a single "balloon" payment. Balloon mortgages are popular with borrowers who expect to sell or refinance their property before the "balloon" payment is due.

Balloon Payment: A lump sum payment of the balance of the loan.

Bankruptcy: Legal relief from the payment of most debts after the surrender of all non-exempt assets to a court-appointed trustee. Assets are distributed to creditors as full satisfaction of debts, with certain priorities and exemptions. A person, firm or corporation may declare bankruptcy under one of several chapters of the U. S. Bankruptcy Code: Chapter 7 covers liquidation of the debtor's assets; Chapter 11 covers reorganization of bankrupt businesses; Chapter 13 covers payment of debts by individuals through a bankruptcy plan .

Cap: The maximum allowable increase, for either payment or interest rate, on an adjustable rate mortgage during a specific period of time.

Cash Out: Receiving money back when refinancing your present mortgage.

Ceiling: The maximum allowable interest rate during the life of an adjustable rate mortgage.

Certified Mortgage Specialist (CMS): A professional sales associate who communicates the needs of the agent and borrower to the operation team.

Client Coordinator (CC): The client coordinator sets the tone throughout the application process and ensures that each customer is kept informed of all needs and status through clear and concise communication.

Closer: The person who coordinates the closing time with the client coordinator and reviews and prepares the necessary closing documents.

Closing: Also known as settlement, closing is the finalization of the process of purchasing or refinancing real estate. The closing includes the delivery of a deed, the signing of notes and the disbursement of funds.

Closing Costs: Any fees paid by either the borrower or the seller during the closing of the mortgage loan. This normally includes an origination fee, discount points, attorney's fees, title insurance, survey fees, and any items that must be prepaid, such as taxes and insurance escrow payments.

Closing Statement: An accounting of the debits and credits incurred at closing. All FHA, VA and conventional financing loans use a uniform closing or settlement statement, commonly referred to as the HUD-1.

Co-Borrower: A party who signs the mortgage note along with the primary borrower and also shares title to the subject real estate.

Collateral: Property pledged as security for a debt (e.g. real estate that secures a mortgage). Collateral can be repossessed if the loan is not repaid.

Combined Loan-To-Value (CLTV) Ratio: The mathematical relationship between the total of all loan amounts (first mortgage plus subordinate liens) and the value of the subject property.

Community Reinvestment Act (CRA): This act requires financial institutions to meet the credit needs of their communities, including those of low-income and moderate-income areas. It also requires banks to make reports concerning their investments in the areas where they do business.

Conforming Loan: Generally this refers to a mortgage loan under $417.000. Qualifying ratios and underwriting methods in such loans are standardized to a large degree.
A loan with a mortgage amount that does not exceed the amount that is eligible for purchase by FNMA or FHLMC. All loans are considered either conforming or non-conforming. Also known as jumbo.

Contract of Sale: The agreement between the buyer and seller as to the purchase price, terms, and conditions necessary to convey the title to the buyer.

Conventional Loan: A mortgage loan that is not insured or guaranteed by the federal government.

Conversion Option: An option to convert an adjustable rate mortgage or balloon mortgage to a fixed-rate mortgage under specified conditions.

Co-Signer: A party who signs the mortgage note along with the borrower but does not own or have any interest in the title to the property.

Credit Limit: The maximum amount that an individual can borrow under a home equity plan.

Creditor: The person or institution to whom another owes a debt.

Credit Rating: A rating given to a person or company to establish creditworthiness based upon present financial condition, experience and past credit history.

Credit Report: A document compiled by a credit-reporting agency that provides information about a buyer's credit cards and payment history, mortgage history, bank loans and public records regarding financial matters.

Deal Structure: An underwriter's review of certain aspects of a loan application that do not meet standard guidelines.

Debt-to-Income Ratio: A comparison of the amount of monthly income to the amount the borrower will owe each month in house payments (PITI) plus other debts. The other debts may include, but are not limited to, car payments, credit cards, alimony, child support, and personal loans. This ratio is commonly used to see if the borrower has the capacity to repay the debt.

Debt Service: The total amount of credit card, auto, mortgage and other debt.

Deed of Trust: Used in many Western states, this is the agreement that is used to pledge a home or other kinds of real estate as security for a loan. Similar to a mortgage.

Default: Failure to comply with the terms of any agreement. In real estate, default is generally used in connection with a mortgage obligation and refers to a failure to comply with the terms of the promissory note. Most often default involves a failure to make mortgage payments. However, there are other means by which a borrower may default, such as the failure to pay real estate taxes.

Depreciation: A decline in the value of property. (The opposite of appreciation.)

Discount Points: A percentage of the loan amount that is either charged or credited to the loan by the lender. Loans that are made at the present market rate, with no points, are considered to be made at "par." Because of this ability to charge or credit points to an individual loan, the lender can tailor a loan program and interest rate to fit the needs of an individual borrower. Discount points can be negotiated in the Purchase Contract to be paid by either the seller or the borrower. Each point equals 1% of the mortgage loan. For example, a charge of 1 point on a $50,000 loan would result in a charge of $500; 1/2 point would be $250 ($50,000 x .50%).

Down Payment: The difference between the purchase price and that portion of the purchase price that is being financed. Most lenders require the down payment to be paid from the buyer's own funds. Gifts from related parties are sometimes acceptable but must be disclosed to the lender.

Due on Sale: A clause in a mortgage agreement that states that if the borrower sells, transfers or (in some instances) encumbers the property, the lender has the right to demand the outstanding balance in full.

Earnest Money: A deposit made by a purchaser on real estate as evidence of good faith.

Effective Interest Rate: The annual cost of credit expressed as a percentage. It includes upfront costs paid to obtain the loan and is, therefore, usually a higher amount than the interest rate stipulated in the mortgage note. The effective interest rate is useful when comparing loan programs that have different rates and points.

Encumbrance: A claim against a property by another party, which usually affects the ability to transfer ownership of the property.

Equal Credit Opportunity Act (ECOA): Also known as Regulation B, the ECOA is a federal law that prohibits a lender from discriminating on the basis of race, color, religion, national origin, sex, marital status, age, income derived from public assistance programs, or previous exercise of Consumer Credit Protection Act rights.

Equity: The difference between the current market value of a property and the principal balance on all outstanding loans.

Escrow Account: An account held by the lending institution into which the borrower pays monthly installments for property taxes, insurance, and special assessments, and from which the lender disburses these sums as they become due.

Fair Credit Reporting Act: Regulates the collection and distribution of information by the consumer credit reporting industry. The Fair Credit Reporting Act also affects the ways in which financial institutions collect and convey credit data about loan applicants or borrowers.

Fair Housing Act: Prohibits the denial or variance of the terms of real estate-related transactions based on race, color, religion, sex, national origin, disability, or familial status of the credit applicant. Real estate-related transactions include mortgages, home improvement loans and other loans secured by a dwelling.

Federal Home Loan Mortgage Corporation (FHLMC): Also known as Freddie Mac, this publicly-owned corporation was created by Congress to support the secondary mortgage market. It purchases and sells conventional residential mortgages, as well as residential mortgages insured by the Federal Housing Administration (FHA) or guaranteed by the Veterans Administration (VA).

Federal National Mortgage Association (FNMA): Also known as Fannie Mae, this privately-owned corporation supports the secondary mortgage market. It adds liquidity to the mortgage market by investing in home loans nationwide.

FHA Loan: More appropriately termed "FHA-insured loan," this is a loan in which the Federal Housing Administration insures the lender against losses the lender may incur due to a homeowner's default.

FICO Score: A credit score given to an individual that establishes his or her creditworthiness based on present financial condition, experience and credit history.

Finance Charge: The cost of credit expressed as a dollar amount. Specifically, it is the total amount of interest and other loan charges paid by the borrower over the term of the loan and at closing. Loan charges include origination fees, discount points, mortgage insurance, and other applicable charges. If the seller pays any of these charges, they cannot be included in the finance charge.

Financial Statement: A summary of facts showing the financial status of an individual or company. For individuals, the financial statement reveals their assets and liabilities as of a given date. For a company, it includes a Profit and Loss Statement (P&L) for a designated period of time plus a balance sheet, which states the company's assets and liabilities as of a given date.

First Mortgage: A mortgage that is in first lien position. The first mortgage takes priority over all other liens that are financial encumbrances.

Fixed Rate: An interest rate or payment amount that is kept at the same figure for the term of the loan.

First Rate Adjustment, First rate adjustment after: In association with an adjustable rate mortgage loan, this is the number of months after the loan has closed when the first interest rate adjustment will occur.

First Rate Adjustment, Maximum rate decrease: In association with an adjustable rate mortgage loan, this is the greatest amount by which the interest rate can decrease in the first adjustment period.

First Rate Adjustment, Maximum rate increase: In association with an adjustable rate mortgage loan, this is the greatest amount by which an interest rate can increase in the first adjustment period.

Fixed Rate Mortgage: The type of mortgage in which the interest rate cannot change during the entire term of the loan.

Floating: The term used when a purchaser elects not to lock in an interest rate at the time of application.

Flood Insurance: Insurance that compensates for direct physical damages due to a flood to the insured property, subject to the terms, provisions, conditions and losses-not-covered provision of the policy. Flood insurance is required for mortgages on properties located in federally designated flood areas.

Gift Letter: A letter or affidavit that indicates that part of a borrower's down payment is supplied by relatives or friends in the form of a gift, and that the gift does not have to be repaid.

Good Faith Estimate: A written estimate of closing costs that a lender must provide the borrower within three days of submitting an application.

Grace Period: A period of time during which a loan payment may be paid after its due date without incurring a late penalty. However, such late payments may appear on the individual's credit report.

Gross Income: Used for loan qualifying purposes, this refers to the income of the borrower before taxes or expenses have been deducted.

Hazard Insurance: Insurance against losses caused by perils that are commonly covered in policies described as a "homeowner policy."

Home Equity Conversion Mortgage (HECM): A special type of mortgage that enables older homeowners to convert their home equity into cash using a variety of payment options to address their specific financial needs. Unlike traditional home equity loans, the borrower does not qualify on the basis of income but on the value of his or her home. In addition, the loan does not have to be repaid until the borrower vacates the property. Sometimes called a "reverse mortgage."

Home Equity Line of Credit (HELOC): A loan that allows the borrower to borrow funds at the time and in the amount he or she chooses, up to a designated maximum credit limit. A home equity like of credit is often used for home improvements, major purchases or expenses, and debt consolidation. Repayment is secured by the equity in the borrower's home. Simple interest (interest-only payments on the outstanding balance) on a HELOC is usually tax deductible.

Home Equity Loan: A fixed- or adjustable-rate loan obtained for a variety of purposes that is secured by the equity in the borrower's home. Often used for home improvement or freeing up equity for investment in other real estate or non-real estate investments. The interest paid is usually tax deductible. Therefore, home equity loans are often recommended as replacements or substitutes for consumer loans in which interest is not tax deductible, such as auto or boat loans, credit card debt, medical debt and education loans.

Home Maintenance: Costs associated with maintaining a home. These costs may include, but are not limited to, general repairs, replacement or repair of the furnace, air conditioning, roof, plumbing and electrical systems.

Home Mortgage Disclosure Act (HMDA): Also known as Regulation C, the purpose of HMDA is to provide disclosure of mortgage lending application activity (home purchase or improvement) to regulators and the public. Information is collected from each home mortgage application and compiled to produce a report on application activity by geographic designation (census tract).

Homeowner's Association (HOA): A non-profit corporation or association that manages the common areas and services of a condominium or Planned Unit Development (PUD).

Homeowner's Insurance: Insurance that covers damage to the insured's residence as well as liability claims made against the insured, subject to the policy terms, conditions, provisions, losses-not-insured provision and exclusions.

Housing Expense Ratio: Ratio used to determine the borrowers capacity to repay a home loan. It's derived by comparing the borrower's monthly income to the house payment (principal, interest, taxes and insurance).

HUD I Settlement Statement: A form used at loan closing to itemize the costs associated with purchasing the home. The HUD I Settlement Statement is used universally by mandate of the Department of Housing and Urban Development.

Index: A number, usually a percentage, upon which future interest rates for adjustable rate mortgages are based. Common indexes include the Cost of Funds for the Eleventh Federal District of banks, and the average rate of a one-year Government Treasury Security.

Initial Interest Rate: The interest rate at the start of an adjustable rate mortgage (ARM). It may be lower than the "going market rate," and it remains constant until adjusted up or down on the adjustment date.

Interest Income: The potential income from funds that would have been used for the down payment, closing costs, and any difference (increase) between monthly rental payment and monthly mortgage payment. Interest income is earnings from savings accounts, certificates of deposits and certain other investments, and that the amount to be earned is usually spelled out in advance, as in 2% interest on money in your savings account.

Interest Rate: The percentage of an amount of money that is paid for its use for a specific time; usually expressed as an annual percentage.

Judgment: A court decree declaring one individual (or company) is indebted to another and fixing the amount of such indebtedness.

Jumbo Loan: Mortgage loans over $203,150. Terms and underwriting requirements may vary from conforming loans.

Late Charge: A penalty charged for failure to pay a regular mortgage loan installment by its due date.

Lien: A legal claim against a property that must be paid off when the property is sold. A lien is created when you borrow money and use your home as collateral for the loan.

Life of Loan, Maximum Rate Decrease: In association with an adjustable rate mortgage loan, this is the greatest amount the interest can decrease over the life of the loan.

Life of Loan, Maximum Rate Increase: In association with an adjustable rate mortgage loan, this is the greatest amount the interest can increase over the life of the loan.

Loan Application: A document which defines the loan contract terms, gives the borrower's name, place of employment, salary, bank accounts, credit references, real estate owned, and describes the property to be mortgaged. The lender uses the information contained in this document as a basis for deciding whether or not to grant the loan.

Loan Balance: The amount of principal owed by the borrower.

Loan Term: The number of years over which a loan is amortized. Most people think of it, the number of years it takes to pay off the loan, generally 15, 20 or 30 years.

Loan to Value Ratio (LTV): A ratio determined by dividing the sales price or appraised value of the property into the loan amount. The ratio is expressed as a percentage. For example, with a sales price of $100,000 and a mortgage loan of $80,000, the loan-to-value ratio would be 80%. Loans with an LTV over 80% may require private mortgage insurance.

Lock or Lock In: A commitment you obtain from a lender assuring you a particular interest rate or feature for a definite time period. This provides protection if, for example, interest rates rise between the time you apply for and close the loan.

Margin: An amount, usually a percentage, which is added to the index to determine the interest rate for adjustable rate mortgages.

Median Income: The middle level of income, with half of the incomes higher and half lower. This is not to be confused with an average income.

Minimum Payment: The lowest amount you must pay (usually monthly) on a home equity loan or line of credit. In some plans, the minimum payment may be "interest only" (simple interest). In other plans, the minimum payment may include principal and interest (amortized).

Mortgage: The document used to pledge the title to a piece of real estate as security for repayment of a loan.

Mortgage Banker: The individual or institution that originates mortgage loans, loaning borrowers the necessary money and closing the loan in their names.

Mortgage Broker: The individual or institution that takes loan applications and processes the necessary paperwork, but does not fund the loan. The mortgage broker works on behalf of several investors, including mortgage bankers, savings and loans, banks and investment bankers.

Mortgage Insurance (MIP or PMI): Insurance purchased by the borrower to insure the lender (or the government) against loss should the borrower default. MIP, or mortgage insurance premium, is paid on government-insured loans (FHA or VA loans) regardless of the LTV (loan-to-value) ratio. If a government-insured loan is paid off in advance of maturity, the borrower may be entitled to a small refund of MIP. PMI is paid on loans that are not government-insured and that have an LTV greater than 80%. When a homeowner has accumulated 20% of a home's value as equity, the lender may waive PMI if the borrower requests it. Note that such insurance does not constitute a form of life insurance (the kind that pays off the loan in case of death).

Mortgage Loan: A loan that uses real estate as security or collateral to provide repayment should a borrower default on the loan terms. The mortgage or deed of trust is an agreement that pledges the home or other real estate as security.

Mortgagee: The lender in a mortgage loan transaction.

Mortgagor: The borrower in a mortgage loan transaction.

Negative Amortization: Amortization in which the payment made is insufficient to fund complete repayment of the loan at its termination. This usually occurs when the potential increase in the monthly payment is limited by a ceiling. The portion of the payment that should be paid - but cannot be paid because of the limit on the increase - is added to the remaining balance owed. The balance owed may increase, rather than decrease, over the life of the loan.

Net Income: The difference between effective gross income minus all expenses, including taxes and insurance. The term is qualified as income before depreciation and debt.

Non-Conforming Loan: A loan with a mortgage amount exceeding the amount eligible for purchase by FNMA or FHLMC. All loans above this amount are considered to be non-conforming or jumbo loans.

Non-Owner-Occupied Property: Property purchased by a borrower as an investment with the intent of generating rental income, tax benefits and profitable resale, rather than as a primary residence.

Note: A written promise by one party to pay a specific sum of money to a second party under conditions agreed upon mutually. Also called a "promissory note."

Note Rate: The interest rate on the mortgage loan.
Origination Fee: A fee paid to a lender for processing a loan application, stated as a percentage of the mortgage amount.

Origination Process: The process in which a lender solicits business, gathers required information and commits to the lending of money for the purchase of real estate.

Owner-Occupied Property: A property that is occupied as a primary residence by the borrower or an immediate family member.

PITI: Principal, interest, taxes and insurance, which taken together comprise the monthly mortgage payment.

Planned Unit Development (PUD): A housing project that may consist of any combination of homes (one-family to four-family), condominiums or various other dwellings. In a PUD, often the individual unit and the land it occupies are owned by the unit/homeowner, while the Homeowner's Association owns the common facilities.

Points: The amount paid either to maintain or lower the interest rate charged. Each point is equal to 1% of the loan amount (e.g., two points on a $100,000 mortgage would equal $2,000).

Pre-Approval: A process in which a customer provides appropriate information on income, debts and assets which is used to make a credit-only loan decision. While the customer typically has not identified a property to be purchased, a specific sales price and loan amount are used to make a loan decision. (The sales price and loan amount are based on customer assumptions.)

Pre-Qualification: A process designed to assist a customer in determining the maximum sales price, loan amount and PITI payment he or she can get. A pre-qualification is not considered a loan approval. Applying for a loan is a separate process.

Prepaid Expenses (Prepaids): The funds required by the lender to be deposited in order to establish the escrow account for taxes and insurance at the time of closing (also refers to prepaid interest).

Prepaid Interest: Interest that the borrower pays the lender before it becomes due.

Prepayment: A loan repayment made in advance of its contractual due date.

Prepayment Penalty: A penalty under a note, mortgage or deed of trust imposed when the loan is paid before its maturity date.

Principal and Interest: The two components of a monthly mortgage payment. Principal refers to the portion of the monthly payment that reduces the remaining balance of the loan. Interest is the fee charged for borrowing the money.

Principal Balance: The amount of money due on a mortgage, not counting interest.

Principal, Interest, Real Estate Tax, Insurance Payment (PITI): The total mortgage payment, which includes principal, interest, taxes and insurance.

Private Mortgage Insurance (PMI): Insurance purchased to cover a loss by a lender in the event of default by a borrower. A private insurance company issues this insurance. The premium is paid by the borrower and is included in the mortgage payment.

Processing: Gathering the loan application and all required supporting documents (including the property appraisal, credit report, credit history, and statement of income and expenses) so a lender can make a decision as to whether or not to grant a loan.

Promissory Note: A document in which the borrower promises to pay a stated amount on or by a specific date. The note normally states the names of the lender and borrower, the terms of payment and the interest rate.

Property Taxes: Taxes assessed on real estate. Property taxes are based on valuations by local and/or state governments.

Purchase Agreement: A written agreement between a buyer and seller of real property that states the price and terms of the sale.

Purchase Price: The total amount paid for a home.

Qualifying Income Ratios: These are ways to analyze a borrower's financial status to aid lenders in deciding whether or not to grant the borrower a loan. One type of analysis compares the amount of the proposed monthly mortgage payment to the monthly income. Another type of analysis compares the amount of the prospective borrower's total monthly payments (for example car, credit card plus proposed mortgage payments) to his/her monthly income.

Rate Index: An index used to adjust the interest rate of an adjustable mortgage loan.

Real Estate Appreciation Rate: The percentage of increase in the value of a piece of real estate expressed as an annual rate.

Real Estate Settlement Procedures Act (RESPA): A consumer protection law that requires, among other things, lenders to give borrowers advance notice of closing costs.

Realtor: A person licensed to negotiate and transact the sale of real estate on behalf of a property owner (as well as purchase on behalf of buyers). A real estate broker or associate must be an active member of a real estate board affiliated with the National Association of Realtors.

Recording Fee: The amount paid to the county recorder's office in order to make a document a matter of public record.

Regulation Z: A Federal Reserve regulation issued under the Truth-in-Lending Act that, among other things, requires that a credit purchaser (borrower) be advised in writing of all costs connected with the credit portion of the loan.

Rental Payment: A payment made to use another's property. The amount of the payment is determined contractually and is typically paid on a monthly basis.

Renter's Insurance: Insurance against perils commonly covered in policies described as a "Renters Policy."

Repayment: The payment of a mortgage loan over a period of time established when the loan is originated.

Rescind: To avoid, cancel or treat a contract or other object of the agreement as if it never existed.

Right to Rescission: The legal right to void, cancel or treat a contract in such a way as if it never existed. Right of rescission is not applicable to mortgages made to purchase a home, but may be applicable to other mortgages, such as home equity loans and any refinance loans.

Sales Contract: A written agreement between parties stating

all terms and conditions of a sale.

Savings Rate: The interest rate a person expects to earn on a savings account or investment account.

Secondary Market: An informal market where existing mortgages are bought and sold. It is the traditional aftermarket for mortgage loans that brings together lenders that sell mortgages with lenders, investors and agencies that buy mortgages.

Security Interest: An interest that a lender takes in the borrower's property to ensure repayment of a debt.

Seller Contribution: The seller may be paying some or all of the borrower's cost (closing, points, etc.). The amount of the contribution has limitations.

Selling Costs: The costs incurred in selling a home. This could include realtor expenses and other miscellaneous expenses such as painting or minor repairs to prepare the home for sale.

Servicing a Loan: The ongoing process of collecting a monthly mortgage payment, including accounting for and payment of the yearly tax and/or homeowner's insurance bills.

Servicing Released: A stipulation in the agreement for the sale of mortgages in which the lender is not responsible for servicing the loan.

Servicing Retained: A loan sale in which the original lender's servicing department continues to service the loan after the sale to a secondary institution or investor.

Settlement Statement: Also referred to as a HUD-1 Settlement Statement. A complete breakdown of costs for the seller and buyer involved in a real estate transaction.

Survey: A measurement of land, prepared by a registered land surveyor, which shows the location of the land with reference to known points, its dimensions and the location and dimensions of any improvements.

Subordinate Financing: An additional lien against real estate which secures the borrower's first mortgage. This lien takes second priority to the first mortgage.

Subsequent Rate Adjustment, Maximum Rate Decrease: In association with an adjustable rate mortgage loan, this is the greatest amount the interest rate can decrease when it is scheduled for reevaluation and possible adjustment.

Subsequent Rate Adjustment, Maximum Rate Increase: In association with an adjustable rate mortgage loan, this is the greatest amount the interest rate can increase when it is scheduled for reevaluation and possible adjustment.

Subsequent Rate Adjustment, Next ARM Adjustment Date: In association with an adjustable rate mortgage loan, this is the date scheduled for the next reevaluation and possible adjustment.

Subsequent Rate Adjustment, Rate Change Frequency: In association with an Adjustable Rate Mortgage loan, this is the frequency with which possible adjustments may be made to the interest rate after the initial adjustment.

Tax Rates: Tax levied by the federal government and some states based on a person's income. Federal income tax rates vary depending on a person's adjusted gross income.

Tax Savings: The amount saved on taxes by itemizing deductions on income tax returns.

Title: Evidence of the right to or ownership of a piece of property. In the case of real estate, the evidence of owner-ship is the title deed, which specifies in whom the legal state is vested. The title deed also specifies the history of owner-ship and transfers of the property. The title may be acquired through purchase, inheritance, devise, gift or foreclosure of a mortgage.

Title Insurance Policy: A contract by which the insurer, usu-ally a title company, indicates who has legal title and agrees to pay that individual (or company) a specific amount of any loss caused by claims or defects in the title.

(a) Owner's Title Policy: Usually issued to the landowner. The owner's title insurance policy is bought and paid for only once and then continues in force without any further payment. Owner's title insurance policies are not assignable.

(b) Mortgagee's Title Policy: Issued to the mortgagee and terminates when the mortgage debt is paid. In the event of foreclosure, or if the mortgagee acquires title from the mortgagor in lieu of foreclosure, the policy continues in force, giving continued protection against any defects of title that existed at, or prior to, the date of the policy.

Transaction Fee: A fee that may be charged each time you draw on a home equity credit line.

Treasury Bills: Interest-bearing U.S. government obligations sold at a weekly sale. The change in interest rates paid on these obligations is frequently used as the rate index for adjustable rate mortgage loans.

Truth in Lending (TIL): The name given to the federal statutes and regulations (Regulation Z) designed primarily to ensure that prospective borrowers of credit receive credit and cost information before concluding a loan transaction.

Underwriting (Mortgage Loans): The process of evaluating a loan application to determine the risk involved for the lender. It involves an analysis of the borrower's creditworthiness and the quality of the property itself.

VA Loan or "VA-Insured Loan": A loan in which the Veteran's Administration insures the lender against losses that may occur due to the borrower's default. Available only to veterans.

Verification of Deposit (VOD): Form used in mortgage lending to verify the deposits or assets of a prospective borrower when monthly bank statements are unavailable or unusable.

About the Authors

Richard Weathington

Richard started in the loan business in 1987 in Sacramento, California. After advancing in the ranks at various banks and mortgage companies, he opened his own mortgage brokerage.

Soon several colleagues approached him for advice on how to venture out on their own and obtain brokers' licenses. Prompted by his success in helping other people become brokers, Richard became a Credentialed Instructor.

Since 1995 Richard has worked as an executive for some of the most prestigious banks in the world, including US Bank, Saxon Mortgage, and Profound Mortgage, where he secured multimillion-dollar deals for several Silicon Valley high-tech companies-all while developing his teaching and mentoring skills.

In 2000, Richard pursued his passion for teaching by instructing full time at multiple Bay Area lenders as well as for the American School of Mortgage Banking. For the past five years Richard has taught courses including: Loan Processing, Loan Officer Training, Mortgage Loan Underwriting, and Loan Originator Sales and Marketing.

Today Richard serves as the chairman of The Loan Broker Academy-a breakthrough program that teaches "everyday people" how to succeed in the mortgage industry and that guarantees its students certification by the State of California in just two intensive days.

Beth M. Ley, Ph.D.

Beth M. Ley, Ph.D., has been a scientific and technical writer since 1988 and has written many health-related books, including the best sellers, DHEA: Unlocking the Secrets to the Fountain of Youth and MSM: On Our Way Back to Health with Sulfur.

She wrote her own undergraduate degree program and graduated in Scientific and Technical Writing from North Dakota State University in 1987 (combination of Zoology and Journalism). Beth has Master's (1998) and Doctoral degrees (1999) in Nutrition.

Beth is dedicated to God and to spreading the health message. She enjoys nature and spending time with her Dalmatian, KC.

Her professional memberships include the New York Academy of Sciences, the American Nutraceutical Association, and Resurrection Apostolic International Network (RAIN).

More Books from BL Publications

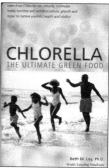

237

OTHER BOOKS AVAILABLE:

Aspirin Alternatives: The Top Natural Pain-Relieving Analgesics (Lombardi) ... $8.95

Bilberry & Lutein: The Vision Enhancers! (Ley) $4.95

Calcium: The Facts, Fossilized Coral (Ley) $4.95

Castor Oil: Its Healing Properties (Ley) $3.95

Dr. John Willard on Catalyst Altered Water (Ley) $3.95

Chlorella: Ultimate Green Food (Ley) $4.95

CoQ10: All-Around Nutrient for All-Around Health (Ley) $4.95

Colostrum: Nature's Gift to the Immune System (Ley) $5.95

DHA: The Magnificent Marine Oil (Ley) $6.95

DHEA: Unlocking the Secrets/Fountain of Youth-2nd ed. (Ash & Ley) $14.95

Diabetes to Wholeness (Ley) $9.95

Discover the Beta Glucan Secret (Ley) $3.95

Fading: One family's journey ... Alzheimer's (Kraft) $12.95

Flax! Fabulous Flax! (Ley) $4.95

Flax Lignans: Fifty Years to Harvest (Sönju & Ley) $4.95

God Wants You Well (Ley) $14.95

Health Benefits of Probiotics (Dash) $4.95

How Did We Get So Fat? 2nd Edition (Susser & Ley) $8.95

How to Fight Osteoporosis and Win! (Ley) $6.95

Maca: Adaptogen and Hormone Balancer (Ley) $4.95

Marvelous Memory Boosters (Ley) $3.95

Medicinal Mushrooms: Agaricus Blazei Murill (Ley) $4.95

MSM: On Our Way Back to Health W/ Sulfur (Ley) SPANISH $3.95

MSM: On Our Way Back to Health W/ Sulfur (Ley) $4.95

Natural Healing Handbook (Ley) $14.95

Nature's Road to Recovery: Nutritional Supplements for the Alcoholic & Chemical Dependent (Ley) $5.95

PhytoNutrients: Medicinal Nutrients in Foods- Revised /Updated (Ley) $5.95

Recipes For Life! 10 Principals of Biblical Nutrition (Spiral Bound Cookbook) (Ley) $19.95

Secrets Banks and Lenders Don't Want You to Know (Weathington/Ley) .. $29.95

Secrets the Oil Companies Don't Want You to Know (LaPointe) $10.00

Spewed! How to Cast Out Lukewarm Christianity Through Fasting (Ley) .$15.95

The Potato Antioxidant: Alpha Lipoic Acid (Ley) $6.95

Vinpocetine: Revitalize Your Brain w/ Periwinkle Extract! (Ley) $4.95

$5.00 shipping in the US

Credit card orders please call toll free: 1-877-BOOKS11

For more information or online ordering visit:
www.blpublications.com

Your Free Gift

As a token of my thanks for taking out time to read my book, I would like to offer you a free gift:

Click Below and Download your **Free Report**

Learn 5 Mental Shifts To Turbo-Charge Your Performance In Every Area Of Your Life - in Next 30 Days!

You can also grab your FREE GIFT Report through this below URL:

http://sombathla.com/mentalshifts

More Books by Som Bathla

The Gift of Grit

The Magic Of Accelerated Learning

The Power of Self Discipline

The Science of High Performance

The Way To Lasting Success

The Mindful Mind

Conquer Your Fear Of Failure

The Mindset Makeover

Living Beyond Self Doubt

Focus Mastery

Just Get It Done

Master Your Day Design Your Life

The Quoted Life

The 30- Hour Day

You may also visit my all books together at

http://sombathla.com/amazon

Table of Contents

Introduction

"The two most important days in your life are the day you are born and the day you find out why.

~ Mark Twain

What do you think the most exciting innovation of the past decade has been?

Yes, you guessed it right!

I'm talking about the smartphone. But why do you call it a smartphone in the first place?

Because you can perform most of your functions at the touch of a finger that otherwise required working on a computer. Also, it serves multiple purposes on just a single device—it's your watch, camera, e-reader, video game console, movie player, and much more. In the nutshell, it makes

you feel smarter by offering you quick solution for your various needs.

When you buy a smartphone, you have a few specific purposes in your mind. For example, when I bought my first smartphone, my primary objective was to read, but I didn't want to carry and manage a different gadget for reading the electronic books. My wife would always buy the smartphone, by looking at the front and rear camera's megapixel capacity, better design, and other cool features.

What purpose do you want to achieve when you buy the latest version of iPhone or your favorite phone? Maybe you want to take the benefit of the latest features and thus have seamless access to your work-related data without needing to open your computer. Or maybe you just want to flaunt your new device in front of your friends or maybe you just wanted this for your infotainment purposes.

It could be any other purpose. But the point is there is some "why" or "purpose" before you incur any expenditure on your smartphone or any other product.

OK, now let's talk about another most exciting aspect of discussion.

Let's talk about YOU.

What's your purpose or utility? I know it's a heavy question, still, let's just dig it.

Have you ever thought about what your purpose in life is? Of course, your parents had a purpose to give you birth. They wanted to experience more joy and fun in their lives and chose to bring you to their lives to meet this objective. Some parents have purpose to bring their child to this world to continue their family and hope their child will earn accolades and make a name for themselves.

We are so clear about the purpose of buying any gadget or appliance. We are also clear about why we were brought to this world by our parents. But here comes the most important question.

Do you know what your purpose in life is? No, we already talked about your parent's purpose—this is a question about your purpose of doing what you have been doing and will continue to do.

The question is what's your why? What makes you wake up every morning and get going with enthusiasm? Have you got it already or are you searching for it yet?

Most people who work day jobs are not as excited on Monday morning, as they are on Friday evenings—and that shows that it's not their work that makes them jump out of the bed. A recent study[1] showed that 68% of the workforce in the United States feels disengaged from their work. And that's why we have restaurants with the name TGI Friday's (acronym for Thank God It's Friday).

However, there is a better way of living. If you want to know about people, deeply engaged in living with joy and fulfillment, let me take you to Okinawa an island in the southern-most region of Japan. It is reported[2] that Japanese people have an average life expectancy of 83 years old, the highest in the world. And the people on Okinawa Island are considered to be the

---

[1] https://www.inc.com/sonia-thompson/68-percent-of-employees-are-disengaged-but-there-i.html

[2] https://www.ncbi.nlm.nih.gov/pmc/articles/PMC2822182/

healthiest people on the planet with "longest disability-free life expectancy in the world".

Do you want to know the reason for their healthy, vibrant and ailment free life?

This is because Okinawans are known for maintaining a highly positive outlook in life. They pursue their "ikigai" (pronounced as 'Icky Guy'), which is a concept that means "reason for being" or "reason for waking up in the morning. It means the very thing that prompts you to wake up in your morning with excitement. It's your prime reason why you jump out of bed and start doing that thing. It is your core purpose of life – your deeper "Why". You'd be surprised to know; the Japanese don't have a word for the term retirement.

In his great book, *The Happiness Equation*, Neil Pasricha talks about "a 102-year-old-karate master whose ikigai is to carry forth his martial art, a 100-year-old fisherman whose ikigai is to feed his family, a 102-year-old woman whose ikigai is to hold her great-great-great-granddaughter."

They got their ikigai—their reason to wake up every morning and get busy with their work, which makes them happiest and longest living people in the world.

Have you got your ikigai yet?

No worries. That's the very objective of this book—to help you find out your purpose that wakes you up every morning and do the things that give you a sense of fulfillment and joy.

What will you find in this book?

If you are skeptical about the whole topic of finding your why, I understand that, because it generally sounds like a bit mystical subject to talk about. But that's not the case—if you stay with me, I'll share with you enough neuroscience and human psychology-based research and studies that will show you how purpose in life drives your behavior and actions to get the best results in your pursuits.

Here is a glimpse of what you will from this book:

- What exactly purpose means and whether you really need it.

- How a life with purpose can give miraculous benefits proven by neuroscience-based studies and a lack thereof will ruin everything you've earned in life.
- What a Purpose-in-Life Scale is and how you too can measure your score.
- Why should you choose pursuing your purpose rather than only focusing on your passion, without caring about your *Why*?
- Learn the most important questions that can activate your purpose and understand the rules of the game for discovering your purpose.
- Discover a 6-step process to get started on your purpose discovery journey.
- How can you stay connected to your purpose every time you drift from it?
- And finally how clarity of purpose will help you to get into a state of flow and seamless high performance.

Doesn't that all sound exciting?

Trust me, the psychological studies, science-based research, and taking cues from philosophy, this book will offer you a

succinct guide and a blueprint to discover your purpose.

Now without further delay, let's get started.

Chapter 1: How Purpose is Your Soul's Oxygen

****

"Your purpose in life is to find your purpose and give your whole heart and soul to it" —

Gautam Buddha

Whatever you do in life, there is a reason. The law of cause and effect—a dominant principle of classic physics is in force everywhere. This law states that for every effect, there is a cause behind it.

Ralph Waldo Emerson went to the extent of saying the law of cause and effect is the "law of laws". The most important lesson involving human conduct and interaction is seen in the law of cause and effect, which states: *"For every action there is an equal and opposite reaction"*. Taking it to a deeper level, every thought, word, and deed is a cause that sets off a wave of energy throughout the universe which in turn

creates the effect whether desirable or undesirable.

Tony Robbins, world-famous life coach and author, explains that every human action is caused by the two reasons—either you want to increase pleasure or avoid pain. No one wants to feel pain and be sad, and of course everyone wants to be happier. Therefore, all your behavior and actions are driven by these underlying reasons. There is a purpose or *why* behind each of your action—whether it's a tiny day to day action or your highest goal.

If you open the refrigerator to chow on a dark brownie, your 'why' is to satiate your desire of instant gratification, to feel happier. If you want to stay in bed late in the morning, your purpose is to enjoy the warmth of the quilt—your why is avoid the pain of getting out in the chilly winter, and enjoy the pleasure of staying in your cozy bed. Your *why* behind both the actions were to seek instant pleasure or to avoid immediate pain, so you accordingly chose your behavior or action.

Now let's take another example that lies on the other end of the spectrum. You wake up

at 5 a.m. in the morning and hit the gym for your intensive workout or run outside winter. Here you also have a reason or purpose behind such action. Either you are preparing yourself for the next half or full marathon, or you simply love to get a feel of a healthy and fit body. Did you notice how changing your underlying purpose or your *why* changes the quality of your actions? The same act of getting out of your bed, which was causing pain in the first example, is giving you a sense of fulfillment here. It's because the quality of your actions changes, depending on the purpose you have set in your mind. This little story will elaborate on it further.

A man was passing through a construction site, where many laborers were doing the manual work. This man asked one laborer, "What are you doing, brother?". The laborer looked grudgingly and said, "Can't you see? I'm doing this crappy work of lifting the bricks to build this building."

The man was shocked to see the rude behavior of this laborer. But he moved on and faced another laborer. He repeated the same question. This second laborer was comparatively in a better state of mind. He

stated he was working hard to earn his livelihood, so he could take care of his wife and children well. Though this laborer was equally sweating and feeling tired from the work, but his approach toward the work had some better reasons, which gave him a sense of fulfillment.

Next the man moved to a third laborer, who had a peaceful smile on his face despite being fully drenched in sweat. He asked the question again: "What are you doing, my friend?" This laborer responded in a way that touched the man's heart. He said, "You see, I am putting brick after brick to construct a temple of God here."

This is a short story, but it leaves us with a profound message. You see three different people doing the same work had different purposes behind their work, which remarkably differentiated the behavior and quality of life of each person.

Martin Seligman in his book *Authentic Happiness* puts it in a very beautiful way. He says:

"Any job can become a calling, and any calling can become a job. A physician who views the work as a Job and is simply

interested in making a good income does not have a Calling, while a garbage collector who sees the work as making the world a cleaner, healthier place could have a Calling."

Have you ever paused and asked yourself the deeper purpose behind your actions?

Now it's a time to introspect and ask: *"Why am I doing what I am doing?"*

And to help you reach to you deeper why, let's first understand what exactly we mean by why or your purpose. Let's try to understand the psychology of purpose. We need to understand our innermost needs and what motivates us for taking action.

What Is Purpose And The Human Psychology Behind It?

Let's start by understanding the meaning and psychology of purpose.

Researchers have defined purpose in life[3] as below:

"Purpose is the psychological tendency to derive meaning from life's experiences and

---

3

https://www.ncbi.nlm.nih.gov/pmc/articles/PMC289717 2/

to possess a sense of intentionality and goal directedness that guides behavior."

According to Kendall Bronk, a researcher at Claremont Graduate University on the impact of purpose on the human well-being, the sense of purpose is defined by its inherent subjectivity- by the core innermost self. She explains[4] that purpose can be broken down into three components.

- It's an ultimate goal that shapes your short-term choices and behavior.

- It is personally meaningful, coming from within. In other words, no one is standing over you and forcing you to pursue your goal; you are self-motivated. The goal imbues your life with importance and value.

- Finally, a purpose in life goes beyond the self, leading you to want to make a difference in the world.

We thrive when we are working for some greater good, which is beyond our own selves. Some people find purpose in making

---

[4]https://greatergood.berkeley.edu/article/item/can_the _science_of_purpose_help_explain_white_supremacy

others laugh, caring for the sick and injured, or just taking care of their families. Others want to protect the environment.

The Theory of Human Needs and How Purpose Is Your Soul's Oxygen:

The moment human being takes birth, he craves for the needs of various things. Our all actions are directed toward fulfilling those needs. Abraham Maslow propounded his famous theory[5] on the hierarchy of human needs and the pyramid below explains his explanation of various types of needs:

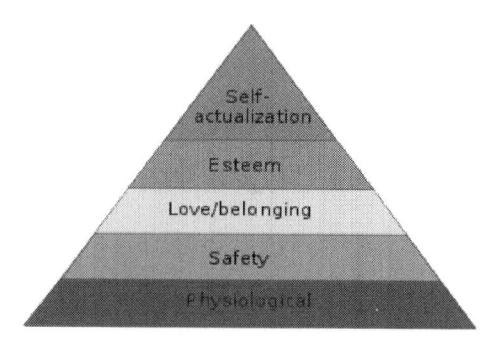

(Image courtesy: Wikipedia)

---

[5]https://en.wikipedia.org/wiki/Maslow%27s_hierarchy_of_needs#Self-transcendence

Maslow explained as part of his initial study that there are five kinds of human needs and they start from the lowest end of the pyramid. However, in the later part of his career, Maslow discovered that all these five needs are related to human's own needs, and he came out with last sixth need of humans. Here's what these needs are:

1. **Physiological**: These needs are limited to the survival of humans and most important for the survival of human body. It includes water, food, clothing, shelter, breathing, sex, etc.

2. **Safety**: Once the physiologic needs of a person are reasonably satisfied, the needs for safety and security govern his behavior. Safety includes safety from war, natural disaster, economic safety, health-related safety i.e. access to healthcare if needed.

3. **Love & Belonging**: After physiological and safety needs are fulfilled, the third level of human needs is interpersonal and involves

feelings of belongingness. It includes the need for family, friends, and intimate relationship with someone.

4. **Esteem:** Esteem needs are ego needs or status needs develop a concern with getting recognition, status, importance, and respect from others. All humans have a need to feel respected; this includes the need to have self-esteem and self-respect.

5. **Self-Actualization**: This level of need refers to what a person's full potential is and the realization of that potential. Maslow describes this level as the desire to accomplish everything that one can, to become the most one can be.

The Maslow Hierarchy of needs theory paper that was submitted in 1943 covered on these five needs.

But Victor Frankl, who wrote *The Man's Search for Meaning* after his torturous stay in Germany's concentration camps during World War II, thought the entire focus on oneself was narcissistic and ultimately detrimental. He suggested real fulfillment

in life occurs only when a person transcends the self.

In the latter part of his career, Maslow understood the importance of Frankl's words. He explored a further dimension of needs in 1969 while criticizing his own vision on self-actualization. He propounded the sixth need of self-transcendence.

6. **Self-Transcendence**: The need for self-transcendence states the self only finds its actualization in giving itself to some higher outside goal. He said that *"The fully developed (and very fortunate) human being working under the best conditions tends to be motivated by values which transcend his self. They are not selfish anymore in the old sense of that term[6]."*

You can see yours or your parent's lives can easily see the pattern of needs that go in the above lines. If you started your life at the lower rungs, you can easily relate to those stages of your life and the prioritization of your needs. You must have started with

---

[6] A. H. Maslow, "The Farther Reaches of Human Nature," Journal of Transpersonal Psychology 1, no. 1 (1969): 1–9.

caring about your basic needs of food, shelter; before moving to your personal safety needs. Once your physiological and safety needs were met, then you'd have moved to love and belonging and then to the need of self-esteem. If you are growth-minded, then you are already on the path of actualizing your full potential by way of learning new skills and implementing in your chosen pursuits.

But the point here is the first 5 needs are related to your own self-needs and once you reach till the apex of your 5-step pyramid, you will still lack fulfillment. It's your purpose that transcends beyond yourself, which will give you a sense of fulfillment.

If you are not able to figure out your life purpose, your soul will be gasping, until it finally gets it. Therefore, finding your purpose that transcends you from yourself is the requirement of your soul—it's your soul's oxygen.

To live a truly meaningful life, discovering your life's purpose is not merely a nice-to-have thing, rather it is a must-have thing. You've got duty to nurture your soul as well, and a life of purpose is soul's oxygen.

How Finding Why Is at the Core of Everything?

In his famous TED Talk, Simon Sinek, author of the great book *Start With Why: How Great Leaders Inspire Everyone To Take Action* explains the concept of Golden Circle.

He explains that the Golden Circle principle is based on the premise that **most people pay way more importance to *How* and *What*, but they don't give the required attention to the *Why*.** He explains that it is not the case with highly successful individuals and companies, because at the core of their work is the deeper understanding about **why they do what they do**.

- In the picture, you see the **outermost circle covers *What***. This shows the outside world what you offer as a product or service or what your job title or function in any organization is.

- The **next inner circle covers *How***. It indicates to the world the actions you take to deliver your products/services and how you set yourself apart from others.

- The **innermost circle talks about *Why***. This addresses the prime question: why do you do something? What is the deepest reason inside you to do that activity?

Simon gives a wonderful example that demonstrates the power of purpose—the power of stronger why. It's a story about the massive failure of Samuel Pierpont Langley, an American astronomer, who after achieving prominence, wanted to make an audacious discovery of making a flying machine capable of carrying humans.

Since he had already shown his prominence, he was well trusted by the US Government. He was given a grant of USD 50,000 to figure out how to make this flying machine. He held a seat at Harvard and was very well connected with all the top-notch minds of his time. He could easily hire and in fact hired the best mind of his time to work on his project. Media was following him everywhere. Langley had everything he needed for any venture to succeed. But no one in the history knows about Langley.

On the other hand, Orville and Wilbur Wright, known as Wright Brothers, had no resources, connections, or people compared to Langley. They had no money, so they pursued their dreams of inventing a flying machine with the proceeds from their bicycle shop. No one from their team had a college education, not even the Wright Brothers themselves.

Then what was the reason the Wright Brothers took off on the first ever flight in December 1903 despite lacking rudimentary resources, while Langley was well funded, and all resources generally

considered as a recipe for success. What made the difference?

The difference was the Wright Brothers were driven by a purpose bigger than themselves. They had a belief if they could figure out how to fly through a flying machine, it would change the world. On the other hand, Langley had a different objective. He was motivated by his drive to be rich, ultra-successful, and famous. He was not in the pursuit of purpose; he was in the pursuit of his personal success. The people who believed in the Wright Brothers' dream worked with them with their passion, their blood, sweat, and tears. While people with Langley just worked for their pay-checks.

There is a further proof Langley was motivated by the wrong reasons. Because the day the Wright brothers took flight, he quit his position. He could have applauded and praised the guys and would have thought of further improvisation through his knowledge and skills. But he didn't do that. Because he couldn't invent, he couldn't be famous, so he decided to quit.

Let's take one more example about the power of *why* and how it impacts people's buying decisions- say buying computers. A regular marketing message for selling computers comes to you like this: "We make great computers. They're beautifully designed, simple to use, and user-friendly. Want to buy one?"

But now look at how Apple communicates its message about selling computers. It says: *Everything we do, we believe in challenging the status quo. We believe in thinking differently. The way we challenge the status quo is by making our products beautifully designed, simple to use, and user-friendly. We just happen to make great computers. Want to buy one?"*

Anyone can see the stark difference in both the marketing approaches. Merely by changing the order of message, people get interested to buy Apple computer. It proves that **people don't buy what you do; they buy why you do it**.

If someone communicates from the '*outside-in*' level, we understand the logical and rational information i.e., feature, pricing, specifications. But this

understanding is at the outer level, and it never drives our behavior. When we communicate from '*inside-out*' we are able to drive the other people's behavior and trigger them to take action.

Therefore, the stronger your why is, the more you are able to connect with the people. If you can connect with the real why of the other person, you don't need to spend much time on communication, and they will convert more.

On the other hand, if you are not able to connect well with your audience, you have to spend much more time on communication, and still they won't be convinced enough by your product or service.

The principle in any kind of persuasion is:

More Connection >> Less Communication needed >> More Conversion (i.e. getting results)

The antithesis of the above:

Less Connection>> more communication needed >> less Conversion

People don't buy only the product rather they buy it because of you, it's because they connect with your *why*.

With that let's move to the next chapter and understand how having a purpose in life can do wonders for your physical and mental health and general well-being.

Chapter 2: Science Proves the Magical Effects of "Purpose in Life"

****

"Many persons have a wrong idea of what constitutes true happiness. It is not attained through self-gratification but fidelity to a worthy purpose."

— Helen Keller

In the last chapter, we talked about how ascertaining and finding your life purpose is like your soul's oxygen. In this chapter, you will understand the above statement is not just an empty rhetoric, rather you will see science-based evidence about how discovering and living your *why* can improve the overall human well-being and

put you on the fast-track to growth and fulfillment.

Let's start by understanding the structure of the brain, its parts, and their primary functions.

Three Types of Brain

In the 1960s, American psychologist and neuroscientist Paul MacLean invented the Triune Brain Model to explain the functioning of different parts of the brain in terms of its evolutionary process. According to this theory, three distinct brains emerged successively during evolution and now co-inhabit in the human skull, as below.

1. Reptilian (instinctual) Brain
2. Mammalian or Limbic (emotional) Brain
3. Primate or Neocortex (thinking) Brain

The reptilian and mammalian parts of your brain are very basic in nature and oldest as part of the evolution. The Reptilian system of the brain is responsible for the most basic survival functions, such as heart rate, breathing, body temperature, and

orientation in space. Also referred to as the "emotional brain", the limbic system is the reactive part of us that initiates the "fight or flight" response to danger.

But now we come to the third—thinking—primate part of your brain- you can also call it 'smart' brain- the executive part of the system. This part is focused on higher functions such as sensory perception, generation of motor commands, spatial reasoning, conscious thought, and in humans, language. It's only this part of the brain that makes you different from animals, as it is responsible for human consciousness. In fact, it is this part of your brain that knows deep down, you need some purpose and meaning behind all the actions in your life.

The point I want to stress upon is that significance of finding purpose is not something that you only hear in motivational speeches or read in any personal development book, rather it is a subject matter of neuroscience research and psychological studies. Now let's get deeper into what psychologists and neuroscientists have explored about purpose in life.

How Purpose in Life positively impacts the quality of your actions?

In his book *The Man's Search for Meaning*, Victor Frankl describes the experiences of prison inmates during the concentration camps during the Second World War. He shared his experience that the inmates who were most likely to survive were those who had a purpose or goal in their life. The people who survived the arduous times during those camps were those who had a dream of meeting their loved ones or finishing other major tasks after they left the camps.

In one 2012 study[7], the role of purpose as a motivator was examined. Undergraduate students were compared based on their self-reported levels of enjoyment, long-term motivation, and their levels of purpose in response to an inherently enjoyable task. It was hypothesized that when purpose was present in an intrinsically motivated task, people would experience increased engagement, positive affect and long-term motivation for their actions. Behavioral observations, including a measure of time-

---

[7] https://kb.osu.edu/dspace/handle/1811/53206

on-task, provided support for the hypothesis that purpose contributed to motivation above and beyond intrinsic motivation (more on intrinsic motivation in next section).

Psychologists state that clarity of purpose has many positive effects on your life; a few of them are listed below:

- **Avoid Psychological Discord:**

Psychological discord is a fundamental sense of unease; humans often experience it whenever their attention isn't occupied by external things, and it can manifest itself in boredom, anxiety, and depression. If you have nothing to focus on that is outside of you, you get constantly engaged in the incessant chatter of the mind, triggering negative thoughts and feelings. By focusing our attention externally and giving us a constant source of activity to channel our mental energies into, purpose ensures we spend less time immersed in the associational chatter of our minds.

Purpose gives us something to constantly look at. We stay guarded from our inner

associational chatter and don't spend much time inside our heads unnecessarily.

• Make us Less Self-Centered

Aligning ourselves to a purpose often makes us less self-centered. We feel a part of something bigger, something outside ourselves, and this makes us less focused on our own worries and anxieties. Our own problems seem less significant, and we spend less time thinking about them, and so our sense of well-being increases.

• Increases Flow

Purpose is very closely linked to the state of flow—the state of intense absorption in which we forget our surroundings and ourselves. The state of flow is a magical state in which you are so immersed in whatever you are doing, time flies by. If you have a strong sense of purpose, you're likely to experience flow more frequently. Mihaly Czikszentmihalyi, the flow researcher, has shown flow is a powerful source of well-being. The more flow we experience, the happier we feel. You will find an entire chapter later in the book on how purpose

can improve the quality of your life by allowing you to enter a state of flow.

- **Improves self-esteem**

Purpose can also enhance our self-esteem. So long as we feel that we are successfully dealing with challenges and moving closer to our goal, our self-confidence increases. We feel a sense of competence and achievement, an enhanced ability to deal with difficulties and challenges.

- **Purpose improves Hope.**

Finally, purpose is closely related to hope. Working toward a goal implies we feel the goal is attainable and that our lives will change for the better once we have reached it. It implies hope—depending on our type of purpose, for example; hope for a better life for us, a fairer and more just society, liberation from suffering and oppression for others, a healthier world, and so forth. And as with purpose itself, a great deal of research has shown the positive effect of hope on well-being. The effect is especially evident with patients suffering from serious long-term illness. For them, a high level of

hope brings both an increased ability to cope, and a greater chance of recovery.

In the 1950s, Curt Richter, a Johns Hopkins scientist, did a series of experiments that tested how long rats could swim in high-sided buckets of circulating water before drowning. Richter found that, under normal conditions, a rat could swim for an average of 15 minutes before giving up and drowning. However, if he rescued the rats just before drowning, dried them off and let them rest briefly, and then put them back into the same buckets of circulating water, the rats could swim an average of 60 hours. You notice that if a rat was temporarily saved, it would put efforts to survive 240 times longer than if it was not temporarily saved.

It was surprising how the same rat could swim for 240 times more in the later session of the experiment. The research concluded that the rats were able to swim longer because they were given hope. In the second time, they swam longer because they remember that they were saved in the first instance from drowning, and that raised a hope that they would again be rescued. Now they had a purpose of staying

alive, which was created by way of rescuing them from drowning and generating hope—and this hope generated energy in them to continue.

- **Purpose in life enhances longevity**

Studies[8] demonstrate that people reporting a strong purpose in life, on average, live longer lives than those with a weak purpose. A recent study following over seven-thousand middle-aged American adults for fourteen years found that even a one-point increase on a seven-point scale of purpose resulted in an over 12 percent reduced risk of dying.

- **Purpose-in-life is core to protect your heart**

Although the heart is not technically part of your nervous system, it is profoundly linked to your brain. Your brain which uses adrenalin to monitor your heart; and it is your heart which delivers oxygen-rich blood to your brain.

---

[8]

https://www.ncbi.nlm.nih.gov/pubmed/24815612

This two-way relationship depends on the health of your blood vessels. A stroke occurs when those vessels fail to provide blood to your brain, which literally kills brain tissue by depriving it of oxygen. While a healthy diet and exercise are ways to reduce the risk of stroke, research suggests that having a high purpose-in-life plays a significant role in preventing strokes.

In one 2015 report[9] by Eric Kim from the University of Michigan, they assessed the Purpose-in-Life scale in almost seven-thousand older adults who had never had a stroke and followed them over a four-year period to determine stroke incidence. They found for each standard-deviation increase in their Purpose-in-Life score, these adults reduced their stroke risk by 22 percent. In another study, researchers followed 1,500 individuals with cardiovascular disease for two years. The researchers found each unit increase in their Purpose in Life score was associated with a 27 percent decrease in

---

9

https://deepblue.lib.umich.edu/bitstream/handle/2027.42/111619/kimeric_1.pdf

their risk of having a heart attack within two years.

- **Other Major Health benefits of purpose in life:**

In his book *Life on Purpose*, based on lot of studies and research, the author Victor J. Stretcher summarizes the amazing health benefits of having purpose in life as shown below:

> "Let's look at another outcome many people are terrified of: Alzheimer's disease. At the Rush Alzheimer's Disease Center, Patricia Boyle and her colleagues followed over nine-hundred seniors for seven years, looking for the incidence of Alzheimer's. The results were startling. Over that period, seniors with a low purpose in life were 2.4 times more likely to develop Alzheimer's disease than those with a high purpose in life.
>
> People with a strong purpose in life also, on average, do better psychologically and socially than those without. They have better sex,

sleep better, are less likely to become depressed, and are more relaxed.

Diabetics with a strong purpose are more likely to have their blood glucose under control.

People who have received drug and alcohol rehab are half as likely to relapse six months later if they started treatment with a strong purpose.

Physiologically, purpose in life is associated with an increase in natural killer cells that attack viruses and cancerous cells.

Purpose is also associated with a reduction in inflammatory cell production and an increase in HDL ("good") cholesterol."

How a life of Purpose can help you make more money?

A 2016 study[10] published in the *Journal of Research in Personality* found that people

---

10

https://www.sciencedirect.com/science/article/pii/S009
2656616300836

who felt a sense of purpose accumulated more wealth than those who feel as though their lives lack meaning. The researchers discovered individuals with a sense of purpose had a higher income and a bigger net worth than those who felt as though their lives lack meaning.

And it was not only for the short-term; rather the difference in wealth seemed to span the test of time. Over the course of ten years, people with a sense of purpose continued to have higher incomes and bigger nest eggs than other people. The researchers suspect people who feel their lives have meaning are goal-oriented. Looking at their long-term goals likely motivates them to develop better financial habits.

Purpose-in-life Scale

You must have heard about Intelligence quotient (IQ). Also, the concept of Emotional Quotient (EQ) is not new to most people. But most people will be surprised to note that there is a 'Purpose-in-life' scale also.

Though earlier, the psychologists were skeptical of purpose in life being measured, but thanks to the research done by the psychologists James Crumbaugh and Leonard Maholick, in 1964, now purpose-in-life scale concept is being used worldwide.

A person's Purpose-in-Life scale is based on three dimensions:

- A belief that life does have a purpose;
- Upholding a personal value system; and
- Having the motivation to achieve future goals and overcome future challenges.

Purpose-in-life scale or questionnaire is a 20-item scale measuring different dimensions of the life purposes. These twenty questions are all about your personal belief system about yourself, how your everyday life is, how is your attitude toward life, boring or exciting, how is your own worth-assessment. Each question needs to be answered to the scale of 1 to 5, where 1 means the lowest and 5 means the

highest in your particular behavior or attitude. And unfortunately, if you score less than 50 in these questions, then it means you are experiencing an 'existential void', meaning a lack of purpose in your life.

You can also assess your purpose-in-life score by accessing the questionnaire through below link: http://faculty.fortlewis.edu/burke_b/perso nality/pil.pdf.

How lack of purpose can destroy lives

The need for purpose is one of the defining characters of human beings. Every human craves purpose of doing anything and suffers from serious psychological difficulties due to lack of it.

An example of miserable life because of lack of purpose is about one of the most famous sportsmen in the 1990s, Paul Gascoigne, an English former football player, also famously known as "Gazza". It is reported[11] that since the end of his football career, he is battling with alcohol

---

[11] https://www.psychologytoday.com/us/blog/out-the-darkness/201307/the-power-purpose

addiction and other mental health issues now for more than 20 years. He has been in and out of rehab, arrested for assaulting his wife, and in the most recent headlines found staggering through the lobby of a hotel, asking strangers to buy him a drink.

One of his ex-teammates and friend, Gary Lineker, reported saying that after the end of his football career, Gazza couldn't find any better purpose of his life so he got trapped into alcohol addiction and other mental problems. Gazza's example shows the ill-effects of lack of purpose in your life. The lack of purpose leads to boredom, anxiety, and sometimes depression.

Having a purpose in life is important for almost every aspect of life, be it physical, mental, psychological, emotional areas of your life. The science and psychologists now have ample studies and research to evidence that a purposeful life is the only way to ensure your overall well-being.

Now let's move on to the next section to understand how finding your purpose is more important than finding your passion.

Chapter 3: What Wins - Purpose or Passion?

****

> *"If we want to feel an undying passion for our work, if we want to feel we are contributing to something bigger than ourselves, we all need to know our WHY."*
>
> *— Simon Sinek*

You might have often heard this advice "Follow Your Heart" or "Go for your passion" or "Do what you love to do".

This is incomplete advice, and that's why it's horrible.

If you simply follow your passion, that's not going to work, unless you find ways to deliver the value to the world out of it.

For example, if you love to play video games, and it's your 'passion', no one is going to transfer money to your bank account merely for playing the games. But if you can deliver value out of your passion of playing video games, maybe by way of designing the games or through teaching the games, you can earn success by following your passion.

Let me give my example. I am an avid reader—reading is my passion, but unless I'm able to deliver value to the world out of my reading, following my passion of reading the books only, isn't going to put food on my table or pay my bills. The way I am following my passion as a full-time author is by way of writing books to impart the wisdom and thus deliver the value to my readers.

Now let's take it to the next level. While following your passion (along with delivering value is a good advice), but without defining your purpose, following your passion is not going to give you a meaningful life.

I know it sounds a bit confusing. But it's important to clarify that following your

passion doesn't mean you have found your life purpose. Finding your passion is just a subset of the finding your purpose. To understand this better, let's try to understand the difference between finding your purpose and finding your passion, as wellness entrepreneur Jessica Lauren DeBry puts it very beautifully. She explains:

"Passion is your compelling emotions behind your dreams. Your feelings drive your passion. Purpose is the why behind it all. Purpose is the deep reason for your existence."

Passion is defined as "*a strong and barely controllable emotion.*" However, the purpose is defined as "*the reason for which something is done or created or for which something exists.*"

Let's understand few key differences between passion and purpose:

1. Passion is about Emotion while Purpose is about Reason

We do things because we like them, because they make us feel good. Passion is

the emotional drive to do what you do; it is the emotional spark that gets you moving forward with what you want to do with your life.

While **passion is all based on your emotions**, your purpose goes behind that. **Purpose is your motivation;** your why behind taking your actions. While passion thrills you, it's purpose that fills you.

Passion without purpose is not going to fulfill you. Therefore, your purpose is the foundation on which your passion should be built.

2. **Passion can be often selfish, but purpose is always selfless**

It's not always, but often following your passion has tendency to be selfish. You can pursue a passion for your own sole pleasure only.

When you follow your passions, you're doing it because it feels good, because it's something you deeply enjoy— even if that means putting yourself before others who really need it. While passion can have

selfish elements to it, purpose is never selfish.

"Purpose is not selfish. It involves serving others, but it's not servitude. It's feeling joyful about creating joy. It's about adding value in the lives of others while creating value in your life. It's win-win" – George Krueger

3. Purpose is more focused

Where passion can be all over the place, wild and exciting, purpose is much more focused. When you feel passion for something, it doesn't matter what it is. Your passion can change at the whim of your own emotions and your feelings.

If you are strongly connected with your purpose, the temporary failures or criticism from your peers doesn't shake you. It's the clarity of the purpose that keeps you focused on your action, despite failing numerous times.

Purpose is singular and very specific, as compared to passion that could be varied and much wider. Our passions often get

changed over a period of time, but purpose is a long-term phenomenon. Passion can come and go, but purpose is forever—or at least until you've completed your purpose and found another one.

4. Passion is about What and Purpose is about Why

Passions is about *What;* while purpose is about your *Why.* You may be passionate about different things like sports, music or anything else, but your purpose is why you get drawn to a particular activity. Purpose is all about motivation—it's all about why you do what you do.

Based on above definition and comparison you'd realize that passion doesn't appear to be a very reliable or stable metric, but on the other hand purpose seems to be a lot more concrete and objective parameter to base our important life activities.

Purpose versus Passion

Ryan Holiday, in his book *Ego is the Enemy* and in one of his articles[12]

summarizes why you should choose purpose over passion. He rather warns against solely following the passion. Here is what he stated:

> "Your passion may be the very thing holding you back from power, influence or accomplishment. Because just as often, we fail because of passion. **To be clear, this is not about caring. This is passion of a different sort—unbridled enthusiasm**, our willingness to pounce on what's in front of us with the full measure of our zeal, the "bundle of energy" our teachers and gurus have assured us is our most important asset. Instead, what we require in our ascent is purpose. **Purpose, you could say, is like passion with boundaries**. Passion is form over function. The critical work you want to do will require your deliberation and consideration. Not passion.

---

[12] https://ryanholiday.net/the-3-ways-ego-will-derail-your-career-before-it-really-begins/

Purpose is about pursuing something outside yourself as opposed to pleasuring yourself. It'd be far better if you were intimidated by what lies ahead—humbled by its magnitude and determined to see it through regardless. Leave passion for the amateurs. Make it about your purpose: what you feel you must do and say, not what you care about and wish to be. Then you will do great things. Then you will stop being your old, good-intentioned, but ineffective self."

In another real-life example, a young basketball player named Lewis Alcindor Jr., who won three national championships with John Wooden at UCLA, used one word to describe the style of his famous coach: "dispassionate." He stated that in the sense of not being passionate. Wooden wasn't about rhetoric speeches or inspiration—he saw those extra emotions (arising from passion) as a burden. **Instead, his philosophy was about being in control and doing your job and never being "passion's slave."** The player who

learned that lesson from Wooden would later change his name to one you remember better: Kareem Abdul-Jabbar, who, if you don't know, is the third-highest-scoring NBA player by total career playoff points scored.

Your purpose is extremely significant to your life and helping you shape who you are as a person. While passions can help shape and form your personality, your purpose will help shape and form your identity.

You should not solely run behind your passions by ignoring the purpose of your life. However, if you are living with passion and also have clarity of purpose in your life; combining these two is the sure-shot recipe to lead a meaningful and successful life.

Steve Jobs didn't merely have passion to build technology or computers, rather he had a bigger purpose behind all that. He had a bigger purpose to bring the joy in the lives of his customer by the clean designs as well as seamless operations of his products. When Jobs said, *'follow your heart and intuition, they somehow know what you truly want to become'*; it wasn't about

following your passion, it was about discovering your purpose and living your identity created through that purpose.

Similarly, Elon Musk is very passionate about the technology and thinking way out of the box, for making rockets and spaceship and creating other innovative products, but again he has a purpose larger than his life. His purpose is to make the lives of people convenient by his novel ideas. Recently, he made an announcement[13] (watch this video) showing his ideas to use spaceship rocket technology to travel between any two parts of the world in less than 30 minutes.

Finding your passion in disregard to your deeper purpose will not give real meaning to your life. Though you might succeed from the material world perspective, but the lack of meaning will make you feel like a failure, as this success will not give you any fulfillment.

With that now let's move to the next section of the book to look at some of the key

---

fundamentals before you start your exploration of finding your purpose.

Chapter 4: The Key Principles Before You Start

****

"There are three things extremely hard: steel, a diamond, and to know one's self."

– Benjamin Franklin

Set the Right Foundation- Identify Your Motivation

You can't build a robust building unless you have put in the time and effort to lay down a strong and deep foundation. Same applies to your life and more particularly to discovering the purpose of your life.

When most youngsters get to their new jobs or set up their new ventures, when asked this question, "What do you want from this job or business?", they end up saying they want to earn a million dollars, or big houses or big cars or other material things or just

earning fame or getting surrounded with cool people.

But that's not the real answer to this deep question. It's merely a surface level answer that has further layers to it. Of course you want these material possessions from the outside world, but you don't want them just for the sake of them only. I understand you'd feel like you just need these things only and once you get there, you'll be fully satisfied. But in reality, you want these things for numerous reasons—maybe you want to impress your parents, siblings or friends—a feeling of proud, maybe you want to gain experience of traveling freely to your favorite locations and broaden your life horizon—a feeling of experiencing adventure. Or maybe you just want to meet different people or reach out to people you admire, and believe that once you are financially free, you can take necessary steps to reach out to such people—again you want to feel and experience something, in this case, it is feeling of connection.

You see, running behind outside things is never merely for these things only, rather you have some assumptions in your mind that if you earn big money and acquire

these material world possessions, then you will be able to enjoy the feeling, you have been longing for. Humans have a deep inner need of feeling certain ways and experience certain things.

So, it's very important to understand our true drives, and not run blindly toward the material world under the false assumption that the outside possession will meet your deeper needs is a sure-shot way to unfulfilled life. You will be successful from the outside, but you won't feel fulfilled in your heart. You need to understand the difference between your **Intermediate Whys** and the **Final Whys**. Let's understand the difference by way of this short story.

One young man was lying comfortably on a swing at a beach. His friend came and asked him what he was doing. The young man replied he was just relaxing. The well-wisher friend told him he should go and get a higher education. The young man asked, "Why should I do that? What's the purpose behind it?" The friend replied, "You will get a degree, which will help you to get a good job and you can earn good money".

The young man asked, "OK, I understand, but again what's the purpose behind all this? What will happen if I do all this?" The friend said, "Then you can buy a big house, a nice car, go on vacation etc.".

The young man again asked with a smile on his face, "And what's the purpose in doing all that?" The friend was getting irritated, but still replied, "Now with all that money and resources, you can enjoy your life and relax. Simple."

Here's how the bomb exploded. The young said laughingly, "That's what I am doing already. Don't you see I am chilling and relaxing? Why would I waste so many years running behind different things only to attain something I am already doing?"

Though this story is generally taken on a lighter note only, but one can get some wisdom nuggets out of it as well. I chose this story here not to undermine the importance of putting hard work toward your goals. I specifically captured this here, as I wanted to show the importance of clarifying the deeper purpose before you take any action. You need to understand that your **Final why** is to enjoy some

feeling or emotions that you want to experience in your life, while your **Intermediate Why** is something that YOU determine as is necessary to achieve your final why. The final why can be compared with ultimate destination, while the intermediate Why is something you think and choose as a path and vehicle to reach that ultimate destination. So remember destination is always more important than the path and vehicle you choose in your journey.

Tony Robbins once rightly quoted, *"Success without fulfillment is the ultimate failure"*.

To have success with fulfillment, one needs to gain clarity about what the true motivation is behind any action. There are two types of motivation namely (1) intrinsic motivation and (2) extrinsic motivation.

Extrinsic motivation is when we are motivated to perform an action or engage in an activity to earn a reward or avoid a punishment. This motivation is primarily focused on the outside aspiration related to money, fame, or beauty. Each of these

aspirations requires validation from the outside world.

On the other hand, **intrinsic motivation** involves engaging in a particular behavior because it is personally rewarding, essentially you are performing an activity for its own sake rather than any desire for any outside reward. It is all about doing or following something personally meaningful to you. This addresses your core needs and wants –they pertain to your core values, personal interests as well as your relationships and your personal growth.

Let's understand by through some practical examples of extrinsic vs. intrinsic motivation:

- Exercise to build muscles to show off to people is EXTRINSIC. On the other hand, exercising to enjoy the feeling of fitness and vibrant health is INTRINSIC.

- Studying solely for the purposes of getting grades and securing a job is EXTRINSIC. But, studying something you love exploring the subject and get deeper because you

are passionate about the subject is INTRINSIC.

The foundational step in discovering your why is to introspect your own thoughts, behavior, interests, to find out something which you personally find fulfilling and you can deliver value to the world out of that. This is one of the most important and fundamental requirements to help you find your true why.

Also, in his book *Why We Do What We Do,* Edward L. Deci explains how intrinsic motivation help to attain more happiness and enhance the quality of life and overall well-being. In his words:

"If any of the three extrinsic aspirations— for money, fame, or beauty—was very high for an individual relative to the three intrinsic aspirations, the individual was also more likely to display poorer mental health. For example, having an unusually strong aspiration for material success was associated with narcissism, anxiety, depression, and poorer social functioning as rated by a trained clinical psychologist...

In contrast, strong aspirations for any of the intrinsic goals—meaningful relationships, personal growth, and community contributions—were positively associated with well-being. People who strongly desired to contribute to their community, for example, had more vitality and higher self-esteem. When people organize their behavior in terms of intrinsic strivings (relative to extrinsic strivings) they seem more content—they feel better about who they are and display more evidence of psychological health."

Therefore, while discovering your purpose you need to pay a holistic attention and not merely choose your why based on the outside world material success factors.

PERMA Model for Happiness: Martin Seligman, also known as the father of positive psychology, proponed PERMA model, which prescribes five core elements for psychological well-being and happiness. Let's have a quick look at what are these five elements in PERMA model:

> **P**- Positive Emotions: Feeling good, optimism, pleasure and enjoyment

E- Engagement: Fulfilling work, interesting hobbies, and flow

R- Relationship: Social connection, love, intimacy, emotional and physical connection

M- Meaning: **Having a purpose, finding a meaning in life**

A- Accomplishments: Ambitions, realistic goals, important achievements, pride in yourself.

You can see that finding a purpose or meaning in whatever you do is one of the important elements of the PERMA model – which means in order to enjoy the true happiness and overall well-being, you need to discover your true purpose.

It Is Never Too Early or Too Late To Begin A Life Of Purpose

People often tend to say they are too young to think of heavy topics like life purpose or meaning. The young people think they needn't even worry about finding life purpose, as age is on their side, so they'd prefer to live life enjoying the pleasures and indulgences of the world.

Then there are people on the other side of the spectrum, who tend to think they are too late to even think about purpose anymore. Their statements seem like "I'm already in my forties or fifties now. I've spent most of my life doing the things in a particular way, even though I didn't like that way, but still I think it's too late to even think about finding a purpose anymore."

Wherever you're in your life, whether age is on your side or you think it's too late, the wisdom from Stephen Covey, the world-renowned author of *7 Habits of Highly Effective People*, which he shared at the end of his life, is the exact piece of guidance needed here.

Below was the question that was asked to him, which was brilliantly answered by him on how we can create the best lives.

"Q: You have said your most important final message is to live life in crescendo. What does that mean?

*A: **It means that the most important work you will ever do is always ahead of you. It is never behind you**. You should always be expanding and deepening your commitment to that work.*

Retirement is a false concept. You may retire from a job but never retire from meaningful projects and contributions.

Crescendo is a musical term. It means to play music with ever greater energy and volume, with strength and striving. The opposite is diminuendo, which means to lower the volume, to back off, to play it safe, to become passive, to whimper away your life.

So live life in crescendo. It's essential to live with that thought. **Regardless of what you have or haven't accomplished, you have important contributions to make.** *Avoid the temptation to keep looking in the rear-view mirror at what you have done and instead look ahead with optimism."*

Your Purpose May Be Just Around the Corner

You don't always need to run around and struggle finding your purpose. Sometime your life's purpose is just under your nose. Therefore, before you embark on your journey to finding purpose, give a pause, give a thought, and you may get your purpose just around you.

Every moment, there are some universal hints already appearing in front of you; you just need to be bit more observant. You need to ask yourself:

- What makes you fully alive?
- What is your uniqueness i.e. your unique talents, skills, capabilities etc?
- What are things you want to do that will connect you to the people you admire?
- What do you imagine or what is your vision about your future?

You need to take clues from these things and start at some point. And purpose is not like you go to a place and they will hand it over to you. It's more of self-observation and exploration. And always the best place to start journey is from the point where you are now. Take stock of you and your situation and start taking action toward what comes to you naturally.

Look Around For Mentors

Every moment of your life, you crave for living a life that matters and fulfils you. And this often beacons you to some persons,

who are already living a life you are dreaming about. You will always find the people around, who you may want to follow. Now with the advent of internet, it's not difficult at all the get guidance from those people. Read about those people. If they can't physically teach you in the real time, they already would have written books or literature that can help you learn from their wisdom.

And the next step would be to model what they have done. Tony Robbins, the strategic life coach, and highly successful entrepreneur offers the modelling principle in his below quote:

"Long ago, I realized that success leaves clues and that people who produce outstanding results do specific things to create those results. I believed that if I precisely duplicated the actions of others, I could reproduce the same quality of results that they had."

Get Support from Like-Minded People

You don't need to struggle alone. You always need to keep in mind you are not the first person on the planet who is on this unique and peculiar quest of finding purpose. If you look around with sincere intentions, you will find some like-minded people, who are on the same journey of discovering their why.

Napoleon Hill coined the term 'Mastermind' in his legendary book *Think and Grow Rich*, which entails that few people who have similar thought process and have common goal to reach meet periodically and brainstorm on the challenges and opportunities of each member, so the whole group can benefit from the experiences of each member.

Through mastermind groups, you are joining hands and minds with people, who are like-minded, so each member of the group can learn from others and also brainstorm the growth possibilities together. Mastermind group holds each other accountable for the deliverables expected from others.

With like-minded people within your reach, you can comfortably discuss your struggles,

your approach, and progress made in your journey and get benefitted by an independent third-party view. Also, you'd be helping the other person in discovering their purpose through brainstorming on different aspects of their life.

Be Prepared for Occasional disillusionment

The greatest journeys are often full of struggles and challenges, though often not visible to the outside world. But the objective of these impediments is not to stop you or turn you back, rather they come in your way to test your willingness and strengths. As Randy Pausch said once:

"The brick walls are there for a reason. The brick walls are not there to keep us out; the brick walls are there to give us a chance to show how badly we want something. The brick walls are there to stop the people who don't want it badly enough. They are there to stop the other people."

If we're stretching toward a noble goal, we will definitely experience unique highs and lows. Instead of worrying about them, be prepared to resist and face them with all

your might. Every time you fall, just get up, dust yourself off, and get back to work.

Let's be anti-fragile as we know that we can handle whatever life throws at us and get stronger with each challenge we face.

Carlos Castaneda in his book *The Wheel of Time* states: "The basic difference between an ordinary man and a warrior is that a warrior takes everything as a challenge, while an ordinary man takes everything as a blessing or a curse." And: "The trick is in what one emphasizes. We either make ourselves miserable, or we make ourselves strong. The amount of work is the same."

Sometimes, you'll have a strong feeling things are not going the way you'd thought earlier, and this will frustrate you, and you'll start accusing everything around you. But it's important to remember what Dalai Lama offered as an incredible insight. He said, "Remember that not getting what you want is sometimes a wonderful stroke of luck".

One real-life story exemplifies Dalai Lama's words. Jan Koum was a poor immigrant from Ukraine. Brian Acton lost a big time in the dotcom bust and was even rejected for

jobs by Twitter and Facebook. They two became friends in 2007 while working at Yahoo and decided to leave the company and took a year off. Later they proceeded to start a new messaging service. And five years later, Facebook acquired their messaging service company, WhatsApp for a whopping stock-and-cash deal of USD 19 billion.

Now had these two guys blessed with steady jobs, they might not have felt the urge to take the entrepreneurial plunge.

The lesson from the story is that you need to have faith that even if the things are not going on your side, the turning of events may come to your advantage.

Now let's get to the next chapter and start with the purpose triggering questions.

Chapter 5: Powerful Questions To Activate Your Why

****

"He who has a Why to live for can bear almost any How."

~ Friedrich Nietzsche

You now know the importance of understanding and living your why. You also know not having a purpose in life can turn an ultra-successful person into a total failure. The significance of a clear 'why' or 'purpose in life' from the perspective of neuroscience and psychology is already explained earlier. Now with all the above information, you are all set to jump into this section and the later sections that will focus on helping you learn the art of finding your why.

Remember, finding your why or discovering your life purpose is not a science, rather it's an art. As you know

science is something, which based on experiment, gives objective results to everyone, means, if you know your input, you can almost 100% expect the outcome based on the scientific principle. If an apple falls from the tree, you know with 100% surety, that it will fall down, thanks to Newton's law of Gravitation. But this is not the case with art.

The art is subjective—unlike science—art is different for everyone. The painting of Picasso will give different meanings and impressions to different individuals, because Picasso has created an art, and this art will be viewed differently by different set of people, based on their personal life circumstances, way of thinking, belief system and lot of other personal factors. The work of art involves enough work of exploration and depends entirely upon your personal thinking, perception, belief, your outlook and everything personal.

Similarly finding your why is also an art. It is subjective and different for every person. There are more than seven billion people on this planet, and each individual has his or her own unique different objective and purpose in life.

The process of discovering your why starts with asking the right set of questions and waiting for your deep, subjective and original thoughts about it. In this section, you will find enough thought-provoking questions, and the idea behind that is to activate your reticular activating system (RAS) of your brain. Activating the RAS of your brain is a pathway to bring clarity and creativity in your thought processes. Ever remember, you've just started thinking of a particular thing, for instance, buying a new car of a specific model, let's say your next Ford or Honda in the color red. Once you start thinking about the red Ford or Honda car, from that day onward, you would notice more of red color Fords or Hondas. It's not that suddenly people have started buying and driving more such cars, but it is your brain's RAS in play. Once you put certain questions or thoughts in your mind and allow them to process in your head, your mind starts taking notice about what is important for you and filters all other information as irrelevant and just presents before you the type of information that you've indicated as important.

But how do you start the process of activating your RAS?

It's pretty simple. You need to ask yourself the right questions – the questions that trigger some actions. Don't ask the questions like, "God, why is it me again?" Rather ask, "What is the best action I can take to get the maximum out of this situation?". Voltaire quoted on the similar lines by saying *"Judge a man by his questions rather than his answers"*.

And that's why most successful people keep asking themselves quality questions. Then in the search of better answers, they consume a lot of ideas and they say, 'let's sleep on this idea". They are simply activating their RAS and waiting for the best solution to come to that.

OK, now without further ado, let's drive straight into some big ideas about how to trigger questions that activate your purpose.

What are Your Life Values?

Our individual life values are our personal compass, which guide us to our true north star. Each of us is a unique creation of God.

Unlike the man-made physical appliances which have an explicit operating manual, there isn't any clear, visible, and concrete manual to operate our lives. But if we give us a chance to explore, we will find that our heart and our intuition serve as the guiding tools. In fact, each of us is guided by some personal life values.

Let me clarify, I'm not specifically talking about any ethical values or teaching something on moral studies. I'm talking about the personal values that give direction to each individual's behavior.

Tony Robbins, in his book, *Awaken the Giant Within* talks about the value system of each individual. He states that each of us different set of value to lead our lives. Some people are driven by the values of freedom and adventure—and these people get into entrepreneurship or any other crazy ideas. On the other hand, few people have their prime values of security and certainty. You will find majority of people doing their regular job their whole life, as this gives them a certainty of income every month and financial and social security.

Finding your why has in its underpinning finding your life values. Let's list out most common values which people often state:

- Love
- Success
- Freedom
- Health
- Comfort
- Intimacy
- Security
- Safety
- Adventure
- Power
- Passion

Now carefully read the above illustrative list for a moment and introspect what is/are your value(s)? What is most important to you?

To help you give some perspective, let me share my personal example.

I worked in a corporate job for 17 years, even if I might have been unaware at that time, but now in the hindsight I realize my values have always been freedom and adventure. I frequently changed my jobs after every two-three years, and the reason

for such changes was primarily that the job started to lack adventure or would become monotonous. Therefore, my obvious next move would be to start posting resume for job to other organizations. My another important life value is freedom – the job which offered me the maximum freedom, I stayed there for longest On the other hand the jobs where I didn't find much autonomy due to unreasonable demands of my superiors or crazy corporate rules, policies or complex structures, I found myself a misfit there and immediately planned to move ahead.

Finally, after realizing that job wouldn't offer me any more satisfaction toward my values, I decided to become an entrepreneur—without any compulsion of reporting to anyone or punching the clock daily–choosing my own hours and moreover every day now is an adventure.

Now I'll give you a metric to compare different values by citing a contrasting set of values to show the importance of values in guiding our behaviors and actions. My wife has her values that are on the other end of spectrum, because she values certainty and security more than anything

else and which means every month secure paycheck and certainty of future is most important to her. So switching from employee to become an entrepreneur was definitely not an easy move for me, because our value systems are the opposite to each other.

I know I haven't arrived yet, it's my hunch I'm on my path. Because I believe that unlike the man-made GPS system, which shows you with certainty where to go, life offers you the wisdom to move one step further. You are never shown the ultimate end destination of life, like you see in your worldly GPS system. The process for discovering you why, therefore, is to just keep taking consistent action by trusting your guts feelings.

You can do this small exercise below to start finding your why. Just take a piece of paper, and write on the top, "What's most important to me in life?"

Now be honest here. Write what's important to you and only you. You might write that your wife, parents, or your kids are most important to you. Or maybe you will say that you love your work.

Before you do this exercise, please remember that your values fall into two categories: Means values and End Values. Therefore, the above values that you just described are merely your means values, but you've to get deeper under the layers and find out your "End" values.

When you say your family or kids are most important to you, in fact, your end value is love and affection. For you love and affection is most important. Now to attain that love and affection, you will change your behavior and actions accordingly. Similarly, if your work is important to you, then it is your "end" value of mastery or expertise, that is driving you toward your work.

After doing this exercise of writing what's most important to you, you'll have an idea about your life values, and that will drive you closer to your purpose or why. Because once you know the deeper cause or End Value, you can explore many opportunities to find your "means values". It opens up many alternatives in front of you to serve your end result.

Would You Still Do It, If Today Is Your Last Day?

Steve Jobs in one of the convocation ceremonies at Stanford University gave a very profound message. He emphasized on the realization that each of us has to die one day and therefore that requires us to decide how we should live each day of our life. He refers to a wonderful quote that changed the way he started to look at his life. here is the quote: *"If you live each day as if it was your last, someday you'll most certainly be right."*

Deeply impressed by the power of his quote, he shared his personal experience that every morning from last more than 33 years, he looked at himself in the mirror and had been asking a simple yet a profound question. He would ask himself if that day was the last day of his life, would he be doing the things he had planned to do that day. And if the answer to that question came in negative for few days in a row, it meant that things have to change.

This is what Jobs stated in his speech at Stanford University:

"Your time is limited, so don't waste it living someone else's life. Don't be trapped by dogma—which is living with the results of other people's thinking. Don't let the noise of others' opinions drown out your own inner voice. And most important, have the courage to follow your heart and intuition. They somehow already know what you truly want to become. Everything else is secondary."

On the similar lines, Simon Sinek in his book *Start With Why* advocates that if you don't get a profound yes for doing anything particular, you should not spend time on that thing.

Legend Warren Buffet puts the significance of finding your purpose and doing what you want in bit different way. He says:

"There comes a time when you ought to start doing what you want. Take a job that you love. You will jump out of bed in the morning. I think you are out of your mind if you keep taking jobs that you don't like because you think it will look good on your resume. Isn't that a little like saving up sex for your old age?"

This formula is based on the principle of listening to your heart. We often suppress

the voice of our heart by paying much more attention to the logical thoughts running in our minds. While we might think we are making intelligent decisions and safeguarding our position, there's a big chance avoiding or not paying attention to the voice of your heart leads to a pretty mediocre life. Now even science[14] has reported your heart is a way more intelligent organ than your brain.

What is Your Onlyness?

Another great way to activate your quest for discovering your purpose is to consistently question about your *Onlyness.* The objective behind enquiring your onlyness is to explore what are the things around you that *you and only you* can do it.

It's entirely irrelevant to compare yourself with others—any comparison is toxic. Everyone has his or her own separate journey and destination, with a unique set of life circumstances and environment. If you get into a habit of comparing your journey with others and start beating up

[14] https://www.warriorforum.com/off-topic-forum/31978-scientific-research-shows-heart-more-intelligent-than-brain.html

yourself for not achieving much, that'll do nothing but frustrate you. You need to find out your own unique voice or strengths, which if put to use can deliver the value to the world.

Someone would argue not everyone is talented or gifted with special abilities; few people are born to be just following others and not doing something on their own. I would caution here. The people who say these someone is not gifted or talented with unique abilities is someone who has probably not yet put enough effort into finding their uniqueness.

Our world is filled with unique examples where some people were at the verge of giving up and even committing suicide— because life started to appear meaningless to them. But somehow they gathered some motivation to take few steps more and eventually were endowed with the gift of awareness about their unique abilities.

Tim Ferriss, the investor, entrepreneur and bestselling author of *The Tools of Titans* and many other books have openly admitted in many interviews that he was at the verge of committing suicide in his

twenties, as he was not able to find the meaning out of his life. But somehow circumstances just turned little bit in his favor. Fortunately, his parents got to know about his intentions. At that moment, Tim realized committing suicide was a very selfish step, as this was not only his life, rather his parents would have been emotionally traumatized, if he chose that path. Then he went in his quest and realized that he lives to explore life and what best he can make out of it. He claims to be human guinea pig, as he realized he loves to experiment and teach people about his learning from those experiments. This drive made him write many bestselling books and start a podcast on how to optimize one's life and succeed.

He continued until he was able to find his Onlyness i.e. the thing that he and only he could do it.

Let me share with you one more example of someone adopting his onlyness, which resulted in turning him into genius. This is the story of Buckminster Fuller, an architect, author, and inventor, who went on his quest by asking this question: "What Is My Job on the Planet with a Capital J?"

Jon Kabat-Zinn, a professor and renowned mindfulness researcher, in his book *Wherever You Go There You Are*, has dedicated an entire chapter titled "What Is My Job on the Planet with a Capital J?" In this chapter, Kabat-Zinn tells the inspiring story of Fuller, who, apparently, before he was recognized as a genius, had failed numerous times by age thirty-two and was contemplating suicide. Apparently, everything he tried didn't work out and he thought perhaps life would be better for his wife and infant daughter if he ended his life.

Fortunately, somehow he thought in some different way and rather he decided to live from that moment on as if he had died that night and decided that he would become an employee of the planet—devoting himself to "asking, ***What is it on this planet [which he referred to as Spaceship Earth] that needs doing that I know something about, that probably won't happen unless I take responsibility for it?*** He decided he would just ask that question continuously and do what came to him, following his nose.

In this way, working for humanity as an employee of the universe at large, you get to modify and contribute to your locale by who you are, how you are, and what you do. But it's no longer personal. It's just part of the totality of the universe expressing itself.

Rarely do we question and then contemplate with determination what our hearts are calling us to do and to be. We should rather frame such efforts in question form: "**What is my job on the planet with a capital J?**" or, "**What do I care about so much that I would pay to do it?**" If we ask such a question and don't come up with an answer other than, "I don't know," then we just need to keep on asking the question."

Most of the time, we just keep asking other people what we should do. Why we do this is because we consider other people as experienced and educated to help us what we should do. But here's the thing. We can take advice from others in terms of what should we do or how should we do it. What and How are only the surface level questions and just require gaining some knowledge about the new subject or

acquiring some skill sets to perform the thing better.

But beware. When it comes to the question of why should you do it? No one else can help you out. It's only you who can answer that question. And the only way is to keep asking yourself what to do.

Find Your Euthymia

Seneca was a great stoic philosopher and he came out with this term euthymia, which is a Greek word. It means believing in yourself and trusting that you are on the right path, and not being in doubt by following the myriad footpaths of those wandering in every direction. This means all about knowing yourself and have the courage to walk your own authentic path.

The English translation of euthymia is tranquility. It's the feeling we have when we *truly* trust ourselves. When we know we're headed in the right direction and we're able to quit comparing ourselves to everyone else and stop second guessing ourselves constantly.

The quality of your life significantly improves, if you develop the ability to listen

the subtle cues coming from your inside. Once you start paying attention, believe me, these voices will start getting clearer and clear. Then you'll be pulled by a sense of faith—a hunch that you'll find the right track, if you just listening to your inner voice and keep moving. Please remember, if you are always ignoring your own inner voice and just going by the norms of society and operating under some fear of what others think or what if you fail, then you've already decided to fail. You've already quit trying the exploration of your true purpose in life. The best course is to keep exploring until you find your euthymia.

Here is what Ryan Holiday explains in his book *Ego is the Enemy* about the Seneca's Euthymia. In his words:

"So why do you do what you do? That's the question you need to answer. **Stare at it until you can**. Only then will you understand what matters and what doesn't. Only then can you say no, can you opt out of stupid races that don't matter, or even exist. Only then is it easy to ignore 'successful' people, because most of the time they aren't—at least relative to you, and often even to themselves. Only then

can you develop that quiet confidence Seneca talked about."

We live in the world of Google and always want to be 100% sure of the final outcome before we take the first step. We're fortunate because we can almost get answers to almost any questions by asking Google. But unfortunately, Google doesn't have answers to complex subjects like finding your life's purpose or meaning. It's a trial and error route. You have to keep exploring, and one day, you're going to get it.

Here is another recommendation from Mark Manson, the author of bestseller book *The Subtle Art of Not Giving a F*ck* for finding your life's purpose or discovering your "why". He states:

"Discovering what you're passionate about in life and what matters to you is a full-contact sport, a trial-and-error process. None of us know exactly how we feel about an activity until we actually do the activity.

So ask yourself, if someone put a gun to your head and forced you to leave your house every day for everything except for sleep, how would you choose to occupy

yourself? And no, you can't just go sit in a coffee shop and browse Facebook. You probably already do that. Let's pretend there are no useless websites, no video games, no TV. You have to be outside of the house all day every day until it's time to go to bed—where would you go and what would you do?"

The only option left is to trust your gut and keep taking action. You may face failures, but you need to have a faith that the failure is there to show you some lesson or do some course correction. Once you have taken enough steps, you'll start to get that hunch of confidence that you are on the way to figure it out, until then, you have to keep taking action to find that clarity.

Discover Your Eulerian Destiny

I heard about this concept of Eulerian Destiny from Tai Lopez, a multi-millionaire entrepreneur, and investor, through one of his programs titled *67 Steps to Getting Anything You Want Out of Life: Health, Wealth, Love, & Happiness.*

Eulerian Destiny name gets its origination from the graph theory, Eulerian path,

discovered by Leonhard Euler. The Eulerian path is the trail in a graph which visits every edge exactly once. In terms of your destiny, this would be equivalent to using the path of least resistance to explore all edges of your life experience, strengths, and skill set. If you can align those things you will have the shortest, easiest, most productive rise to the top of your chosen field.

Tai describes it as a way to determine what you should be doing with your life using information you already have or have experienced.

He explained the four specific factors, which will help you to find your Eulerian destiny:

1) What did you grow up around?

2) What do strangers say about you?

3) You have you been doing for the last five to ten years?

4) What is something you can talk about effortlessly for hours?

So, if you answer these questions about yourself, looking at your living environment, your connection and

interaction with people around you, what you have been doing in recent years, etc., you will find that all these answers will overlap together in some area — and that overlap, where the four aspects combine will form your Eulerian Destiny.

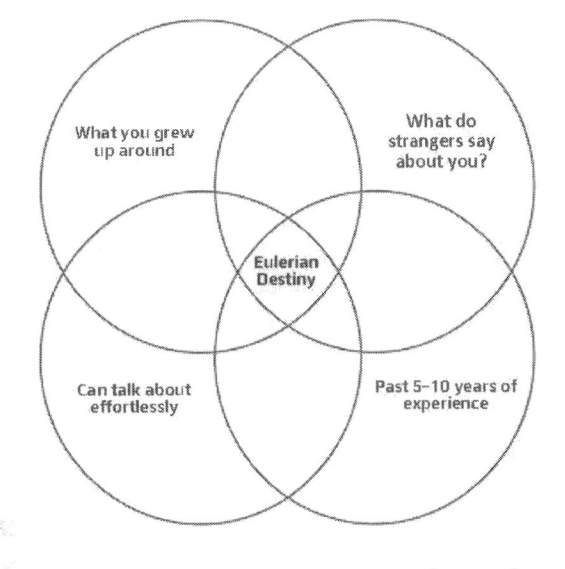

I will try to explain it to you through my own example. I realized reading about personal development, business, and entrepreneurial literature is something I had been doing for more than ten years. I found myself obsessed with personal development and finding the answers to all these questions about human psychology, neuroscience, how people succeed, their

traits, their growth trajectory, etc.

In fact, I often treat myself as a guinea pig i.e. a subject for research in testing the human potential and like to keep experimenting with different things in my life. I also personally tested this "talking effortlessly" trait and noted that, if I was among like-minded people who love and believe in self-mastery and enhancing performance, as I do, I could talk for hours and hours!

This introspection to assess my eulerian destiny also helped me to form some views about my strengths and helped me to choose my career as an author and online entrepreneur.

You should try to draw the four circles with the help of questions and find your own answers, and that will move you closer to determining your eulerian destiny.

Your Life GPS: The 3 Essential Questions

Finding your purpose is a journey, you have to travel from where you are to a specific destination. And as you do on any journey,

you take the help of a map or GPS to see your route and the ultimate destination.

To activate your life GPS, Michael Hyatt in his book *Living Forward* recommends asking three powerful questions, which he terms as *Your Life GPS*. Here's the three essential questions your need to ask yourself to clarify your purpose.

Question 1: How do I want to be remembered?

In planning anything, the best place to begin is at the end. What outcome do you want? How do you want the story to end? How do you want to be remembered when you are gone?

The other way of asking this question is **what do you want to be engraved on your headstone?** This is such a powerful question and if followed through by your heart has the potential to transform the way you lead your life. Here is the story of Jerry Hirsch, an engineer-turned-entrepreneur-turned-lawyer-turned-real-estate-developer-turned-philanthropist, which exemplifies how this question can change the life trajectory of someone.

Jerry Hirsch turned out a philanthropist; he was developing shopping malls in Arizona at such a pace as if he were popping corn. He made tons of money and seemed to have everything he wanted, until his wife left him. This led him to severe depression and he was even hospitalized. That's when he discovered Viktor Frankl's book, Man's Search for Meaning. "It completely changed my life," Jerry said: "I envisioned my tombstone would say 'Before there was Hirsch there were 423 Kmart's and now there are 667.'" Is that what I wanted my legacy to be? And I said, "No. There must be something more meaningful than that."

He quit what he was doing and founded the Lodestar Foundation, which leverages philanthropic impact through volunteerism and collaboration among nonprofit organizations. One of Lodestar's philosophical tenets is, "Happiness can only be found by identifying and striving to achieve a meaningful purpose for one's existence." In 2010, Barron's named Jerry one of the "25 Most Impactful Philanthropists."

Question 2: What matters most?

Maybe you have never given yourself permission to ask this question... what's important to you? What matters most in your life? This is a question about priorities. No one else can decide what they are for you.

Question 3: How can I get from here to where I want to be?

If you are going to improve your life and realize your potential, you will have to figure out where you are now; where you want to be; and how you get from one to the other. Once you've honestly tried and found the answers to the first two questions, this "how" questions become the easiest one. You'll soon come across right set of people, right circumstances, which will show you the way to go toward your purpose.

This chapter was full of questions, which have the power to alter the direction of your life. Hope you've been pausing enough and asking these questions to yourself. My humble request is to treat this chapter as your own interview with yourself—with a condition that you have to be honest in your responses.

Ask these questions and wait for the answers to come. Of course, you want the answer in the perfect and final shape, but that's not the way life works. Life rarely gives the direct answers—the real answers evolve over time. Trust your intuition and take action based on your own answers, as per the level of your current awareness and consciousness- and once you start moving, your answers will start taking shape and bring you closer to your why.

Chapter 6: Never Miss These Rules

****

"If you deliberately plan on being less than you are capable of being, then I warn you that you'll be unhappy for the rest of your life."

~ Abraham Maslow

If you've already spent some time in introspection of your life based on the questions in the previous section, I sincerely hope you'd have already struck some chords in your heart. I hope you have already done the experiment by asking yourself the quality questions because you now know very well by now the powerful questions have the potential to deliver life-changing answers.

Now let's change the gears and get ready to take some action. You won't be able to find your why simply by brainstorming or

sitting at home doing nothing. You have to get into the zone now. Go out, start exploring. However, before you move out, you need to understand the rules of the game. If you know the rules before you get into the game, you will be better prepared to cope up with the situations that might arise later. Finding the purpose is also like a treasure hunting game, where you don't know the end results, but if you follow the rules, sooner or later, you will find the way to your treasure. Therefore, let's get started to understand the key rules for finding your why.

Bid Goodbye To Your Comfort Zone

"Before anything great is really achieved, your comfort zone must be disturbed."— *Ray Lewis*

Your comfort zone is like your personal bubble. It's sort of some self-created wall around you; it's your personal boundary, which you've created over time by doing the same things over and over. This personal bubble feels very comfortable. Why? It is because you know everything within this comfort zone and it gives you a sense of safety. Each activity in this personal bubble

almost feels like brushing your teeth—so comfortable and just on autopilot basis. Have you ever become uncomfortable brushing your teeth? No, you wouldn't because, it is known, it is certain, and you've done it zillions of times in your life so far.

Life seems easy here, but easy doesn't mean meaningful or fulfilling. Someone has rightly said: *"A comfort zone is a beautiful place, but nothing ever grows there."* Though, you might be doing your regular job, or running your small business or delivering professional services, or whatever you do for earning your livelihood, you know that you are doing almost same things over and over each day. And before you realize, these things put you into a zone of comfort. We don't require any attention or don't feel any challenge in doing those activities.

But you'll never be able to find your true purpose, unless you try new things. Because like any other exercise of finding anything, you need to explore many opportunities, you need to meet different people, you need to do things that you have never done. Only once you experience new

and different things, you can determine the best out of those alternatives or options explored by you. The comfort zone of known has its own boundaries, and it will never go beyond that.

Therefore, your objective should be to expand the boundaries of your comfort zone, gradually, by doing things out of your comfort zone. A short real-life example explains the limitlessness of human potential how far one can go by stretching one's own boundaries.

Roger Bannister, a British athlete was the first person in the world to break the record of running a mile in less than 4 minutes in 1952 Olympics. But when he initially expressed his commitment to achieve this seemingly insurmountable goal; everyone around laughed at him and told him it was never done in the past and wasn't humanly possible.

But the man was full of faith and dreams and strongly believed in greater human potential. To achieve that dream, he immensely stretched his comfort zone. He started following a very rigid training

program and started minutely observing his diet, his performances, the size of his long steps, etc. in very diligent manner. And the result is now history, as he broke the world record of running a mile in less than 4 minutes. Once Roger did that seemingly impossible task, the other sprinters also achieved similar or better results.

Look at your life from the perspective of just playing a game. Ralph Waldo Emerson once made profound statement as:

> *"All Life is an experiment, the more experiments you make the better"* ~ *Ralph Waldo Emerson*

Whenever, you face challenges in getting out of your zone, then just think about the bigger picture of what you wanted to explore or become in life. And if you are sincere toward your dreams and evolving into a higher version of yourself, then your dreams and ambitions will pull you out of your comfort zone.

Purpose Comes by Practice

Now coming to the next rule of the game—of course, you've to be out of your comfort zone. But that's not where the story ends. In fact, getting out of your comfort zone is just a starting point of your purpose exploration journey.

First and foremost, your purpose won't emerge straightforward as you start. It generally doesn't come as fully formed. You will get some initial glimpse of purpose, but then you have to start working on it. Purpose evolves over time, and it happens only if you keep taking action. Also, it doesn't have a fixed duration or timetable that when it will arrive to you. But it depends on your intentions and deliberate efforts you put toward.

Let me take example of my personal journey as an author. When I started out, I never saw a fully emerged figure of my purpose of writing. While the broad understanding was clear to me that if I deliver amazing value to my reader, only then I'll be entitled to any kind of reward be it financial or sense of fulfillment due to work. While one limb of purpose was to deliver valuable information to the readers, but there was another purpose of earning

my livelihood out of choosing writing as my career. Another sense of purpose was to experiment and prove to myself there are much better ways of living a life on own terms other than doing a job which I didn't like and couldn't see it doing for the rest of my life.

That's how I started with my purpose. But over time I got a deeper sense of clarity that my purpose is to enrich my audience with unique and life-changing information in an engaging manner. And all that is getting clearer after writing more than a dozen books on the various aspects of human psychology and behavior. Moreover, I feel there is still some much bigger purpose, which will only evolve, if I keep putting myself to work toward my purpose so far evolved. I'm now deeply convinced that I just have to keep moving forward to gain more clarity of my purpose.

I could relate to the words poured by Victor Frankl in his great book *Man's Search for Meaning*, when he said you should never run behind happiness or success, because these are by-products of following a purpose that is greater than you. He stated:

"Don't aim at success—the more you aim at it and make it a target, the more you are going to miss it. For success, like happiness, cannot be pursued; it must ensue, and it only does so as the unintended side effect of one's personal dedication to a cause greater than oneself or as the by-product of one's surrender to a person other than oneself. Happiness must happen, and the same holds for success: you have to let it happen by not caring about it. I want you to listen to what your conscience commands you to do and go on to carry it out to the best of your knowledge. Then you will live to see that in the long-run—in the long-run, I say success will follow you precisely because you had forgotten to think about it."

Just remember, purpose takes time and effort in evolving. Therefore, just keep practicing and soon it will starts taking shape over a period of time. Once you are moving inch by inch closer to your purpose, you're indirectly inviting the success, happiness and fulfillment in your life, sooner or later.

The Principle of Activation Energy

If you've have read chemistry, you might remember the term *activation energy*. Activation energy means: *"the minimum quantity of energy that the reacting species must possess in order to undergo a specified reaction."*

Let's take some examples: The activation point when water starts boiling is 212-degree Fahrenheit or 100 degree Celsius – water will never boil below that temperature. Even if you go to 210 degrees or say 211 degrees, it will not boil. It will start boiling only at 212 degrees.

Also activating fire has a similar rule. The activation point of triggering fire when you rub two sticks together is 451 degrees—therefore, you cannot produce fire at any level below 451 degrees. To get the magic of production of fire, you need to increase its activation energy to 451 degrees and nothing less.

In the similar fashion, you can't activate your purpose, unless you put in the necessary efforts to it. Unfortunately, there is no scientific number or metric to define the activation point of triggering the fire of your purpose, but taking cues from water

and fire examples, you get an idea that this number has to be pretty higher. In other words, if you look at the lives of people, who live purposeful lives, their trigger point of activating the purpose was not anything small. When Mahatama Gandhi, an Indian lawyer, was thrown out of the train compartment in South Africa merely because of his black color, it was the activation point of energizing his life's purpose—to force British people to quit India.

As I said, unfortunately, nobody knows the activation energy factor to awaken their purpose, therefore the only solution is to keep pushing forward with more and more energy on your current pursuits based on the level of clarity you have today. For example, if you feel miserable with your day job, but you need to continue doing it because you have bills to pay, then the best option left is to put your evenings or mornings (outside of your office time) to do something that is meaningful to you. And while doing that meaningful stuff, just increase your energy, keep pushing hard and this will expedite the chances for evolution of your purpose better and

clearer. And sooner or later, you will be able to find out the ways to quit your job and live your chosen purpose. In fact, this is how I chose my path toward quitting my job and moving toward a full-time content creation career. You must understand simmering is not the way to go; you have to go to the boiling point. And if you keep pushing yourself hard then you will start getting closer to that.

The moot point here is not to think too much about how much you have to work or practice toward finding your purpose. It doesn't matter how long it takes, because once you find it, you will be living most meaningful and rewarding life. In fact, there is no other way of living a better life. Life has to be purposeful, and you have to find that purpose, so whatever time it takes to find it, it's worth putting in time and energy in exploring that.

Vernon Howard, an author and spiritual teacher puts it very succinctly in below words:

"No one can tell you what is right for you except for yourself. So start telling yourself what to do. If you blunder for ten years

while thinking for yourself, that is rich *treasure when compared with living these ten years under the mental domination of another. The only true, honest and enriching authority is the internal authority of your own Supermind."*

The Law of Diminishing Intent

The Law of Diminishing intent was propounded by renowned thought-leader Jim Rohn, when he said the longer your delay in doing something, the less probability you'll have of doing it. With the passage of time and just thinking over it longer before deciding, you start losing all your emotional energy that you could have otherwise put in the project itself.

If you get some idea or thought about your life purpose, that warrants you to take some action in any given direction, you shouldn't spend too much time sitting over it. You need to take action on that idea sooner, before the Law of Diminishing intent comes into play. I'm not saying you have to take a big life decision with huge financial implications in a spur of moment or in a hurried way and repent later. But that's

doesn't mean that you need to get into the disease called paralysis by analysis. Your analysis shouldn't be at the cost of compromising with your purpose.

Take action before the law of diminishing intent comes into play and spoil your momentum.

Mel Robbins, the bestselling author of *5-Second Rule* states that in normal circumstances our mind operates in two ways (1) on autopilot basis; and (2) applying emergency brakes. It means that we keep on doing the things the way we have always done it, due to our mind being on autopilot basis. Whenever we get inspired to take some different action or try something new, and if we take a longer time to take action on it, our mind applies emergency brakes. She, therefore suggests we need to take prompt actions, if we are trying to do something out of our routines, else we will simply get lost in paralysis by analysis situation.

Use the First Law of Physics

You learned about one principle from chemistry earlier, now let's take another

principle from physics. Do you remember what the first law of physics is?

It was proposed by Sir Isaac Newton as the law of motion or law of inertia, which reads as:

'An object at rest stays at rest and an object in motion stays in motion with the same speed and in the same direction unless acted upon by an unbalanced force."

Now, let's not do injustice with this law by limiting its application to physics only. This law applies everywhere in our lives. Once you started taking action on something, you end up doing that activity for a longer time. I'm sure you must have many examples in your life, where you'd have already experienced this. Maybe you didn't want to start on any project because it seemed difficult initially. However, since there was a deadline, you had no choice but to start it and boom, you realized within short time, you were into the full action mode. Here the Newton's first law of physics was helping you out.

In business, and generally in any area of life, momentum is the key. Though, you have to break the initial inertia. Don't

remain stuck in whatever you have been doing in the past. If you are sincerely looking forward to finding the things that bring meaning to your daily life, you need to try out many things—and not once, not twice, rather many times, before you arrive at final conclusion about what connects better with you. Just keep breaking the inertia with a belief that once you get started, you will soon be in momentum, even before you realize this.

Stephen King, the bestselling author beautifully put the way he brings momentum in his game in the words below:

"Amateurs sit and wait for inspiration, the rest of us just get up and got to work."

King knew by his experience once you set yourself to work, soon you will get into it, thanks to this Newton's law. Upon asking how King could write so many novels at a faster pace, he confirmed he would sit on his writing desk between 8 a.m. to 8.30 a.m. every morning and didn't get up until he wrote six pages every day.

I've personally experienced that many times myself, when I didn't feel like writing, but I followed this principle of AIC (Ass in

Chair) to get into the momentum, and soon I realized I've gotten into the zone and started generating the content for my book or other writing projects.

The Best Advice- Don't Take Advice From Everyone

This sounds a bit absurd, doesn't it?

But there is truth to it and we need to expound it a bit further.

I'd say that only for certain things, it's better to take advice, but for most of other things in life, it's not a good advice to seek advice. For example, if you are a 3-year old kid, who doesn't know fire can burn you or if you don't know deep water can be a problem for you, then it's really a good idea to listen to advice from your elders. Advice is important for a while. Like watch out for cars. Don't eat worms. Flush the toilet, etc.

But when you are grown up and can think about yourself, then it's not the right approach in most cases. Let' talk more specifically about this in the context of your life's purpose. You see there are more than 7 billion humans on the planet and no two humans are alike in all respects. You know

already that while the faces of two people might resemble each other, but the fingerprints of two people will never be same—the same is true with eye retinas and tongues.

God didn't think about the way Ford, Apple, or any other company thought and designed their products. All cars of the same model or all phones of the same model will look exactly similar. Because Universe loves uniqueness, novelties and variety and therefore nothing created by nature is alike. Everything is different.

Not only physical appearances, but there are vast differences between thoughts, emotions, and feelings of different persons. Everyone is different in some way. The same applies to your purpose or you why behind what you do.

You won't have similar reasons to get motivated, as your parents or your siblings have, even if you are part of the same family. Different things motivate different people. Therefore, if your elder brother is motivated to become a CEO of a big company, it doesn't mean your heart can't beat for creating new songs or writing a

romance novel. Both of you have different reasons, different ikigai in your lives. Now would it make sense to take advice about a new adventure program from your brother, who is probably the last one on this planet to ever think about your crazy adventures? Absolutely not!

Successful people know when it's important to stop taking advice and start listening to yourself. Stop taking advice from people, especially from those who are not motivated by the similar drives as you are. The answers are all inside you. Think deep and decide what's best.

Having said that if you wish to take advice from outside, then be selective in taking advice. Take advice from only the people, who are ahead of you on the same journey as you are; who are your role models for level of success you want to achieve. If you want to be a best basketball player, go and listen to what Michael Jordan has to say you. However, if becoming a social media entrepreneur is what pulls you, then listen to what Facebook, Twitter, and Instagram folks are talking about.

Chapter 7: Follow This Six-Step Process

****

"There is no greater gift you can give or receive than to honor your calling. It's why you were born. And how you become almost alive."

~ Oprah Winfrey

You know by now finding your why behind what you do is not some straightforward simple formula, rather it's an exploration.

I read an article recently and it was intriguing to note that in ancient Hawaii, there were certain family members or masters whose expertise was to discover by intuition or insight a young person's purpose. Parents would take their children to these experts early on, so they could raise each child according to his or her true purpose. The child's purpose wasn't determined by test scores, or aptitude

assessments, or based on who the child's parents were. Instead, the experts would sense each child's true nature, the very core of who the child was and who he or she could become.

Once a child's true purpose was identified, their upbringing was tailored to match it. They were sent to a teacher who could teach them the skills and knowledge connected to their purpose. If a child was identified as a builder, she was given tools of her craft. If he was revealed to be a healer, he was given herbs and taught to identify medicinal plants. A little drummer was given drums and sent to play with other musicians. A mini-fisherman was given a net and sent to learn about the ocean.

Unfortunately, we don't find such mystical people around, who can magically tell us our life purpose for us to simply follow that. And assuming for a moment that we had such people, then also, neither our modern school system, nor today's parents would allow their child to pursue any kind of crazy dream.

No one else outside is really interested in you discovering your real purpose. Only if you are sincere about living a fulfilled life, where you could see meaning in life, then there are certain ways to explore your purpose.

OK! You learned enough aspects of discovering your why, now is the time to bundle up everything together and offer you a recipe with the ingredients and instructions to discover your purpose. In his great book "Life on Purpose", author Victor J. Stretcher has specifically stated six unique steps that can help you discover your purpose in life.

By now, you've done enough introspection by looking at a variety of questions about your life; and this is going to help you follow this six-step process of finding your purpose. If you put in the required time, energy and efforts in following the steps below, these steps have the potential to bring your way closer in your search for your purpose.

With, let's get started to learn these steps:

Step 1: Ascertain Your Life's Core Values

In one of the previous sections, you already learned in detail about the different types of values that different human beings can have in their lives. Below I have again stated a list of the most common values that people have (as a ready-reference, to help you avoid referring back to the previous chapters). You can choose your three top values of life. If you think you have some different life values, which is not on this list, you can write down that below and choose that as your core value, to complete your list of three core values:

- Love
- Success
- Freedom
- Health
- Comfort
- Intimacy
- Security
- Safety
- Adventure
- Power
- Passion
- Creativity

To give an example, my top three values are freedom, adventure, and love, which I have followed for many years unknowingly. Now I am mindfully taking only those actions that meet the tests of these values.

Have you selected your three values now? Now is the time to put some pressure on pre-frontal cortex area of your brain (your thinking brain). You need to think about these three values and find instances in your life where you followed these values and were most happy. Try to back up your top three selected life values with the data in your real life. This will strengthen your belief that you have chosen and already followed some set of values.

Step 2: Find a Role Model and Emulate

Now select any person, who you think should be your role model in the pursuit of your chosen values. This person could be anyone, your family member, or any historical figure. It could be one person or a combination of more than one person who've pursued similar values, as you've chosen for yourself. You can be influenced by the adventures lifestyle of Richard

Branson, or the selfless services of Mother Teresa or maybe Mahatama Gandhi could be your role model. Whosoever, you choose your role model you need to emulate these persons and take such actions as your role models have taken to live a purposeful life.

This association with such role models will help you mold your identity.

Step 3: Take the Headstone Test

The next step comes on the similar lines of Steve Jobs' death question i.e. what would you want to do today if today was your last day of life? In this step, you have to draw your headstone and write your name on it. Write your date of birth there. Your date of death needs to be written as of "TODAY'. Now think about it what's going to be your one-line epitaph (what is something special by which you want to be remembered after you have gone)?

What do you want to people say about you at your death ceremony? Think about it. This is the deepest question that you can ask from yourself. And the answer to this is going to be your way to live.

Step 4: Decide Your Goals Now

At this stage, you are now deeply connected with your own inner self at the deepest levels– because you know your life's core values, you have identified your role models and gone through your headstone test. It's time now to ask yourself about what are the goals in your life that matter most to you? To make the job easier, you need to break these goals into different parts of your life like personal, family, work, society. For example, if you value a relationship with your family as most important, what are you going to achieve in the next three months, six months or one year?

Maybe you will target meeting your closest friends once in a month or maybe you can set a goal to travel to somewhere outside your town with your closest family members and spend intimate moments with them. Same applies to your other values, be it adventure, success, freedom, creativity, whatever it is. Set time-bound specific goals that will help you to move further toward your values.

While deciding your goals, you need to be mindful that your goals address your core needs. According to Tony Robbins[15], we

have six human needs that drive everything we do:

1. Certainty — knowing you'll be able to avoid pain and feel pleasure.
2. Uncertainty/ Variety — the need for change and new experiences.
3. Significance — feeling special and needed.
4. Connection/ Love — feeling a close bond with others.
5. Growth — the ability to change and improve.
6. Contribution — the feeling that you are helping others and making a difference.

Robbins identifies the first four needs as those that shape our personalities- they are connected solely with your own individual needs. On the other hand, the last two are our spiritual needs—these needs require you to expand beyond your own selves. Remember, if you focus only on your own individual needs, you will become successful in the material world; but it is only the last two spiritual needs i.e. the

---

[15] https://www.tonyrobbins.com/mind-meaning/do-you-need-to-feel-significant/

need for growth and contribution to the world; that will give you a sense of fulfillment. And as you know very well, what Robbins said: *"Success without fulfillment is the ultimate failure."*

Step 5: Assemble These Most Valuable Goals Into An Overall Life Purpose

Now is the time to ask yourself whether your most valuable goals formed based on your core values really add up to your bigger purpose. Ask yourself, "Is this purpose bigger than myself?"

This question is very important, because human beings feel happy and fulfilled when they know that they are growing. Limiting your life's purpose to your own needs will ultimately lead you feeling empty from inside and unfulfilled, because just fulfilling your own needs of food, travel, and entertainment only will start to lose its meaning. Only if your purpose is bigger than your own individual needs, you'll have an assurance of your own evolution as a human being and growth- because humans have the apex need of self-transcendence, as you already read earlier in the book

Therefore, plan your most valuable goals and assemble them into your life purpose keeping in mind all your human needs, that makes your purpose bigger than yourself.

Step 6: Practice the Purpose

Now is the time to practice and live the purpose day in day out. Post your why on a place you'll see every day. Talk about your life purpose with people close to you. As you noted earlier that purpose evolves with practice.

Keep practicing your purpose. If sometime later, you realize this purpose doesn't fit with your core values, don't hesitate to change the purpose. You must keep exploring and finding the purpose, as you know already the rules of the game—the purpose keeps on evolving over a period of time.

If you follow the above steps to ascertain your why, you will progress faster in your purpose discovery journey.

Chapter 8: How Not to Drift and Stay Connected

****

"The very first condition of lasting happiness is that a life should be full of purpose, aiming at something outside self."

— Hugh Black

I hope you've been able to make progress to find your why based on the triggering questions and the steps explained in the previous sections. At least this helps you to get moving in a direction with an assurance you are going on the right path.

But hang on. I want to caution you here. Don't assume you got a lifetime certification badge on your collar with engraving *"Purpose Discovered"*. As you know the principles of purpose discovery— you will come across different things and obstacles, which can drive you from your

path. You will feel often feel disillusioned and wonder whether the path you've chosen is right or not. You might sometime feel that something is not right, though deeper inside there is a nudge to keep going. This is a frustrating situation, as you don't know whether to move on or change the course. You're not pretty sure how should you handle this.

I would like to explain it with a small story of Paula.

Paula was a CEO of a medium-sized business and quite instrumental in running the entire business operations. She was intelligent, quick decision taker and people in the organization would often say, Paula was everywhere (they said Paula Front-and-Center).

But recently, Paula was confused why she was not able to focus well on the key activities. She delayed taking decisions and also avoided confronting certain important issues. She knew something was definitely wrong, but she was not able to figure out where the lapse was. In fact, she got remarks from the staff that she was not paying attention to them. She missed

appointments and forgetting to discuss the focal points at the key stakeholders' meetings.

Since she was a bright and intelligent person, and was sincerely looking for it, she finally stumbled upon the core reason of her problem, which she was least expecting. Paula had a secretary Amy, who managed the complete flow of information to and from Paula to every in and out of the organization. But lately Amy was feeling too burned out that she was not managing the flow of information and communication to Paula well. Amy was communicating half-information to Paula or forgetting to deliver the message about some urgent action. And Paula bore the brunt of all this, as it was she who appeared stupid in front of others.

After this revelation, Paula knew Amy needed a break to regain her concentration to handle the things well.

OK, now let's connect this story with our own brains.

In fact, this story is all about how our brain works. Our brain has a part called Prefrontal Cortex or "PFC" (equivalent to

Paula Front-and-Center). PFC is one of the most important portions of our brain, as it controls all the executive functions of the brain. It directs our attention, focuses on most important activities, help us to make the best decisions after analyzing the complex information, and coordinate millions of bytes of information in the brain to arrive at logical conclusion. In the nutshell, if your PFC doesn't work, you're into a big trouble. And this can happen if there is brain damage, and another reason to disturb your PFC is stress.

When we are stressed due to our day to day challenges or difficult timelines, it hampers the proper functioning of another part of our brain called Amygdala (compare it with Amy in above story). Amygdala is also called the fear center of our brain. It's responsible for survival of human beings since primitive ages, as it is Amygdala that generates the 'fight' or 'flight' response to any situation. It alerts the PFC to either fight at a given situation or avoid the situation by fleeting away from that place. But, when you're in stress, Amygdala starts malfunctioning and starts generating unnecessarily fight or flight response. And

the result is that you start getting into unnecessary arguments with people around you or you start procrastinating working on your important deliverable.

The whole point is the stressed Amygdala disturbs your PFC and you start getting disconnected from your purpose and the most important actions needed to move toward your purpose.

Now, when you are working toward your most important goals, directed toward your purpose, there will be uncertainties or difficult situations coming in your life. And in those time, you start getting disconnected from your purpose or why of what you wanted to do. In the toughest times, when you don't feel that energy to move toward your goals, it's very important to reconnect with your purpose.

Great advice. But you would ask, how do you get reconnected with your purpose?

And the answer is through brain breaks.

Brain Breaks

No, we are not talking about some long-weekend break here to rejuvenate because

that will not be a long-lasting solution. Of course you'll feel good on Monday, but as the week progresses you will start feeling down and by mid-Wednesday, you're again in the trap of misbehaving Amygdala.

I recently came to know about this concept of brain break[16]. It means every morning before you start your day, you just sit down at your workstation and relax for ten minutes. Remember you don't have to look at your smartphone, watch the news or do anything. Simply close your eyes; focus on your breath—inhale and exhale—nothing more. Then ask yourself the most important question, *"What activities do I need to focus today? Which will take me a bit closer to my purpose?"*

This simple break helps you to wash away your all distractions and silences your inner critic. This brain break exercise by way of focusing on your incoming and outgoing breath is a form of mindfulness meditation. The good part, you don't need to sit in any particular lotus or other difficult body

---

[16] https://lodestar.asu.edu/blog/2011/11/neuroscience-purpose-recharging-nonprofit-world

position. You just need to focus and make your breath as anchor.

The Magical Effects of Mindfulness

The neuroscience proves that this simple exercise does the job of calming down your Amygdala and which helps it to pass on the right set of information to your PFC. With proper functioning of Amygdala, your PFC focuses better on its executive functions and enables you to take best judgements and you can better focus on your purpose.

In her book, *The Willpower Instinct: How Self-Control Works, Why It Matters, and What You Can Do To Get More of It,* the author Kelly McGonigal, psychologist and researcher describes the overall benefits of this mindfulness exercise on humans. She states that you don't need a lifetime of meditation to see the results and explains intense meditation for few hours shows great results. In her words from the books, she explains that:

> Some researchers have started to look for the smallest dose of meditation needed to see benefits... One study found just three hours of

meditation practice led to improved attention and self-control. After eleven hours, researchers could see those changes in the brain. <u>The new meditators had increased neural connections between regions of the brain important for staying focused, ignoring distractions, and controlling impulses</u>. Another study found that eight weeks of daily meditation practice led to increased self-awareness in everyday life, as well as increased gray matter in corresponding areas of the brain. It may seem incredible that our brains can reshape themselves so quickly, <u>but meditation increases blood flow to the prefrontal cortex, in much the same way that lifting weights increases blood flow to your muscles.</u> The brain appears to adapt to exercise in the same way that muscles do, getting both bigger and faster in order to get better at what you ask of it.

If you have problem, sit down for 10 minutes in the beginning. You can take the help of some guided meditation, which is

available for free on many smartphone apps like Headspace, Calm, Welzen, etc. In my book _The Mindful Mind_, I have captured various aspects of mindfulness, including the benefits as confirmed by neuroscience and the best ways to get started immediately

The Best Way to Do Breathing Exercise

The above technique of focusing on breathing for ten minutes gives many enhanced benefits if you learn to take slow breathes. You'd ask: how slow; is there any metric to measure that?

Yes, here is what you need to do. Breathe so slow that it is just four to six breaths per minute only. Each breath in and out will take ten to fifteen second. It will be initially little difficult, but you can master it with some practice – it's not that hard to learn.

Explaining the benefit of this technique of slow breathing, Kelly McGonigal states the slowdown of breathing activates the prefrontal cortex and increases heart rate variability, which helps shift the brain and body from a state of stress to self-control mode. A few minutes of this technique will

make you feel calm, in control, and capable of handling cravings or challenges.

Just breathe in for a count of four, and then breathe out for a count of six. Do it few times, and you will start getting the benefits of relieved from any anxiety but geared up for taking the next action.

Therefore, to enable you to stay connected with your purpose, take brain breaks regularly, and don't allow your Amy to malfunction and distract Paula in delivering her best work.

Let's continue the momentum and I'll see you in the next chapter.

Chapter 9: Use "Why" to Trigger Flow & Skyrocket Your Performance

****

"The happiest people spend much time in a state of flow - the state in which people are so involved in an activity that nothing else seems to matter; the experience itself is so enjoyable that people will do it even at great cost, for the sheer sake of doing it."

~ Mihaly Csikszentmihalyi

The clarity of purpose is such a wonderful gift that it has the potential to lead you to the state of ultimate flow. Have you ever experienced a state of flow in your life? I believe every person must have felt a state of flow at some point of time in their life i.e. the state in which they would have had immersed so much in the activity they didn't realize the time simply flew away. It could be doing the work your love, it could be playing the sport you've always loved, or it could be sitting with your loved one since

morning, and you didn't realize when the sun had set.

What is Flow and What People Experience in Flow State?

Flow happens when you are engaged in something you are passionate about. Different names are given to this state of consciousness like 'runner's high', 'being in the zone' or 'peak performance'.

To define, 'flow' is the term used by researchers to indicate the optimal state of consciousness, those highest moments of total absorption by the activity we are into, in such a way that we lose our own sense of existence. In such states, time seems to fly, and the performance of such person goes through the roof. The flow state has been described by the world's greatest thinkers as the most productive and creative state of mind in which work doesn't remain work anymore, rather it becomes a joy.

Flow obviously doesn't sound to be a sober scientific topic to be explored. Still there had been few people who were curious to explore about this concept of flow – to understand the science behind this and

how does it feel, when someone experienced that state of being.

A Hungarian psychologist Mihaly Csikszentmihalyi was one such person who embarked upon this journey to dig deeper into this state of being that generates the highest levels of performance by an individual. He recognized and named this psychological concept for this heightened state of consciousness as "flow".

In one of his talks[17], he described that based on his studies and interviews of more than *eight thousand* people around the world – from Dominican monks, to blind nuns, to Himalayan climbers, to Navajo shepherds – who enjoy their work, regardless of the culture, regardless of education or whatever, he found that below are the seven conditions that are present when a person is in the state of flow:

1. They are completely involved in what we are doing – focused, and concentrated.

17

https://www.ted.com/talks/mihaly_csikszentmihalyi_on_flow

2. A sense of ecstasy – of being outside everyday reality.

3. Greater inner clarity- knowing what needs to be done, and how well we are doing.

4. Knowing that the activity is doable – that our skills are adequate to the task.

5. A sense of serenity- no worries about oneself, and a feeling of growing beyond the boundaries of the age.

6. Timelessness – thoroughly focused on the present, hours seem to pass by in minutes.

7. Intrinsic motivation – whatever produces flow becomes its own rewards.

If you can relate to it and even imagine such scenario, this is a state of ultimate joy. The best part is that in such a state, the levels of performance undoubtedly are of the highest quality and at excitingly fast pace. That's why scientists have been trying to get deeper into the subject and examine exactly what happens inside the human brain that leads to such a state of heightened performance.

Sounds quite interesting, doesn't it?

Yes, it is the ultimate joy, when you are deeply immersed in something and delivering your best shot.

Good news. If you've got the clarity of purpose, you're closer to attaining the state of flow. With clear purpose, you can direct your attention solely to that dream, the way Arjuna, in Mahabharata was focusing on the eye of fish moving in the water, with the objective to pierce its eye with his arrow. That's the power of clarity of objective.

Attention is the Psychic Energy

In his book, *Flow: The psychology of optimal experience*, Mihaly Csikszentmihalyi explains that attention is the psychic energy. He states that the mark of a person who is in control of his consciousness is his ability to focus attention at will, to be oblivious to distractions, to concentrate as long as it takes to achieve a goal. And the person who can do this usually enjoys the normal course of everyday life.

Csikszentmihalyi describes our attention as "psychic energy" and concludes the fact that those of us who can control this energy tend to enjoy life more. Further we have a

limited number of stimuli we can attend to at any given moment. He explains that assuming a life of seventy years, with sixteen waking hours every day, it amounts to 185 billion bits of information over the course of our lives. Therefore, the quality of your attention and where you choose to put it essentially dictates the quality of your life.

Therefore, if you are curious and sincere enough to discover and then let your purpose evolve, you better make sure that you're effectively utilizing this psychic energy to your utmost advantage. With the power of purpose and mastery of your attention, you'll experience the state of flow in your life more frequently.

How to Activate and Ensure You Stay In Flow?

Who wants to live happily just for few fragments of life only? Everyone wants to experience the state of happiness and joy consistently. The question arises: is there a way to ensure you enjoy the state of flow more often, which increases over time and then it becomes a continuous affair?

Yes, it's possible. Again, Mihali in his book flow gives a clear and tested principle to achieve that state. He explains that the game of flow is all about the level of your skill and the challenges you come across. Depending upon what your level of skills and what kind of challenges you face in life, you have different types of experiences in your life. In Mihali's words, the principle works like this:

"In all the activities people in our study reported engaging in, enjoyment comes at a very specific point: whenever the opportunities for action perceived by the individual are equal to his or her capabilities. Playing tennis, for instance, is not enjoyable if the two opponents are mismatched. The less skilled player will feel anxious, and the better player will feel bored. The same is true for every other activity. Enjoyment appears at the boundary between boredom and anxiety, when the challenges are just balanced with the person's capacity to act."

So the heart of the principle to enter into the state of flow is: *to engage in such activities where our skills match our challenges.* The principle goes like this:

1. If your skills are far greater than the challenges, then you will feel boredom;
2. If your skills are far less than the challenges you face, you will be in the state of anxiety.

Therefore, the mantra to enter in the state of flow is to match our skill level with the level of challenges. How would you prefer to do it?

There are two ways to do it. I remember a personal example from my school days and it goes something like this: Suppose you draw a straight line on the whiteboard, and then someone else comes and draws a bigger line on the board. Now the question is how you would make your line bigger. Most people will choose the answer, "I'll rub off the other person's bigger line to make it shorter than mine". But there is another approach that very few people take – they choose to make their line bigger by drawing if further.

I know your choice. You and I are in the journey of personal development, so the obvious approach would be to increase the

level of skills over time to make it equal to the level of challenges we want to face. I believe you wouldn't want to choose the lower level of challenges. Though you might choose to play at a bit lower level, only for the short run, but ultimately you'd want to grow and improve your level of skills.

The clearer you are about your purpose, the more it will help you assess your level of skills as compared to the challenges you are facing in your life. And bigger your life purpose, more you will be inclined to improve the level of your skills level and be in the state of flow.

Csikszentmihalyi puts this in his beautiful words as below:

> The optimal state of inner experience is one in which there is *order in consciousness*. This happens when **psychic energy—or attention—is invested in realistic goals, and when skills match the opportunities for action**. The pursuit of a goal brings order in awareness because a person must concentrate attention on the task at hand and momentarily forget

everything else. **These periods of struggling to overcome challenges are what people find to be the most enjoyable of their lives**. A person who has achieved control over psychic energy and has invested it in consciously chosen goals cannot help but grow into a more complex being. By stretching skills, by reaching toward higher challenges, such a person becomes an increasingly extraordinary individual.

Therefore, understand the importance of setting realistic goals that, again, match our skills with our challenge; and of course, we need to keep improving at our skills. By doing so, we focus our psychic energy/attention in a way where we'll often experience the matching of our skills with challenges – and that's where we'll invite flow in our lives more often.

Closing Thoughts

****

The life we receive is not short, but we make it so, nor do we have any lack of it, but are wasteful of it.

~Seneca

Every journey comes to an end, and so it's no different for this book too. The only differentiating point is that while you've come to the end of this book, this itself triggers the beginning of implementation of wisdom nuggets that you'd have handpicked for you.

I'd like to thank you for being part of this journey, where we traveled together to learn what the purpose is, from layman perspective and then explored it further from neuroscience and human psychology and philosophical perspective as well.

I'm sure that you won't have any doubts about the role our purpose plays in designing our lives. I also hope that the

provoking questions, the fundamental principles and the steps to explore the purpose have helped you to do enough introspection and bring much needed clarity. And lastly, the objective of this book is to inspire you reach into the ultimate state of flow that you attain by following your life purpose and become the best version of yourself.

You started this book with a purpose, because you wanted to explore why you do what you do. Now, you are equipped with enough tools to identify what you are meant to do.

With all this knowledge and information, the next step is of course to start taking action. You need to start listening to the subtle voices originating from your heart. Just follow this voices and act upon them. Don't worry about any guarantees about where you will reach. Have faith in what unfolds after you take steps and decide next action thereafter.

I sincerely don't want you to over analyze and then plague yourself with the law of diminishing intent. Hit the iron when it's hot.

Just take the action that you feel right and allow the universe to hold your hand and take you toward the best possible solution for you.

Just go ahead and take inspired action.

As Martin Luther King, Jr. rightly said:

> *"Faith is taking the first step, even when you don't see the whole staircase."*

I wish you a life of purpose and fulfillment.

Cheers

-Som

Your Free Gift:

Did you download your Free Gift already? Click Below and Download your **Free Report** Click Below and Download your **Free Report**

Learn 5 Mental Shifts To Turbo-Charge Your Performance In Every Area Of Your Life - in Next 30 Days!

You can also grab your FREE GIFT Report through this below URL:

http://sombathla.com/mentalshifts

DISCLAIMER

commands. The reader is responsible for his or her own actions.

The author makes no representations or warranties with respect to the accuracy or completeness of the contents of this work and specifically disclaims all warranties, including without limitation warranties of fitness for a particular purpose. No warranty may be created or extended by sales or promotional materials. The advice and recipes contained herein may not be suitable for everyone. This work is sold with the understanding that the author is not engaged in rendering medical, legal or other professional advice or services. If professional assistance is required, the services of a competent professional person should be sought. The author shall not be liable for damages arising here from. The fact that an individual, organization of website is referred to in this work as a citation and/or potential source of further information does not

mean that the author endorses the information the individual, organization to website may provide or recommendations they/it may make. Further, readers should be aware that Internet websites listed in this work might have changed or disappeared between when this work was written and when it is read.

Adherence to all applicable laws and regulations, including international, federal, state, and local governing professional licensing, business practices, advertising, and all other aspects of doing business in any jurisdiction in the world is the sole responsibility of the purchaser or reader.

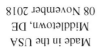

DISC

YOUR

WHY

Unleash the Power Of Why, Find Your
Strengths, Use Obstacles to Your Benefit, and
Lead A Purpose Driven Life

SOM BATHLA

www.sombathla.com

75 feet of empty space—to break one of his records—hit his landing spot, and then sailed 23 feet and five inches over a 27-foot quarter-pipe—to break another of his own records.

"Setting these records kind of pushes the envelope, makes the statement that, ok, anything is possible," explained Danny. "I want to keep progressing the sport, moving it in new directions. This just proves that we haven't really scratched the surface of what can be done."

When the video of Danny's mind-blowing run was premiered to an elite group of action sports performers at a Hollywood theater, the audience was totally stoked by what they had just witnessed. "The public is about to see something they've never seen before," said skateboard pro, Colin McKay. "*It will blow people away.* It will make a vert pipe contest look like lawn mowing."

After seeing the video, the executives at ESPN, the network that originated the X Games, decided that they wanted to tag along on Danny's ride, and worked with him to create a Big Air event for X Games X in August, 2004. Following the designs that Danny had laid out, a monster known as the Mega Ramp was constructed, which stood *nine stories* above the ground. After Buddy Lasek took a practice run, he explained what it felt like to take a ride on the huge ramp. "If you've ever been on the ninth floor of a hotel, imagine riding a skateboard out the window," said Lasek, who didn't take part in the actual Big Air event. "It's what skateboarding should feel like—*flying*."

> *"I have always been self-driven, and never allowed myself to be pressured by other people."*

While the Mega Ramp created exhilaration, it also inspired fear, and only six skateboarders opted to even enter the Big Air contest. "Make no mistake, it is dangerous," cautioned Tony Hawk, who served as a television analyst at the games. And even Danny wasn't immune to the dizzying height of the ramp, which had one drop-in point at 50 feet above the jump off point, and another one at 70 feet. "It's no joke, I have a fear of heights, to some degree. So when I'm up at the top, at 100 feet, I feel like I want to get down as quickly as possible. And rolling down is the quickest way possible. It's faster than an elevator, although it might be a little more dangerous."

While Danny's background includes snowboarding and motocross racing, those exhilarating sports don't come close to matching the adrenaline rush that he gets from flying down a super ramp.

"Having done motocross and snowboarding helped me to gain the confidence that I could actually make a jump of that magnitude, but, really, nothing compares to going down the Mega Ramp. When you snowboard, you can slow down, but on a skateboard there are no brakes. Once you drop in, there's no turning back. It's by far the fastest I have ever been on a skateboard—nothing compares."

Although there were five other skateboarders in the Big Air contest, everyone knew that the event belonged to Danny. "Second place is winning here," acknowledged Bob Burnquist, who wound up finishing sixth. "No one else can do what Danny does.

Danny is the light behind this whole thing," Burnquist continued, as he stared at the top of the ramp. "You look at Danny and go, 'Wow!' If he can think of it and materialize it, then you can see that it's possible. And if you have the skills and the courage, you go and follow him. But it's not just a matter of looking at Danny and blindly following him, because it's a pretty heavy place to be — where Danny is."

Big Air Results
1. Danny Way, San Diego California-91.66
2. Pierre-Luc Gagnon, Montreal, Québec, 86.33
3. Andy Macdonald, San Diego, California-85.00
4. Jake Brown, Sydney, Australia 83.33
5. Jason Ellis, Carlsbad, California-79.33
6. Bob Burnquist, Rio De Janeiro, Brazil-47.66

In fact, when it came to going for the *really* Big Air, no one else even *tried* to go to the place where Danny did. All the other contestants were so intimidated by the 70 foot drop-in, that they opted to do their runs from the lower perch, set at 50 feet, and even then, the ride down was so daunting, that of the 24 runs that the six competitors took, only eight were landed cleanly.

On the first of his four runs, Danny launched a backside 3 over the channel, landed solidly then rode up the huge vert ramp and dialed a humongous backside air over the quarterpipe, which just missed breaking his own height record. But that was just a warm-up for his Gold Medal-winning second run, which he began by dropping in from the 70-foot ledge. After he had nailed another backside 3 over the large gap, he soared high over the quarterpipe with his arms outstretched in a massive Christ Air, offering a salute to one of his early skateboarding heroes, Christian Hosoi, the originator of the trick, who watched it all from the safety of ground level.

"This just proves there are no barriers," said Danny afterwards, the cheers of the other competitors and the nearly 17,000 fans still seeming to echo in the parking lot of the Staples Center. "This was my dream, to take skateboarding to a new level, where everyone could see it.

"We took the Mega Ramp to the X Games, because we wanted to look beyond where we are with competitions, to look into the future and figure out what the next step in skateboarding might be. We're changing the environment so that we can put skateboarding on a level where there is an unlimited amount of possibilities. It's not just to show what can be done on a mega ramp, but also to show that we have barely begun to experiment with what we can accomplish."

TWO
BUCKY LASEK

Like Barry Bonds, the slugging left-fielder of the San Francisco Giants, Bucky Lasek seems to be defying the natural order of sports by getting better as he gets older. And for Lasek, who is 32, the victories keep getting sweeter.

"I've appreciated every victory I've ever achieved, valued every contest I've ever competed in," said Bucky, who was born December 3, 1972, and grew up in Baltimore Maryland. "But as I get older, the time feels more precious. The older I get, the better it feels to be winning and to still be competing at the highest level in skateboarding." Although watching Bucky glide through his routines as if the board was attached to his feet makes it seem as if he was born to skate, he might never have taken up the sport if a thief hadn't copped his bike when Bucky was 12 years old. As a result of the loss of his bicycle, Bucky needed a new set of wheels, and wound up getting a skateboard to replace his stolen bike.

When he isn't skateboarding or spending time with his family, Bucky likes to unwind by racing go-carts.

"I was miserable at the time," recalled Bucky. "But it turned out to be the luckiest thing that ever happened to me. It also taught me a good lesson about learning how to cope with the disappointments that are a part of every life."

Bucky entered his first amateur competition two years after he had first picked up the skateboard, and realized that he wanted to make skating the major focus of his life.

"I started keeping a journal for my ninth grade English class," recalled Bucky. "I was good at expressing myself, and I liked writing essays. That time of your life can get pretty confusing, but when you write things down, you can organize your thoughts better. I wrote about everything. Mainly I wrote about my dream of becoming a pro skater and pretty much living the life that I live right now. I was dead-on-even down to having a white sports car. Back then, it was a white Volkswagen Cabriolet, and now it's a white BMW."

But the road to success, as measured in dollars and victories, wasn't a quick or easy route for Bucky. Unlike some of the current child prodigies of Extreme Sports, such as Shaun White and Takeshi Yasutoko, who have come onto the scene when competitions are televised nationally, and sponsors sign million dollar paychecks, Bucky started his career when money and big wins were scarce. Even after the X Games began in 1995, Bucky mostly remained on the outside looking in, and had only a single Silver medal, in Vert

Doubles, to show for his efforts.

While Bucky was skating on the outer edges of fame and fortune, however, he continued to work at his craft, tuning his techniques and lifting the level of his talent. "I worked out all the time," recalled Bucky, who was trying to break into the top rank of skaters, which included Tony Hawk, Andy Macdonald and Bob Burnquist. "I worked out 3 to 4 hours a day, and I still do."

> Tony Hawk landed the first-ever 900 spin on a skateboard at X Games V.

All that hard work paid off in a huge way for Bucky in 1999, when he stepped out of the competitive shadows and basked in the sweet sunshine of success. In that break-through year, Bucky took first place in the Vert World Championships, grabbed a Silver Medal at the Gravity Games, and snared the Holy Grail of Vert, when he rode to a spectacular come-from-behind victory in X Games V, in San Francisco.

It was a cool San Francisco night, and the

winds were whipping across the Bay, playing havoc with the skaters whenever they went for big air.

"I was hyper enough to start, then the cold made me jittery," said Bucky. "It was hard to control myself. So I just did the Lamaze breathing I had learned in a child-birthing class. Wind was a major factor. But I just tried not to go too high, so the wind wouldn't blow me away."

The finals turned into a duel between Bucky and Hawk and Macdonald, the two skaters who had split the Gold Medals in the four previous X Games. Both Macdonald and Hawk went all-out to retain their perches at the top of the pecking order, with Hawk hoisting up a 92.0 on his final run, and Macdonald maxing out at 93.0. But Bucky *wailed* against the plywood walls, spinning off 540's and kick flips which sent the sparks shooting through the shivering crowd, and earned him a 94.25 and his first X Games Gold.

"I really had something to prove to

myself," noted Bucky. "I just wanted to skate like I skated every day and not fall on stupid stuff. Back home I'd ride well, but then I'd fall in competitions on tricks I do in practice all the time. Skating my best was more important to me than actually taking first place.

"But that was, far and away, my greatest professional achievement," continued Bucky, the importance of that win still reflected in the intensity of his voice. "That first X Games Gold gave me a *huge* sense of accomplishment. Everything fell into place, and my life has changed so much as a result of that win."

"The vert ramp is like an artist's canvas," said Bob Burnquist. "I drop in and paint a picture with my skating."

Although that victory was important to Bucky, because he proved to himself that he could run with the big dogs, it turned out to be a springboard for even better days to come. Bucky began confirming his place at the apex of skateboarding the following year by defending his title with one of the best and most dramatic performances in X Games history.

Although Bucky had had the lead going into the third and last run, Pierre-Luc Gagnon surged into first place on his final skate by scoring an eye-popping 95.00. But Bucky took a few deep breaths and then *burned up the boards* and scored a near-perfect 98.5, and his second successive X Games win.

"I was pretty sure I had the Gold," said Gagnon. "But Bucky just dialed one for the ages."

Bucky found out just how Gagnon felt the following year, when Bucky uncorked a flawless final run at X Games VII. He filled the air with gorgeous tricks, including front side heel flip 540's, and a heel flip indy to fakie on the extension, which put him in first place with a 95.0. But Bucky's Gold feeling faded away, fast, as Bob Burnquist, the last skater in the finals, went off the charts with a 98.0, and bumped Bucky down to Silver.

"Now I know how Pierre must have felt,"

said Bucky, with a wry smile. "But I don't have any regrets about my performance, I did what I wanted to do. Bob's a great skater, and he was really on fire today."

Although Bucky skates to win and earn a living for himself and his family, he also has a passion for the sport, which pushes him to seek excellence even when nothing is on the line except his own sense of pride and self-expression. Bucky demonstrated that quality in his final run at the 2002 Gravity Games. Although he already had first place wrapped up, Bucky went all out, skating as though he was fighting for a medal.

> *On his final run at X Games VII, Bob Burnquist posted the highest skateboarding score in X Games history.*

"I always go into contests with a plan and I try to better myself in each run," explained Bucky. "I just hadn't done the run I wanted to do, so I went out to try to nail that last one. Winning is only half the story."

Bucky, however, has continued to win

Gold medals with such frequency that he could go into the jewelry business, should he ever grow tired of skating. In 2003, alone, he scored the Shiney Yellow at Vans Slam Jam City, Global X Games, the Gravity Games, *again*, then became the first skateboarder in X Games history to garner three Gold medals for Vert, when he notched first place at X Games IX. Bucky then teamed with Bob Burnquist, and added to his collection of bullion by picking up a Gold Medal for their work in Vert Doubles. After his second successive win at the Gravity Games, Bucky showed what he was all about when he was asked if he was happy with his performance.

"Yes, I definitely skated the best I possibly could tonight. Win or lose, I would have walked away from here a happy man."

Bucky stayed jolly throughout the 2004 season, as he repeated his first place finish at Vans Slam City Jam, in Vancouver, Canada, North America's largest and longest-running pure skateboarding competition, and put on another *blistering* come-from-behind win at the tenth anniversary of the X Games. Bucky started the last of his three runs out of the money, in fourth place, behind Gagnon, Rune Gilfberg, and Macdonald, but he faced down the pressure with an amazing display of acrobatic skating, and again aced out Gagnon for the Gold Medal.

Bucky, whose given name is Charles, lives in California with his wife, Jen, and their two daughters, Devin and Paris.

"Bucky is *the* man," said Gagnon. "I stepped it up, but he stepped it up a little bit higher."

"Kids out there should just pick up a skateboard," said Lasek. "It's the best thing I ever did. They may get into a competition one year and be where I am, and feel exactly how I do now."

THREE
NATE
ADAMS

Nate Adams started riding dirt bikes in 1992, when he was eight years old. "My dad got me into it, and I loved it right from the start," recalled Nate. "He bought me a 1983 Honda CR-60, and I loved riding from the moment I got on the bike, and I still do. There are too many hassles and too much danger in the sport to do it for any other reason. You have to love it enough to be willing to put your body, health and, in some circumstances, your life on the line."

Although fans may think that the freestyle riders are crazed cowboys, fearlessly flying through the air with a 230-pound motorcycle nestled between their legs *when they aren't actually flying alongside or behind the machine*, the fear factor is a definite presence in their lives.

"Oh, yes, I'm always afraid," Nate admitted. "I guess people think we're, like, out of control, and just *going for it* all the time. The truth is, there is fear, I always have butterflies before I rev the engine, but I manage to keep the fear in check by knowing what I'm doing and knowing what I'm capable of doing."

> *"It would be fun to do stunts for movies someday. It would be a cool opportunity that not a lot of people get to do with their life."*

Although Nate isn't able to entirely eliminate the fear, he is able to keep it in the background by constantly practicing his tricks, so that doing most of them becomes almost second nature. "I practice *all the time*," said Nate. "And I practice *hard*. There isn't room for any error when you're flying through the air, grabbing for the seat on your motorcycle, so I don't like to leave *anything* to chance."

Nate likes to think tricks through in his

mind, before he gets on his dirt bike and kicks up the dust in his Arizona backyard.

"I break down all the steps of a trick s-l-o-w-l-y," explained Nate. "Once I get about half way through the steps of the trick, it usually just comes together for me. It may take me two or three tries to get it down, or hundreds of tries, but once I can do it, it starts to feel comfortable. From there I just focus on doing the trick bigger and bigger each time."

For the basic tricks, Nate just rides his bike on a dirt track, but when it comes to the backflip or the 360, Nate and the other riders rely on foam-pits for increased safety. But even though the foam-pits have allowed riders to go after gnarlier tricks, the increased safety doesn't come cost-free.

"Foam-pits really make you sore," explained Nate. "You go from 30 MPH to a sudden stop when you land, and it makes your neck ache. It's like whiplash every time."

When Nate decided to start practicing the backflip a couple of years ago, he went to Travis Pastrana's house to work out the kinks with his friendly rival.

"There's no question which sport is the gnarliest," said Brian Deegan, one of the best riders in the world. "Ask any kid, and what do they say? Motocross. We don't have to prove which is the most hard-core sport."

"He didn't have a foam-pit yet, but he had XR70's—Honda Mini Bikes—and we put plenty of layers of bark on top of a huge pile of dirt, to cushion the landing, and flipped onto that. When I started flipping the big gaps, I went back to his house, and by that time he had the foam-pit, so I started flipping big gaps into the foam-pit."

Nate not only practices the individual tricks that he plans to use in a competition, he also practices entire routines, so that when he's out on the track, he's free to concentrate on the details involved in doing the tricks. Although the average fan might not be aware of it, the tricks they see aren't thrown out on an ad-lib basis, like Wynton Marsalis improvising some hot licks on his golden trumpet. With the potential for serious injury, or even death, a constant reality, Nate makes sure that every trick he does during his runs has been carefully worked out in advance, and the entire routine of 16-20 tricks intricately plotted out like a Beethoven string quartet.

"I memorize all the tricks I'm going to do during a run," Nate said. "If I mess up a landing, it can throw the whole routine off."

Nate, however, doesn't mess up many routines, and is, in fact, considered by many people to be the most precise rider in freestyle. Unlike Pastrana, who always rides with lots of style and pizzazz, Nate rides with a cool precision that often seems effortless.

"Nate does things that should be *impossible*," noted Pastrana. "The crowds, and even the judges, don't always respond to the smooth way that Nate rides. But he's the best rider in the world."

"I don't *try* to be smooth," replied Nate, sounding almost defensive. "I just go out and practice and ride. I'm not conscious of doing it. That's just how I ride."

The way that he rides has been good enough to propel Nate into the top rank of freestyle performers during his first four years as a pro. He was named the IMFA Rookie of the Year in 2000, as a 16-year-old, and finished second in both the IMFA Series and the Vans Triple Crown Series in 2001. Although injuries, including a broken collarbone and a dislocated shoulder, sidelined him early in the 2002 season, Nate finished the year in high style by sweeping up the WFA World Freestyle and

> *"The down side of all the traveling is that I don't get to see my friends as much, and do normal stuff. I miss that. I used to just go and ride, and as much as I love this, now I am aware of all my sponsors, and how important it is for me to do well for them. It's a lot more pressure than I had when I was just riding for myself."*

WFA World Big Air Championships. "I just feel good that I was able to ride really well at those events. I didn't actually make it my goal to win those championships, that wouldn't have been very realistic. But I'm really stoked that I did."

Although he had no way of knowing it at the time, Nate was on the verge of having a breakout year, one that would propel him to the very top rank of freestyle riders. Nate stunned the other riders and a packed auditorium at the Vans Triple Crown event in Minneapolis, in early in April of 2003, when he executed the first-ever backflip to a no-hander in a competition. Mike Metzger Wyatt had performed the first backflip in competition a year earlier, but Nate the Destroyer took the trick to an entirely new and outrageous level.

"When I got into freestyle, I didn't think the backflip was possible," said Nate, seeming as giddy about his trick as everyone else who had seen it. "People said never, not in a million years. I know that backflips are something you have to do to win, now, but they're not as much fun to do as some of the other tricks, they're more like high risk. That's not a trick I'll just go out and keep doing for the fun of it."

Nate continued rolling right into X Games IX, where he picked up his first ever X medals, finishing second in Moto X Freestyle, to Pastrana, and also pulling a deuce in Big Air, behind Brian Deegan's ace. Although there was a large contingent in the audience who thought that Nate's run (which included a perfect heel clicker backflip, followed by a clickflip to a no-hander) had destroyed Deegan's, Nate was thrilled with his pair of Silver Medals.

In April of 2002, Mike Metzger Wyatt became the first rider to land a successful backflip, although not in competition. Later in the year, Mike Metzger took the trick to the next level by landing consecutive backflips, a trick he dubbed the Double Fritz.

DANNY WAY

BUCKY LASEK

TAKESHI YASUTOKO

SHAUN WHITE

EITO YASUTOKO

TRAVIS PASTRANA

"I thought I rode the best I've ever ridden in the freestyle, so I go second, so no complaints. I was so excited. And the next day in Big Air I got second again. It was awesome, all my sponsors were punked, and so it's good!"

But Nate was even better at the Gravity Games, when he became the first person to ever take the Gold away from Pastrana in a freestyle competition. Nate put on a dazzling come-from-behind performance, which included a pair of early backflips, and then, with time ticking down, he dialed up a daring backflip over the transfer that sealed the deal.

"The best moment of the year was winning the Gravity Games," exulted Nate. "It kind of felt, like, unreal, and for days afterwards I still was, like, in shock. It was awesome, an awesome feeling."

But, as good as Nate felt then, he felt even more juiced the following year, when he took the Gold on the biggest stage of all, at the tenth anniversary of the X Games.

"I can relax a little," said Nate, who went on to add another pair of Gold Medals at the 2004 Gravity Games. "I've finally made my mark. I mean, my win at Gravity in 2003 helped, but now I feel I've really done it. But I won't let it get me lazy. I have to keep my guard up, and keep practicing. I love riding too much to give it anything but my best."

> *"That loss to Travis at the X Games in 2003 just served as motivation for me. I knew that I had ridden well, but I also knew that I could ride better."*

FOUR
TAKESHI
YASUTOKO

"What I am most attracted to about in-line skating is *speed*," said Takeshi Yasutoko, who was born June 25, 1986, in Osaka, Japan. "As soon as I start running, I pick up speed and feel exhilarated. I also like the feeling I get while *floating in* the air."

Takeshi was a child prodigy, who took to his skates like Mozart took to music, and began to establish himself as a world-class skater at a ridiculously young age. When he was 11 years old, in 1998, he became the youngest athlete ever to compete in the X Games.

The following year he started to establish himself as a credible force in Aggressive In-Line Skating by winning four comps and finishing in the money in seven of the 14 individual contests that he entered. Although he showed he wasn't quite ready for prime time by taking his lumps at X Games V, finishing 8th, while his brother was streaking to a Gold medal, Takeshi took third place at the Asian X games and also pocketed a pair of Gold medals in Thailand, by winning Street and Best Trick contests at the Asian Junior X Games.

> *Unlike his brother Eito, who likes to takes notes while he practices, Takeshi prefers to use mental imaging to help him learn.*

"I think that my brother was born to skate," said Eito, Takeshi's older brother. "I always have to practice to accomplish my goals, but Takeshi seems able to do tricks without practicing very much."

Although Takeshi had started to successfully compete in the international sporting scene, he was still a modest schoolboy, who didn't take his growing fame too seriously.

"I don't talk much about my skating at school," he explained. "And after school, I practice about three hours a day, so I don't have a lot of time to hang out with my friends.

Most of them don't know that I do this."

Takeshi took a giant step toward the top ranks of in-line skating in 2000, when he finished in the top three in 10 of 11 contests, and failed to medal only at the Gravity Games, where he finished just out of the money, in fourth place. Included in his medal haul were a pair of Golds, a trio of Bronzes, and five Silvers, all of which would have been Gold, if Eito hadn't taken those top spots for himself.

One of the second-place finishes occurred at X Games VI, in San Francisco, where Takeshi became the youngest vert skater ever to medal at an individual X Games event.

"This is my third time at the X Games and this is the first medal I've won," said Takeshi, as a broad grin spread across his face. "And on top of that, having the two brothers finish first and second, it's *such* a big deal.

"There is no one trick that I did real well but especially the second run in the finals, everything that I did went well and that was my best run."

Although Takeshi had been modest about

his accomplishment, he left no doubt that he had already set his target on higher goals.

"Regarding the X Games I would like to get the first next year," he said, as the sun glinted off his green fluorescent glasses. "And I would like to get to the top of the skating world."

After some uneven results early in 2001, Takeshi finished the year on a tear, and took another large step toward his goal. Although he stumbled by finishing out of the money in three of his first eight comps, he caught fire at an Aggressive Skating Association Pro Tour event in Italy, and closed out the year by finishing either first or second in nine of his final competitions. It was a year of seconds for Takeshi, who finished as the runner-up in both the Gravity and X Games, as well as in the ASA World Tour Rankings.

Unlike Eito, who scores points with his

Takeshi listens to hip-hop music and sings karaoke, and he also likes to play other sports, including baseball. But he's afraid of heights and doesn't like roller-coasters.

explosive style and inventiveness, Takeshi relies more on the perfect execution of the tricks he does to compile points. And while Takeshi is mild-mannered and somewhat shy, he becomes absolutely assertive the moment that his wheels touch the plywood.

"My philosophy is that I will never be conservative at competitions," explained Takeshi, who has been nicknamed Samurai. "Eito, I think, has a different idea, so it helps me to observe my brother's attitude. I get good feedback from him all the time."

Because Takeshi relies more on a subtle, stylistic approach, and hasn't worked as hard, nor developed the upper-body strength of his brother and the other older skaters, his accomplishments rankle some people.

"If ever there was an example of how little conditioning and strength has to do with success in rollerblading, it is young Takeshi Yasutoko," declared Arlo Eisenberg, who had won the Gold Medal for Street at X Games II. "His success is testament to the importance of technique and confidence over conditioning and strength."

As good as Takeshi had been in the past, 2002 was the year that he leap-frogged to the pinnacle of the skating world. After he finished second at Asian X, Takeshi raised the level of his skating to an entirely new level, as he swept to victory in nine of 12 comps, including his first-ever Gold at the X Games, and finished the top-ranked skater on the ASA Pro Tour.

> "I don't have a strong sense of rivalry with my brother. But if Eito's performance is really good, I feel more motivated. I cannot perform well without being motivated."

"It is difficult for me to express the joy I feel at winning a Gold Medal at the X Games," said Takeshi, who had soared over 14 feet and landed one perfectly styled trick after another, while relegating Eito to the runner-up slot. "I know I am only 16, but it seems to me as if I've been a waiting a long time."

Papa Yasutoko was right there in Philadelphia, applauding his sons' accomplishments, but he also made sure that Takeshi kept his prize in perspective.

"Takeshi is a good skater because of his brother," said Yuki Yasutoko. "They are healthy rivals, pushing each other to be better skaters and to be number one."

Although the brothers do compete against each other, they are friendly rivals. Eito had demonstrated that quality earlier in 2002, at a comp in Cincinnati. Although he had been the top-ranked skater in the world, Eito knew that the little Samurai was rapidly gaining on him. But that did not stop him from giving his brother a boost after Takeshi had fallen twice in his first run, and was in 10th place at the start of the finals.

"I told him it was OK," said Eito, who was in position to win the event with a high score of 91.75. "You have one more run, forget about the first one. No pressure. You just have to cool out and think about the second run."

After hearing Eito's pep talk, Takeshi put on a dazzling routine that earned him a 94.0

score and the Gold Medal. Although Takeshi was thrilled to take the top spot on the medal stand, he remained very humble toward Eito. "He always gets so high, and spins so much," said Takeshi. "This time I was lucky."

> *"Eito and Takeshi have done more to help rollerblading stay alive and attract new people than anyone in the last three years,"* said Mark Shays, Vice President of Aggressive Skating Association Events. *"They're the torchbearers."*

Takeshi also soared over Eito the following year, at the Global X Games, where he hit spins and technical grinds that had the audience, and even the other skaters, up on their feet and cheering.

"It feels good to beat Eito at an X Games, especially because it is the second time," said Takeshi, sounding a little surprised at his accomplishment. "Maybe I am starting to catch up to him."

It looked as though Takeshi was about to make it three in a row over Eito, when he took a commanding lead in the Summer X Games, with a routine that included a sky-reaching

900 above the channel. Although Big Brother came through with a heart-pounding last run that scored him the Gold, Takeshi spoke as if he was just as happy to take home the Silver.

"I am so excited to win with my brother," said Takeshi, whose 95.75 score was good enough to win most comps. "I love coming to X Games. I have so much fun."

But the fun was just beginning for Takeshi, who turned the 2004 season into his personal play thing by sweeping to victories at all the major events, including the Asian X Games— where he finally nailed a Double Flatspin—the LG World Championships, the Gravity Games and the Summer X Games.

Takeshi threw down the gauntlet in his run at X Games X, and neither Eito, who finished third nor Marco di Santi, who finished second, could answer the challenge of his 95.75 score.

In his exquisite run, Takeshi had huge set-up runs, which saw him soar 15 feet above the deck and allowed him to land an amazing new trick, the Double Viking Flip.

"I'm so happy," said Takeshi, who has now staked out his claim to be the world's best in-line skater. "Before the competition I was so nervous, and after my first run I was still nervous because my brother still had to go.

"My first run was perfect for me. I had a lot of speed going into it, and when I did the Double Viking, I felt like I was floating."

Although he is only 18, and is at the height of his skating powers, Takeshi has already begun to think about a life after competitions.

In the Men's Skateboard Vert Best Trick contest at X Games X, Sandro Dias took the Gold with a 900, only the second skater to do so in X Games history. Tony Hawk landed it in 1999 and again in 2003.

"I would like to take over my father's business, Good Skate, Inc. and expand the business around the world," said Takeshi. "I also have a dream of training the skaters of the next generation."

FIVE
SHAUN
WHITE

Like a character out of the movie *Crouching Tiger, Hidden Dragon*, Shaun White seems able to defy the laws of nature and command his body to perform acts of aerial magic. Invariably, he seems to be in *the zone*, that fabled place of consciousness where the lucky few are able to view the high-speed, frenzied action of big-time athletic events through a slow-motion lens, as though their brains were hot-wired by TiVo.

"I can ride with that much speed because I already know what I'm going to do," explained Shaun, as if genius was a simple matter of planning. "Then I just kind of do it. I go into every competition *knowing* that I'm going to stick *every-*

thing I go for. When I can see it in my head, it just works out."

Shaun, who was born September 3, 1986, in San Diego, California, started snowboarding at the age of six, right after he had watched his older brother, Jesse, swooshing down the slopes, as if he was sailing down a slide. Although Shaun took to the sport with incredible swiftness, he can still recall some of the spills he took that first day.

> *"I remember the first time I boarded, it was really slow and sticky that day. My board was huge, but I had so much fun anyways just catching my edges."*

"On my first day on a board, I was like everyone else," said Shaun. "I fell backward, forward, sideways. You name it. I looked like a snow bunny."

Shaun was such a natural, racing down the slopes with courage and grace, that by the following year, 1993, he had already started entering and winning comps.

"The only thing I cared about when I first started snowboarding was a hat I had with a little tail that came out of the back," said Shaun, smiling at the recollection of his old hat. "When I *aired,* as long as the tail flipped up in the back, it was *legit*. It was a good air. Seriously, I didn't care about anything, *all* I wanted to do was hit jumps and get ruined. If I could go *big* and get *rocked*, it was the *best*."

Shaun became so good, so fast, that two years after he had first picked up a board, he won the first of *five* consecutive National Amateur Championships, and the year following that fifth National Amateur, 1999, at the age of 13, he decided to turn pro.

"Shaun White is just a freak of nature," said veteran snowboard pro Dave Downing. "On two feet, he's just a goofy freckle-faced kid with a mop of red hair, but on a snowboard, or even a skateboard, he's absolutely amazing."

Shaun didn't win any comps that first season, going up against older and more experienced pros, but he did have some top-ten finishes and was dubbed *Future Boy* by his fellow boarders. The nickname wasn't, primarily, about Shaun being young, but more about him reaching *nasty* heights and sticking tricks in ways that *nobody* else had ever done.

Shaun continued to improve at a rapid pace over the course of the next two years, earning a bunch of Silver Medals in 2000, and winning his first comp, the Artic Challenge, in 2001.

"That was awesome, because I wanted to be recognized more for my riding talent than my age," said Shaun. "I wanted to make that step from being the cute little kid to being associated with the older riders."

"I dropped out of team sports about nine years ago, because the soccer moms became too heavy. There's nothing worse than having someone else's mom yell at you."

Because he spends so much time traveling around the world to competitions and demonstrations, Shaun spends very little time at Carlsbad High School and relies instead on an independent study program to gain the credits he needs to graduate.

At first, his parents were concerned that he would miss out on educational opportunities, and the shared social scene that most adolescents experience. But Shaun quickly put their fears to rest.

"I'm actually learning *more* this way," explained Shaun. "When we were studying Japanese history, I was actually *in* Japan, standing in a temple. I went to Hiroshima after Sept. 11, which allowed me to better understand the devastation of bombs, world wars and terrorism.

"There are *so many* more experiences to be gained by going on the road and around the world," he continued. "I don't think I'm really missing out on too much. The only thing I missed so far was sixth-grade camp. I was disappointed at first, but then my friends said it wasn't that great."

As Shaun continued to grow and get stronger, his talent level exploded, and he really started to *rock* the slopes. In 2002, he won four events, and finished second nine times, including his Silver Medal-winning efforts at Slopestyle and the SuperPipe at Winter X Games VI.

"He's just naturally talented—*insanely* so," said Peter Foley, head coach of the U.S.

Olympic snowboarding team. "He loves to work at it really hard. He's practicing every day, trying to learn new tricks, trying to get faster and go higher. He gets so much *joy* out of riding."

In an amazing display of talent and determination, Shaun won 10 of the 15 snowboarding contests he entered in 2003, and established himself as the unchallenged king of the slopes.

> "It's fun to ride at contests and stuff.
> But I have the most fun snowboarding when it's just my brother and me."

Shaun started the new year at Aspen, Colorado, where he watched Markku Koski score a hard-to-beat 96.33 in his first run on the SuperPipe at the Winter X Games. As Shaun stood in the start deck, waiting to begin his run, the sun broke through a cloud bank and sat like a precious jewel in the icy blue sky. And then, his mind cleared of Koski's run, Shaun *scorched* down the snowy mountainside and *soared* into a huge McTwist, a 900, and a dizzying array of big air tricks, which earned him a 97.67 and the Gold Medal.

"I just wanted to have some fun, and it turned out *sick*," said Shaun, a smile spacing out the freckles on his face. "I practice 1080s all the time, so it made 900s super easy."

When Shaun showed up for the Slopestyle Finals, he had what had become a trademark red bandana wrapped around his face. He had the look of an old-west outlaw out to grab the loot, which is *exactly* what he did, as he broke away from the rest of the field and rode off with his second Gold of the Games.

"I've always wanted to come to the X Games and do well," said Shaun. "So I guess this is my year....I'm *stoked*."

After becoming the dominant snowboarder in the world, Shaun decided that he also wanted to set his sights on becoming a top-flight skateboarder. Shaun, who had joined Tony Hawk's Gigantic Skatepark Tour in 2002, made his pro skateboarding debut at the 2003 Slam City Jam. Although some people shook their heads, Shaun showed that he could skate with the top pros by copping a fourth place finish. Although he had failed to medal on the plywood, he did make an impression. "He *ripped,* he held his own, I was very impressed," said first-place finisher Bucky Lasek.

> "Shaun is capable of doing anything on a snowboard or a skateboard," declared Tony Hawk. "He has always had the motivation and the talent, but he now has the strength and confidence to push the perceived limits of what is considered possible. My best advice to him now is to enjoy the ride."

"Every pro snowboarder desperately wants to be a pro skateboarder, but no one's done it before," said former pro rider, Cody Dresser. "It's bad enough that Shaun White destroys everyone whenever he enters a snow contest, but now he's a pro vert skater and living out every rider's dream. How sick is *that?*"

Shaun approaches competitions with a sense of yoga-like serenity and utter fearlessness. Although he always expects to win, he's not crippled by the fear of failure.

"The way I feel right now is, going in there, I don't really know what's going to happen," said Shaun, on the eve of the 2004 Winter X Games. "But I have a good feeling

I'm going to be able to do pretty well. But, you know what? I'm really happy with whatever I get. It's not like I've never lost before, so I really don't care."

Although he talks about doing just what comes naturally and having fun, Shaun is also a dedicated athlete, who is intent on discovering the outer limits of his talent.

"This year, I'm almost more determined to do better than last year," said Shaun. "It's going to be tough, but I just feel confident. My motivation is just fun, basically. I just want to make sure I get better every year, so that's kind of what's pushing me."

Shaun took all the drama out of the Slopestyle comp at the 2004 Winter X Games VIII, when he put down a 95.0 on a first run that left him three points ahead of his closest competitor, Danny Kass. Although Shaun could have taken a victory lap on his second run, he went all out and dazzled the shivering crowd and the other pros, and upped his final score to 96.

"He can do anything," said Kass, who also

pulled down Silver in the SuperPipe. "Maybe ten years from now, someone will knock him off, but right now, he's just unbeatable."

Although an injury prevented Shaun from defending his title in the SuperPipe, none of the other riders had any doubt as to what the outcome would have been.

"Competition pushes me to improve."

"If I see someone do a big trick, I try it."

"That just made it possible for us," said Mason Aguirre. "All of us knew that if Shaun could have landed his run, he was going to win."

Although he's sitting on top of the world, Shaun likes to keep life as sweet and simple as it was when he was six.

"Landing a new trick, that's what it's all about for me," explained White, who seeks fulfillment in the arc of a new stunt. "I just won't walk away from a trick until I nail it. If I do, it eats away at the back of my mind, and ruins dinner and everything else. But learning a new trick, that's makes for a perfect day!"

SIX
EITO YASUTOKO

Although Eito Yasutoko enjoys winning every vert contest he can, he is even more interested in maximizing his own unique talents. For Eito, competitions are less about the other performers, and more about his trying to attain the goals he sets for himself.

"My biggest fear is not losing to another skater, but in losing to myself, by not practicing as hard as I should, or not focusing correctly when I am skating at an event."

In competitions, Eito is aggressive in his performances, always appearing to be actively straining to free his body from the grab of gravity. He's an explosive and dynamic skater, who is always trying to increase the altitude on his leaps off the vert, willing himself to sky as high as he can fly. When asked what his favorite trick is, Eito just smiled and said, "Big Air. Whatever trick I do, I want to soar, like an eagle."

Ironically, when Eito was younger, he had very little interest in skating. But his parents had been professional roller-disco skaters and owned a skating rink, so Eito and his younger brother Takeshi were on wheels almost before they started walking.

Eito's nickname is Eight, because his father was especially good at executing a figure 8, and Eito is the Japanese pronunciation of the number eight.

"I grew up at the skate rink," explained Eito, who was born July 23, 1983 in Osaka, Japan. "Everybody around me were skaters, and I thought everybody needed skates for life in the world. I didn't know anything outside the skate rink.

"We didn't really want to skate, but we had to because of our parents. We mostly ignored the half-pipe, though, and focused on speed skating and ice hockey. Then, in 1995, when I was 11 or 12 years old, we went to our first competition in the United States. I saw many good skaters, and I really got hooked."

Although Eito had become stoked on Aggressive In-line Vert Skating during that first visit to America, he didn't enter very many competitions until 1998. But as soon as he started competing more regularly, Eito showed that he would be a force to be reckoned with in the international skating community. In that first year, when Eito was still only 15, he took home Gold Medals from comps in Brazil, Australia, and at the Asian X Games in Thailand. Eito also had his first experience at the X Games in the U.S., where he finished fourth in Vert and in Vert Doubles, with Takeshi as his partner.

"Even then, you could see the explosiveness in his performance," recalled Matt Salerno, who had taken the Silver Medal at X Games IV. "He was a little bit shy, because he only spoke a few words of English back then, but you could see how focused he was, and how determined he was to hit the heights."

Eito showed just how accurate Salerno's assessment had been the following year, when he decimated the X Games V field, with a performance that was highlighted by back-to-back 720s in both directions, and which earned his first X Games Gold.

"I can't believe how high he was able to go in this wind, and still keep his balance," said second place finisher Cesar Mora, who had won the event in 1998. "This may have been his first win at the X Games, but it definitely won't be his last."

Eito went from being a surprise winner to a totally dominant performer throughout 2000, and wound up with more metal than a Barbary Coast pirate. He finished in the top three in each of the ten individual Aggressive In-line Vert contests that he entered, and took home the Gold in seven of them, including a second successive win at the X Games, which he

At the 1996 X Games, Fabiola da Silva of Brazil won a Gold Medal for a run that included the first-ever backflip by a female in-line skater.

ended with such a huge 1080 that the fans jumped right out of their seats. In winning the event, Eito had aced out his little brother, who had quickly become a force on the boards as well. It was the third time that year that Takeshi had finished second behind Eito, but his brother wasn't boastful about those outcomes.

"Sometime I teach him, but sometime he teaches me," said Eito. "But we're different in everything. I usually think a lot before I do my tricks, and I spend so much time practicing. Takeshi doesn't think so much before he does things, or practice as much as I do."

Eito is as dedicated to practicing as he is to performing. He spends hours a day training, improving old tricks and inventing new ones, such as the California Roll and the 1440 Flat Spin, in which he does four full spins while his body is laid out horizontally to the ground. During his practices he stops to take notes on the session, and then reads them at night, before he turns out the light.

"I was lucky that skating comes natural to

me, because I don't have abilities in any other sport." Said Eito, "I am happy that I have skating as a way of expressing my feelings."

Although Eito is single-minded about athletics, he is anything but when it comes to engaging the life around him. In his spare time, Eito takes photographs and sketches, and he is very appreciative of a lifestyle that allows him to interact with many different people.

Taig Khris is the first in-line skater to land a double backflip in competition. He pulled the trick during his gold-medal run at the 2001 Summer X Games VII.

"I've traveled around the world and have had the chance to learn many different cultures," said Eito. "And I've met so many fans that said they know me from television. That makes me happy. To me, that's amazing."

Eito has continued to maintain his place in the top tier of skating, finishing in the top three with almost total regularity and, more often than not, dueling with Takeshi for first place in competitions all around the globe.

"They're the best two vert riders in the

world, period, of any of the three sports," declared Mark Shays, the vice president of Aggressive Skating Association Events. "I've emceed demos where the more celebrated names of skateboarding and BMX are there, and their jaws are on the floor watching the Yasutoko brothers soar."

In-line skating judge, Chris Mitchell, who gets to see Eito perform on a regular and up-close basis, agrees that the Yasutokos are in a league of their own when it comes to Aggressive In-line Skating.

"When he's on, Eito can really dominate," said Mitchell. "They both have a wow factor that we look for, a factor that other skaters don't have."

In 2003, Eito took wow to a new level, when he compiled what might have been the finest season ever recorded by an in-line skater. In an amazing display of unswerving excellence, Eito finished first in eight of the nine contests he entered, and in the only event that he didn't win, he finished second, behind Takeshi, at the Global games.

Eito was especially brilliant at the X Games and the Gravity Games, the twin Meccas of Extreme Sports. In the X Games, Eito entered the last round trailing Takeshi, who had posted a usually unbeatable 95.75 score in the first round. With adrenaline racing through his blood stream, Eito laid down an astonishing 97.25 run, during which he uncorked his patented California Roll and three outrageous double backflip combos.

Eito has invented some of the most exciting tricks, including the Double Flat Spin, the 1440 Flat Spin, and the California Roll.

"I was nervous, but I had to try the backflips," explained Eito, who made X Games history by becoming the first male aggressive in-line skater to win three X Games Gold Medals in his career. "I'm the big brother," he added, with a smile and a wink, "so I have to beat him."

Eito was also trailing before his second run at the Gravity Games, after having taken a first-run spill. But he again smoked through his routine with an awesome array of big air tricks, including a rainmaking double backflip at the buzzer, which earned him another Yellow Medal.

"The competition was so exciting for me," exclaimed Eito. "The crowd, the people, so much noise, so much pressure tonight, competing with such great people."

"Eito is the most feared competitor in the world of in-line vert," said former pro and Extreme Sports announcer Arlo Eisenberg. "When he's at his best, no one can beat him."

A great portion of the crowd at the Staples Center in Los Angeles thought that Eito had been unbeatable at his performance at X Games X in 2004, but the judges thought otherwise, and Eito had to settle for the Bronze Medal. Although there was good reason for Eito to think that he had made the top run, he took the judgment with his usual modesty and sportsmanship.

"I thought I skated as well as I could today, but maybe the others skated better," said Eito, who had moved to the United States during the summer of 2003. "I can't argue with the judges' decision. But watch out for next year, I'll be back with some new tricks."

But, in his usual fashion, Eito has already begun to look beyond 2005, to contemplate his legacy in in-line skating, and his life beyond the vert ramp and half-pipe.

"I want to make history," said Eito, who has done everything within his power to help him realize his ambition. "I want to become a legendary skater. That's my dream."

> *"Feeling scared is no excuse for not doing things. I have a sense of responsibility, because I am influencing the world of skating."*

"I also would like to contribute to the spread of in-line skating worldwide. I don't know when I will retire, but I would like to build a skating facility where I can train skaters of the next generation. And I would like to study design, film directing or song writing. Other than that, I would like to live my life in a quiet, rural place."

SEVEN
DAVE
MIRRA

For Dave Mirra, riding his BMX has always been about doing what he loves and testing the limits of what can be accomplished on a bike.

"The money and fame are welcome, but that's not what it's ever been about for me," said Dave, who is featured in his own video game and stars in the Dave Mirra Supertour, which puts on demos all around the U.S. "For me, it's always been about simply loving to ride and extending the boundaries of my imagination and capabilities."

Dave Mirra came into the world on April 4, 1974, and grew up in the small town of Chittenango, New York. When he was five, Dave's parents divorced, and he and his older brother, Tim, continued to live with their father, while his mother moved to nearby Syracuse. Although Dave's mother had moved out of their house, she didn't move out of the lives of her sons, and saw them on a regular basis.

> "I hope BMX can continue to grow, so that we can see the kids of the future having a blast, getting more opportunities to ride than we had when we were kids."

Dave and Tim spent most of their free time riding around town on their bicycles, whenever there wasn't snow on the ground of their upstate New York town. One day when the brothers were out riding, they saw some older boys driving BMX bikes, having a ball riding down staircases, jumping curbs and any other obstructions that came into their path. That was a magical moment for Dave, who was eight years old at the time.

"I was, like, what is *this*," recalled Dave. "It was as if a light bulb had gone on; I just knew I needed to get a BMX bike and start jumping and doing all the *gnarly* things I had seen those boys doing."

After Dave and Tim got their BMXs, they started popping wheelies, and then raced around their town, riding on and jumping over whatever they could find. Soon, the brothers were building their own home-made backyard ramps, using dirt, scrap wood and anything else they could find that would let them launch themselves skyward and *catch some air.*

"I think kids need to remember to start slow, have fun, and not do anything that they're not capable of doing," said Dave. "I mean, the best way to stay healthy is to stick with what you know you can do. They should take their time, and just let it happen."

Dave and Tim eventually outgrew their backyard construction, but there weren't any ramps to really groove on in Chittenango. So, the two boys and their riding buddies from the town decided to build their own 10-foot high, 16-foot wide vert ramp. And once Dave, who by then was 15 years old, got a taste of *that* big air, he was hooked.

"My heart was in it from Day One," recalled Dave, whose nickname is *Miracle Boy*. "I didn't spend a lot of time thinking about turning pro. I just spent my time being the best rider that I could be, and stuck with it."

> *"On a good day, I try to wake up early, go to the gym, run some errands and then go ride for the rest of the day with my friends. That is a good day for me."*

Dave proved to be such a good rider that he was selected to tour the U.S. doing demos, and was also featured in the BMX video, *Dorkin' in York 2*. When he was 18, in 1992, three years after he and his friends had built their ramp, Dave had become so proficient at riding that he decided to turn pro. Just as he was hitting his stride as a rider, however, Dave, while crossing a street, was run down by a drunk driver, and suffered a life-threatening skull fracture.

It was a long, painful and frustrating

recovery, and, for a while, Dave was depressed by the thought of not being able to pursue his riding career. Then, Dave went to visit Tim, who was attending college in Greenville, North Carolina, and discovered that his brother was living right across the street from Jaycee BMX Park. Riding with Tim helped Dave recover his determination to continue on with his career, and also convinced him to make Greenville his home.

"Riding with Tim really restored my self-confidence," recalled Dave. "I had been thoroughly miserable, and really down on myself."

Once Dave was back in shape and in the saddle, he roared into Windy City for his first comp since the accident, and captured the Gold Medal for Street and a Bronze Medal in Vert at the 1994 Chicago Bicycle Stunt Series. That new beginning pumped up the volume on Dave's confidence and helped launch him into becoming the most honored rider in X Games history.

Dave started his amazing run in 1995, the year the X Games began, when he scored a second place finish in Bike Stunt Vert. The following year, he repeated his Silver in Vert, and also took home the Gold in the debut of Bike Stunt Park. But Dave was just warming up. Between 1997 and 1999, Miracle Boy finished first in both Park and Vert, and made it triple Gold in 1998, when he teamed with his boyhood riding idol, Dennis McCoy, to take first place in Vert Doubles.

> *"I was going to get a dirt bike to mess around with, but I think I decided to devote the rest of my competing life to bike riding. I want to do one thing the best I can, not five things mediocre."*

"Winning Gold never gets old," said Dave, after he had bagged another pair in 1999. "Winning the X Games is the biggest accomplishment that anybody can have in this sport. I'm on a streak right now, but it could end at any time, I guess. I'm just going to keep coming back every year and keep doing the best I can."

Jay Miron, who had finished second in both the Vert and the Park, threw up his hands in surrender and salute.

"*Dave rules,*" said Miron. "He's the ultimate pro. When it counts, Dave steps it up."

Miracle Boy stepped it up big at the 2000 Games, when he won the Park title with an awesome routine, which included a Decade Air, a trick in which he rotated 360 degrees around the headtube with the handlebars, and the first Double Backflip in X Games Bike Stunt history. Although most riders save their best tricks for the last run, Dave decided to go for broke right from the git-go.

"I just went for it on first run with the thought that, whatever happens, happens," said Dave, moments after collecting his 11th X Games medal, *nine* of which were Gold. "I'm kind of on the *meant-to-be policy.* If it's meant to be, then you'll pull it. If not, *oh well.*

"If I'm not going to win, I at least want to put pressure on the other riders," he continued. "If I don't, I get bummed."

Although Dave had gone all out to stick the trick, he wasn't shy about acknowledging what was on his mind in the moments before he roared into it.

"I want to be safe," he reminded himself. "I want to walk away healthy."

Though Jamie Bestwick had ended his three-year reign as King of the Vert Ramp, Dave wasn't feeling bent about his second place finish.

Mat Hoffman, aka The Condor, landed the first-ever no-handed 900 spin in the Bike Stunt Vert competition at the 2002 X Games in Philadelphia.

"I got a Silver in Vert and a Gold in Park, so I can't complain," said Dave, who didn't look as if he were feeling any pain. "I'm happy."

Dave continued to pile up the medals through the following three years. He picked up Golds in Vert in both 2001 and 2002, and then upped his total X Games medal count to 16, by picking up a Silver and his first X Games Bronze in 2003. With those two medals, Dave had tied the legendary Tony Hawk for the most medals in X Games history.

"He has always been a great rider," declared Dennis McCoy. "Long before the X Games, he was always one of the top riders. Back then he didn't win as much, but he started to put everything together mentally. He has always had the hardest tricks out here. He has just gotten to the point where he knows, from a competitors standpoint, when he needs to step it up."

Dave showed that ability to step up big in 2004, when he uncorked a perfect Tailwhip Flair high into the air that sealed the deal on the Gold Medal in Vert.

"I'm just psyched," said Dave, more excited about his accomplishment than the medal. "It's taken me a year to take the Flairwhip from the practice to the ramp. I held back a few things I've been working on, so just wait till the next contest."

The next contest was the Bike Stunt

Finals, and Dave immediately got in trouble when he decked against the wall on a backflip, and finished the first run in last place.

> "You pump the ramp, push down at the right time, and it's almost like being in a swing. You have to land exactly perfect and compress all the way. The better you land, the higher you go."

"I was psyched with the overall run," said Dave, as he just shrugged off his fall. "The backflip off the wall? It's going to happen."

Then he went out and delivered the complete package on his second run, banging out a spectacular Gold Medal-winning performance, which he ended with a Wallride to a Tailwhip, before raising his hand in triumph.

The two wins pumped Dave's X Games medal haul to a record-setting 18.

"I'm stoked about winning the medals," said Miracle Boy, who showed that he was still the King of BMX. "And if I can create history, that's good, because I love history."

EIGHT
TRAVIS PASTRANA

Although it seems as though Travis Pastrana was born on a motorcycle, he actually didn't start riding one until he had reached the ripe old age of four. Travis, a native of Annapolis, Maryland, has always been in a hurry, whether he's riding cycles, jumping off them, graduating from high school at 15, or just zipping through his life at what seems like supersonic speed.

"That's just who I am," explained Travis, as he spread his arms out wide. "I love racing and competing, and having as many experiences in life as I can grab. I don't want to miss out on anything."

That first motorcycle, a one-speed Honda Z-50, was a gift from his father, Robert, and for

Travis, it was love at first sight.

"For some people, it almost seems as though they were born to do a certain thing. For me, it seems as if I was born to ride and race motorcycles."

By the time he was 14 years old, Travis had already won five National Amateur Motocross racing Championships, and had become the youngest ever IMFA World Freestyle Motorcycle Champion. But it wasn't until the following year, 1999, that Travis rocked the world of freestyle riding, and wrote his name large and bold into the history of extreme sports legends.

> "To talk to Travis, you wouldn't know that he was an athlete of any special caliber," said Travis's dad, Robert. "He's just Travis. Always has been, hopefully, always will be."

When Travis showed up in San Francisco for the debut of Freestyle Moto X at the 1999 X Games, he was the youngest of the nine competitors in the event. But that didn't stop him from putting on one of the most amazing riding performances ever seen. On the first of his two runs, Travis dazzled the screaming crowd and the judges by soaring 35 feet into the air, while performing a high-energy series of tricks, which included a Cliff-hanger, a No-handed Hail-click, an Indian Air, and a pair of Superman seat grabs, in which he flew through the air with the greatest of ease. That stunning performance earned Travis a nearly perfect 99.0 score and the Gold Medal.

But Travis wasn't through adding to the excitement of X Games IV, and, at the end of his second foot-stomping run, he jumped the dirt ramp at the end of the course, and flew about 100 feet through the air, splashing down into San Francisco Bay on the seat of his Suzuki.

"All the riders thought it would be really cool," recalled Travis. "Since it was on my last run and wouldn't hold up the competition, I decided to do it.

"This is so awesome and I can't believe I just won the Gold Medal," continued Travis, a wide smile stretched across his face. "I have never seen this many people before in my life at a motocross race, and I'm just excited to be at the X Games."

Travis might not have seen that many people at the racing events, because he was going too fast to see much of anything. He started his racing career with a bang, by taking the checkered flag at the first pro race he entered, and went on to be named the 2000 AMA Rookie of the Year.

"Last year I was 41 points down and struggling in the title chase immediately before the X Games. However, I did the X Games and had so much fun that when I went back to the 125cc series, I caught fire and ended up winning the title."

Although some people on the motocross racing circuit criticized him for not devoting his full attention to his racing career, Travis didn't have any intention of letting anyone put his life into a pigeonhole.

"They just don't understand who I am or what I'm about," explained Travis. "I've devoted myself to being the best racer in the world, but if I have the time to do something else when I'm not racing, then I'll go ahead and do that. Freestyle is a real breath of fresh air for me, and doesn't take anything away from my racing."

And, racing obviously didn't take anything away from his performance in Freestyle Moto X, because Travis returned to the scene of his crime, aka San Francisco, in 2000, and captured his second successive X Games Gold Medal.

Afterwards, he spoke about his winning run as if he were seeing it on the replay screen.

"I had the SuperMute," said Travis, as smooth as an ESPN TV analyst. "The one-handed Indy air, which had never been done on a motorcycle. I also pulled a Superman to Heelclicker, which had also never been done on a motorcycle."

Although Travis had a clean run in the finals, he barely avoided disaster in the prelims, when he bailed out of a backflip that had doom written all over it.

"I was fortunate to be safe on that one,"

acknowledged Travis, who gets dizzy on a Ferris Wheel. "My strengths and weaknesses are the same: I've got the willingness and stupidity to try anything. If I think it's even remotely possible, I'll do it."

Travis amplified that message the following year, when he fulfilled a childhood dream and parachuted into the Grand Canyon while sitting on a motorcycle.

> "Everyone told me that this was the hardest, roughest track in the outdoor series, but I like diversity. Give me mud, or sand, or something that's really rough, and I like it and can usually do well."

"I've wanted to do that since I was 10 years old," said Travis, who had taken two weeks off to study with the best skydiver in the country. "I was able to do a backflip and a Heelclicker, jumped off the motorcycle, and had three seconds of free-fall. It was a quick rush, but it was the best feeling in the world."

As Travis arrived in Philadelphia to try for an X Games three-peat, he was told that a couple of big-name rivals, Brian Deegan and Tommy Clowers, had said that he couldn't stay away from the sport for a year and expect to win.

"They've been saying that for the last three years," said Travis, shrugging his shoulders. "They do get closer and closer, though, and last year was really close. I can't expect to keep going undefeated, but I think I can hold them off one more year."

Then he went out and burned up the course, starting with a Tailwhip, and ending with a backwards flip off his motorcycle, and another Gold Medal. And it wasn't even close.

"I was just out there having a good time, this is unbelievable," said Travis, who had notched a 96.33 and then been whisked off to the airport to compete at the AMA Nationals. "Everyone was yelling for the backflip, so I had to give them one."

The desire to please the fans and constantly test his limits is a dangerous combination, however, and hasn't always ended so painlessly. Travis was sidelined by injuries for large chunks of 1992, including the X Games, although he did manage to make it to the Gravity Games, where he picked up his third Freestyle Gravity Games Gold. But when he tried to take away the Gold in the Step-Up competition, he went down hard, and tore up his knee.

"I've had a lot of injuries, but I can't let that interfere with my life," he continued. "Competing is hard on my body—and my parents—but it's what I do."

Although Travis is stoic, even fatalistic about injuries, they started to mount up and take their toll. When he came to Los Angeles for X Games IX in 2003, it was the first comp he had been able to enter since the previous year, and he knew he faced a stiff challenge to his undefeated streak in Freestyle Moto X.

"Guys have taken the backflip and run with it, pushing it to the limit, which is pretty awesome," noted Mike Metzger. *"But it's a matter of practicing something until it becomes comfortable. It's a matter of taking baby steps until you have it down cold."*

"There are a lot of great riders here, and I haven't been able to train as much as I would have liked to," he acknowledged. "But I'll make my runs and we'll see what happens."

After Brian Deegan had laid down a line in the dirt by taking the lead with a 93.33 score, Travis answered the challenge by pulling out the stops and finishing his routine with a pair of 360 backflips, which put him in the lead at 94.67. But, it wasn't until after a spectacular run by Nate Adams fell just short, at 93.33, that Travis could let out his breath and claim his fourth X Games Gold.

"I knew if Nate had a great run he could still have taken it, and he pretty much did," acknowledged Travis. "He probably had the best collection of tricks. But he didn't have the 360."

One month later, at the Gravity Games, Travis crashed so hard at the end of his first run, that he was knocked out of the competition. But that first run was good enough to put him in first place, until Nate Adams had a great ride and handed Travis his first loss in an FMX comp.

"I hate getting knocked out," joked Travis,

who took his loss as gracefully as any win. "Nate had a super run."

Injuries also played a part in the 2004 Summer X Games, when Travis, riding with a concussion and vision in only one eye, couldn't match the spectacular, Gold Medal-winning ride that Adams had laid down. On his last run, Travis knew that his only chance to cop the win was to pull out all the stops, and dial up a double Backflip. But that day, he realized, wasn't a time for grabbing for Gold.

"Travis is the best rider in the world," said Nate Adams. "He rides with so much style and excitement. He's the only person I watch ride."

"I would have loved to do the double, but staying alive was more important to me today," said Travis, who had to settle for second place. "You need everything you have to compete at this level, and I didn't have it today.

"I'm happy for Nate, but I just want to go home and sleep for a few weeks and heal up from these injuries. Then I want to come back next year and kick butt."

GLOSSARY

GENERAL TERMS

360   A move in which the athlete leaves the ground and spins around one full rotation before landing.

540   A move in which the athlete spins one-and-a-half rotations before landing.

720   A move in which the athlete spins two full rotations before landing.

900   A move in which the athlete spins two-and-a-half rotations before landing on the ramp.

1080   A trick of extreme difficulty in which the athlete spins three full rotations before landing.

Air   Whenever athletes and their equipment are off the ground at the same time.

Backside   A turn or trick executed with the athlete's back towards the surface.

Fakie   To skate or ride backwards.

Frontside   A grind variation performed with the athlete's face towards the surface.

McTwist   An upside down 540-degree turn performed on a ramp, named for skateboard legend Mike McGill.

COURSE TERMS

Gap   Usually, the "empty" section between the take off and landing of a double, step-down or step-up.

Half-pipe   The ramp used in the Vert competition that is "U" shaped. Tricks are done while flying over or off it.

Lip   The top part of the front of a jump, which can send an athlete into the air over the obstacle. The lip is also known as the takeoff.

Quarter-pipe   A single wall of the half-pipe, used in park courses.

Roll-in   A portion at the top of a ramp that athletes can use to roll into the ramp, rather than dropping over the vertical section of the ramp, often used to gain speed.

Vert   A term that is short for vertical, meaning a 90-degree ramp, pool or wall.

AGGRESSIVE IN-LINE SKATE

Flat spin   The skater gets air, turns on the axis of the body nearly horizontal to the ground or ramp and lands.

Grind   To slide along a surface on the skate frames between the wheels or on the outside or inside base of the boot.

BICYCLE STUNT

Can-can   A trick in which the rider takes one foot off the pedal and kicks the leg over the top tube of the frame, then returns the foot to the pedal before landing.

Flair   A trick in which the rider does a backflip to a 180-degree turn and lands forward.

Grind   When a rider slides along the coping on the axle pegs, sprocket or pedal.

Double peg   When both pegs on one side grind simultaneously.

Manual   A trick which a rider does while the front wheel is in the air across the top deck before returning to the ramp.

Seat grab   A trick in which the rider throws the bike
One-hander   In front, takes both hands off the handlebars and then grabs the seat with one hand and lands with both hands back on the handlebars.

Superman   A trick in which the rider takes both feet off the pedals and one hand off the handlebars in the air and stretches the legs as far behind the bike as possible.

Tailwhip   A trick in which the rider maintains body position, holding the bars steady and whipping the frame 360 degrees round the head tube.

MOTO X

Can-can   A trick in which the rider moves one leg over the gas tank to the other side of the bike and back.

Hart Attack   A trick in which the rider performs a Superman Seat Grab with legs thrust straight up from the bike. Named for Carey Hart.

Double Handed Hart Attack   A trick in which a rider performs a Hart Attack with both hands gripping the seat.

Indian Air   A trick in which the rider does a scissors kick integrated into another trick, such as a Superman Seat Grab. Adapted from Bicycle Stunt Dirt Jumping.

Lazy Boy   A trick in which the rider lies back on the seat with hands in the air.

Lean Air   A trick in which the rider grabs the front fender with one hand and the other stretches out to the side or back.

Nac Nac   A trick in which the rider brings one leg over the rear fender to the other side of the bike, as if he's dismounting in mid-air.

No-hander   A trick in which the rider lets go of the bars during a jump.

Saran Wrap   A trick in which the rider passes one foot between his hands and back to the peg, removing one hand from the bars to let the leg pass through.

Superman   A trick in which the rider releases both legs from the pegs and throws his legs back, elevating himself over the bike.

SKATEBOARD

Grind   A term used when one or both axles are scraped on the coping or an obstacle.

Lipslide   To force the tail over the lip and slide on the surface before re-entry.

Manual   Another name for a Wheelie.

Varial   An aerial where the board is spun from backwards to forwards beneath the feet.

RICHARD J. BRENNER is the author of more than 50 best-selling sports books for children and young adults. Brenner, whose books have sold nearly 22 million copies, has spoken at many elementary and middle schools, and was featured at a children's day promotion at the Baseball Hall of Fame.